Teaching and learning in the early years

Edited by David Whitebread

London and New York

First published 1996
by Routledge
11 New Fetter Lane, London EC4P 4EE

Simultaneously published in the USA and Canada
by Routledge
29 West 35th Street, New York, NY 10001

Typeset in Palatino by M Rules

Printed and bound in Great Britain by Redwood Books, Trowbridge, Wiltshire

British Library Cataloguing in Publication Data

A catalogue record for this book is available from the British Library

Library of Congress Cataloging in Publication Data

Teaching and learning in the early years / edited by David Whitebread.
     p.   cm.
   Includes bibliographical references and indexes.
    1. Early childhood education—Great Britain.   2. Early childhood
education—Great Britain—Curricula. 3. Language arts (Early childhood)—
Great Britain. 4. Learning. I. Whitebread, David, 1948–
LB1139.3.G7T43 1996
372.21'0941—dc20   96–2574
                                          CIP

ISBN 0–415–13532–X

DEDICATION

I would like to dedicate this, my first book, to Dorothy Glynn (née Gardner), who was the professional studies tutor on my PGCE course at Clifton College, Nottingham, during the academic year 1973–4. It was Dorothy who persuaded me to focus on the early years, and who was an inspiration to myself and all her students with her deep love and enthusiasm for young children. She had been inspired, in her turn, by the work of Susan Isaacs. I thus like to think that we are continuing a long tradition of recognising that early years education must start with the needs and potentialities of the young child, and that this book will help to inspire others to continue it further.

Teaching and learning in the early years

CONTENTS

LIST OF FIGURES

CONTRIBUTORS

Tandy Adlam did a BEd at Homerton College and has since taught a variety of age groups in Cambridge primary schools. She currently teaches at Colleges Nursery School, Cambridge.

Holly Anderson is a senior lecturer in language and professional studies at Homerton College. A nursery and infant teacher for 18 years, she became a primary language advisory teacher before moving into initial teacher training in 1992. Her publications are in the area of early years language education and she has been UK leader of a cross-cultural research project looking at early years provision in Norway and the UK.

Helen Arnold currently works part-time as a senior lecturer in language and psychology at Homerton College. She has written extensively for children and educators over many years. Her publications include *Listening to Children Reading* 1982, (Hodder & Stoughton) and *Reading for Learning* 1990, (Macmillan/Nelson). She is consulting editor of the Scholastic's *Literacy Boxes (Information)*.

Helen Bromley has taught throughout the early years age range for 16 years, most recently as deputy headteacher of Sunnymede Infant School, Billericay in Essex. She currently works on language courses at Homerton College and contributes to inservice courses for educators throughout Essex. Her publications include chapters on picture books and early reading in *The Politics of Reading* (edited by Morag Styles and Mary Jane Drummond, 1993, University of Cambridge Institute of Cambridge/Homerton College), *Talking Pictures* (edited by Morag Styles, Barbara Jordan and Victor Watson,

1996, Hodder Educational) and *Potent Fictions: Children's Literacy and the Challenge of Popular Culture* (edited by Mary Hilton, 1996, Routledge).

Penny Coltman did a degree in agricultural zoology at Leeds University before originally training as a secondary science teacher. She has worked as a Key Stage 1 teacher at Great Chesterford C of E Primary School, Essex for the last 8 years, where she is currently the maths and science co-ordinator. She is also a part-time lecturer in early years science at Homerton College. She has contributed a number of 'project files' to *Child Education* concerned with carrying out enterprise projects with young children.

Dianne Conway studied geography as a special subject alongside her early years education course at Whitelands College, London (now part of Roehampton Institute). She has taught for 12 years across all the early years age range and is currently teaching a Year 1/2 class in Stapleford Community Primary School, Cambridgeshire. She is the school's geography curriculum co-ordinator, and teaches on geography and integrated human-ities courses for early years students at Homerton College.

Emma Cotton followed a BEd(Hons) degree from Goldsmiths' College with a year's teaching in London before moving to Cambridge. She has worked in a large primary school in the centre of Cambridge for the past 6 years and has been early years team leader for 4 of these.

Jenny Daniels is currently a senior lecturer in English at Homerton College. She has an MA in language and literature from the London Institute of Education. At Homerton she devised and has taught an early years lan-guage course for the last 5 years. Her publications include chapters on narrative, gender and language in *After Alice* (edited by Morag Styles, Eve Bearne and Victor Watson, 1992, Cassell) and *The Prose and the Passion* (edited by Eve Bearne, Morag Styles and Victor Watson, 1994, Cassell).

Ros Daniels works at Hare Street Infant School in Harlow. She has worked at Homerton College on the BEd professional studies course and now also lectures with a colleague on behaviour management. She has published an article on planned activity time (PAT) in *Child Education* (1995, with Jackie Lamb and Debbie Barnes) and an article on behaviour in Bill Roger's latest publication *Behaviour Management* (1995, Scholastic Australia).

Mary Jane Drummond taught in infant and primary schools in London and Sheffield, and was headteacher of an infant school. She has been a tutor at the University of Cambridge Institute of Education since 1985, where she has developed a range of multi-disciplinary early years courses. She is a member of the Board of Managers of the National Children's Bureau and an editor of the *Cambridge Journal of Education*. She has acted as external evaluator for the Bedfordshire 'Expansion of early years education project'(1989–90) and the Hampshire 'Earlier admissions programme'(1993–5). Her publications include *Making Assessment Work: Values and Principles in Assessing Young Children's Learning* (with Dorothy Rouse and Gillian Pugh, 1992, NES Arnold/National Children's Bureau) and *Assessing Children's Learning* (1993, David Fulton).

Jane Edden is currently senior lecturer in music education at Homerton College. She has taught music to children in a variety of schools both in this country and in Trinidad. As primary music specialist for Cambridgeshire she was co-author of *Managing Music with Infants* (1989, Cambridgeshire County Council).

Lesley Hendy is a senior lecturer in drama and professional studies at Homerton College, specialising in the early years. Before retraining as a drama specialist, she worked as a nursery and infant teacher and was headteacher of a first school. Her publications include a chapter on active storytelling in *After Alice* (edited by Morag Styles, Eve Bearne and Victor Watson, 1992, Cassell) and (with Patrice Baldwin) *The Drama Box* (1994, HarperCollins).

John Lewis has taught for about 18 years in London schools. He is currently a part-time senior lecturer in art education at Homerton College. He combines this with freelance lecturing and writing for the National Gallery. He is a painter and print-maker whose work has appeared regularly in major exhibitions.

Patricia Maude is head of the physical education department at Homerton College. She has taught physical education for many years to children in primary schools, students and teachers and has contributed to conferences in this country and abroad. Her recent publications include *The Gym Kit* video and handbook (1994, Homerton College) the gymnastics section of *Teaching Physical Education at Key Stages 1 and 2* (1995, Physical Education Association) and a chapter concerned with differentiation in physical education in Eve Bearne's book *Differentiation and Diversity* (1996, Routledge).

Annie Owen is a senior lecturer in mathematics and the primary mathematics co-ordinator at Homerton College. She worked as a classroom teacher for 9 years, and then as an advisory teacher. She has written several mathematics books for the primary years and contributes regularly to *Junior Education*. Her present research explores the role of pattern recognition and structure in young children's understanding and use of number.

Pam Pointon worked as a classroom teacher for 13 years and then as a research fellow at the Centre for Global Education, University of York. She is currently a senior lecturer in primary geography at Homerton College.

Sallie Purkis was formerly a senior lecturer in history at Homerton College and is now a freelance educational writer and consultant. She is a regular contributor to both *Infant Focus* and *Junior Education* and reviews for a number of journals. She has been a consultant for the BBC (*Watch* and *Radio History*) and for Thames TV (*Seeing and Doing*) . She has published extensively in the field of primary school history including a major series of books entitled *A Sense of History* for Key Stage 1 and Key Stage 2 (1991, Longman Educational).

Laurie Rousham was a teacher and a headteacher in primary schools in Suffolk from 1972–90, teaching children aged four to eleven. He is currently senior lecturer in mathematics education at Homerton College. He has published articles and reviews for the *Times Education Supplement, Child Education* and *Junior Education* and is currently researching the effects of calculator use on the mathematical education of young children.

Rachel Sparks Linfield is a senior lecturer in primary science and co-ordinator for professional studies at Homerton College. Before that she worked for 8 years as a primary school teacher. She has published articles in *Questions, Junior Education* and *Primary Science Review* and recently collaborated with Lesley Hendy on a Key Stage 1 pack entitled KS1 *Science Through Stories* (1995, Pearson).

Babs Sweet was born and educated in Manchester. She has had 35 years' involvement in children's education from supervising kindergartens to running international guide camps. She is currently working at St John's College School, Cambridge where she teaches design and technology to four to nine-year-olds.

Paul Warwick is currently the primary science co-ordinator at Homerton College. Before coming to Homerton he worked as deputy headteacher of a primary school and then as a primary science support teacher for Cambridgeshire LEA. He has published articles in *Questions* and *Primary Science Review*.

David Whitebread is a senior lecturer in psychology and professional studies at Homerton College, specialising in the early years. Before coming to Homerton he taught in several primary schools, mostly in Leicestershire, for about 12 years. His current research interests include the development of children's problem-solving abilities, their mathematical strategies and their road safety skills. He has contributed a number of 'project files' to *Child Education* concerned with enterprise projects with young children, has recently co-ordinated an edition of the journal *Early Years*, and has also published on emergent mathematics (in Julia Anghileri (ed.), *Children's Mathematical Thinking in the Primary Years*, 1995, Cassell).

Sally Wilkinson taught in primary schools in Suffolk for 8 years, teaching children aged four to nine. She now works as an advisory teacher for English with Suffolk LEA and is currently studying for an MA in language and literature at the London Institute of Education.

PREFACE

The impetus to write this book originally came from local events within Homerton College. The college has a long history of training teachers for the early years. There is, indeed, a nearby local authority nursery school which bears the college's name because it began life just over 50 years ago within the college grounds as a training nursery school. Training for the early years had been phased out, but was recommenced in 1989, both within the undergraduate BEd course and the postgraduate certificate course. Since then the small number of early years enthusiasts on the college staff has grown steadily, and links have been made with local teacher colleagues. As we worked together on developing courses slowly the idea developed for this book.

As it turns out, however, we find ourselves publishing at a time of critical importance for early years education in the UK and maybe in other parts of the developed world as well. At long last the crucial importance of good quality early years education is finally being recognised. Research evidence that children's success in school and other aspects of their life can be significantly enhanced by quality educational experiences when they are very young is being taken seriously.

As a consequence, a number off changes are taking place in the educational provision for young children. Within the UK there has been a move in recent years to provide places in school for four-year-olds. However, there has been mounting concern that many of these children have finished up in over-large and poorly resourced reception classes, and with teachers who were not originally trained in the early years. As I write, OFSTED inspectors, educationalists, teachers' representatives and politicians are all debating evidence that smaller class sizes can significantly affect the quality of learning for children in the first few years at school. There is also much talk currently about expanding the provision of nursery education for three- and four-year-olds.

All these concerns and developments may, it is to be hoped, lead to an increase in the status and numbers of well-qualified early years teachers working with our young children. It is also to be hoped that this welcome publicity will encourage more able young men and women to enter into this most worthwhile of professions. I would also like to think that this book will help to enhance the quality of their preparation for the endlessly fascinating and challenging task of educating three- to eight-year-old children.

The original impetus to produce this book arose from a perceived absence of published material written in a way which would interest and serve the needs of our early years students. We wanted to produce a book which introduced and discussed general principles of early years education, but at the same time showed how these translated into practical activities in the classroom.

In recent years we have experienced unprecedented turmoil in British primary education. In England and Wales we have a new national curriculum. We do not share the view of some early years educators that this national curriculum is fundamentally in conflict with principles of early years education. The spirit of this book is that with thought and imagination young children can be taught in ways which incorporate the national curriculum, but which do much more. The book is intended to convey the strong research base related to children's learning and development upon which all good early years teaching must be founded. It is also intended to demonstrate that the best teaching of young children must have a strong element of fun and wonder and excitement.

All sound teaching of young children is based upon understandings about how young children learn, and the book begins with an analysis of current research in this area. Principles which derive from this research inform the subsequent sections of the book concerned with different aspects of early years teaching and the early years curriculum.

There follows a section on basic principles and approaches which discusses issues related to the management of the early years learning environment. This is followed by a series of chapters concerned with play and language, the basics of early years education. A further section examines the wider curriculum of the arts, maths, technology and science, the social sciences and physical education. Each chapter examines basic principles and illuminates them with inspiring, practical examples of classroom activities.

This book is principally directed at early years student teachers, but it is also hoped that it contains material which will be of interest to the whole range of teaching and non-teaching professionals and other adults concerned with the education of young children. The term 'educator' has been used throughout the book in preference to 'teacher' in an attempt to include and recognise this wider group of adults working in early years education.

British nursery and infant education has long enjoyed an international reputation for high quality. This book is most of all a re-affirmation of this tradition, and an attempt to help maintain and improve the quality of the education offered to our young children.

David Whitebread
November 1995

ACKNOWLEDGEMENTS

Vygotsky's model of the 'zone of proximal development', Figure 1.1, is reproduced with permission from *Understanding Children's Development* (2nd edition) (p. 353) by Peter K. Smith and Helen Cowie, 1991, Oxford, Blackwell Publishers. **Bruner's nine glasses problem**, Figure 1.2, is reprinted with permission from *Studies in Cognitive Growth* (p. 156) edited by J.S. Bruner *et al.*, 1966, New York, John Wiley & Sons Ltd. **The regular sequence of motor development in infants** (p. 192) from *Understanding Child Development* (p. 202) by Spencer A. Rathus, 1988, is reproduced by permission of Holt, Rinehart and Winston, Inc. Orlando. **A beginning thrower**, Figure 10.2, and **A beginning and advanced runner**, Figure 10.3, are reproduced from *Life Span Motor Development* (pp. 145, 128 and 129) by Kathleen M. Haywood, 1993, by permission of Human Kinetics Publishers, Champaign, Illinois, drawn from film tracings from the Motor Development and Child Study Laboratory, University of Wisconsin Madison. **An advanced 6-year-old kicker**, Figure 10.4, and **The leap**, Figure 10.5, 1994, are reproduced by permission of PCET Wallcharts Ltd., 27 Kirchen Road, London W13 0UD and Jan Traylen. Photographs are by Jan Traylen from wallcharts entitled *Games Skills* and *Gymnastic Skills*. We would also like to thank Birmingham City Council, Curriculum Support Service for allowing us to use Figures 16.4 to 16.6. This material comes from *Harborne Infant School Local History Project*. **Goodey's (1973) model of geographical experiences** is reproduced by permission of the University of Birmingham Centre for Urban and Regional Studies. The diagram, originally titled *Child in information space*, is from *Perception in the Environment: an introduction to the literature*, occasional paper no. 17 by B. Goodey, 1973 (p. 7). The extract on p. 313 from *Geography in the National Curriculum: Non-Statutory Guidance for*

Teachers, 1991 (p. 4) is reproduced by permission of the copyright holder, the Curriculum Council for Wales, Cardiff. The extract on p. 315 from *Geography for ages 5–16*, DES, London, 1990, extract from *Geography from 5–16*, DES, London, 1986, and p. 316 **Aims for geographical education**, from *Geography for ages 5–16*, DES, London, 1990 are all reproduced with permission. Crown copyright is reproduced with the permission of the controller of HMSO, Norwich. **Exploring the seaside: a geographical enquiry** from *Response to the Draft Orders for the Geography National Curriculum in Wales*, 1991, is reproduced by permission of the Geographical Association.

CHAPTER 1

Introduction

YOUNG CHILDREN LEARNING AND EARLY YEARS TEACHING

David Whitebread

There has traditionally been a strong association between understandings about child development and early years teaching. This book is written, however, at a particularly exciting time in this regard. The relationship between developmental research and the practices of teaching young children is currently a rich area of growth and development. This book is an attempt to distil the current state of knowledge about the ways in which young children (up to the age of eight) develop and learn, to show how educational principles derive from this, and to illustrate these principles with practical examples drawn from work in early years classrooms. In this introductory chapter I want to show how psychological research concerned with child development informs the principles of practice exemplified throughout the rest of the book.

There is a long tradition of ideas about children and their learning in early years education. In the nineteenth and early twentieth centuries these were largely developed by a number of outstanding and inspiring educators. Tina Bruce (1987) has provided an excellent review of the ideas of Froebel, Montessori, Steiner and others, derived ten common principles of early years education and attempted to show how these relate to modern research. These principles emphasise the holistic nature of children's learning and development (as distinct from learning separated out into subjects), the importance of developing autonomy, intrinsic motivation and self-discipline through the encouragement of child-initiated, self-directed activity, the value of first-hand experiences and the crucial role in children's development of other children and adults.

As we shall see, many of these ideas have been reinforced by modern psychological research; they have also been extended and developed in interesting and important ways. Much of current thinking about children's learning has been influenced by the work and ideas of three outstanding developmental psychologists – Jean Piaget, Lev Vygotsky and Jerome Bruner – and so it is with their contributions that we begin.

Piaget

The first major developmental psychologist to influence classroom practice was, of course, Jean Piaget. His ideas were welcomed enthusiastically in the 1960s because they were a reaction to the 'behaviourist' view of learning current within psychology and education at the time, with which people were increasingly unhappy. The behaviourist view placed the child in a passive position, and viewed learning simply as a combination of imitation and conditioning by means of external rewards and reinforcements. This model works quite well as a way of explaining how you can teach parrots to roller-skate, but it is a woefully inadequate explanation of the range and flexibility of the achievements of the human child.

A huge amount has been written about Piaget's theory and its influence upon primary education. Brainerd (in Meadows 1983) and Davis (1991) provide good reviews of the impact on education. On the positive side, the most important contribution of Piaget's work was to alert educators to the child's active role in their learning, and the importance of mental activity (see Howe 1984). Piaget showed how children actively attempt to make sense of their world and construct their own understandings.

On the negative side, Piaget's emphasis on stages of development appears to have been ill founded and resulted in serious underestimation of the abilities of young children (see Wood 1988). The work of Margaret Donaldson (1978) and many other developmental psychologists subsequently has demonstrated that Piaget's tasks (such as his famous conservation tasks) were difficult for young children for a whole range of extraneous reasons unconnected to the child's understanding of the underlying concept. These tasks were too abstract and did not make sense to young children, they over-relied on rather sophisticated linguistic competence, and they were embedded in misleading social contexts. Interestingly, one of the major areas of discovery as regards young children's learning in recent years has related to their peculiar sensitivity to these kinds of contextual factors. This is an issue to which I want to return later in the chapter and, as we shall see, it has important implications for early years teaching.

More recent evidence has suggested that young children arrive at school with many more capabilities than was previously thought, and than was suggested by Piaget. The pioneering work of Tizard and Hughes (1984) in the area of language, and of Gelman and Gallistel (1978) in relation to young children's understandings about number, are good examples here. Both suggested that children's abilities were being systematically under-appreciated by teachers, for much the same reasons as they had been by Piaget. In school, children were being faced by ideas or tasks taken out of any meaningful context, and for no clear purposes, and they were finding them difficult. In the home environment, when the same ideas or tasks occurred naturally, embedded in real meaning and purposes, the same children understood and managed them with ease.

Vygotsky

Piaget has also been criticised for under-emphasising the role in children's learning of language and of social interaction with other children and with adults. The ideas of the Russian psychologist, Lev Vygotsky, have been an important influence in this area (see Smith and Cowie 1991, for an introduction and Moll 1990, for an extensive review of educational implications).

Piaget had emphasised the importance of the child interacting with the physical environment, and his followers in the educational sphere argued that the role of the teacher should be that of an observer and a facilitator. The general view of this approach was that attempting to directly teach or instruct young children was a mistake. It was claimed that whenever teachers attempted to teach children something, they simply deprived the children of the opportunity to discover it for themselves.

This view was partly a reaction against the simplistic 'behaviourist' model that children only learnt what they were taught. To some extent, however, it can be seen to have thrown the baby out with the bath water. More recent research inspired by the work of Vygotsky has argued that there is a much more central role for the adult, and, indeed, for other children, in the processes of learning. This role is not as an instructor delivering knowledge, however, but rather as a 'scaffolder' (a metaphor suggested by Jerome Bruner; see Smith and Cowie 1991, pp. 356–8) supporting, encouraging and extending the child's own active search for understanding.

Perhaps the most significant idea within Vygotsky's model of human learning is that of the 'zone of proximal development', as illustrated in Figure 1.1. Faced with any particular task or problem, a child can operate at one level on their own, described as their 'level of actual development'. But they can perform at a higher level when supported or 'scaffolded' by an adult or more experienced peer, described as their 'level of potential development'. The 'zone of proximal development' (or ZPD) is that area of learning described by the difference between these two levels of

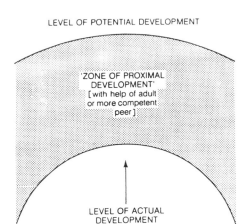

performance or understanding. Vygotsky and his followers have argued, therefore, that children learn most effectively through social interaction, when they are involved in jointly constructing new understandings within their ZPD.

Figure 1.1 *Vygotsky's model of the 'zone of proximal development'*

Bruner

This view has been supported by evidence of the significant role of language within learning. The work of Jerome Bruner has been influential in regard to this issue (see, for example, Wood 1988, for a discussion of Bruner's ideas on language and thought). Bruner described language as a 'tool of thought', and demonstrated in a range of studies the ways in which language enables children to develop their thinking and perform tasks which would otherwise be impossible. In his famous 'nine glasses problem' (see Figure 1.2), for example, he showed that children who could describe the patterns in a 3×3 matrix of glasses (which were taller or shorter one way and thinner or fatter the other) were also able to transform the matrix (i.e. arrange the glasses in a mirror image pattern). Children without the relevant

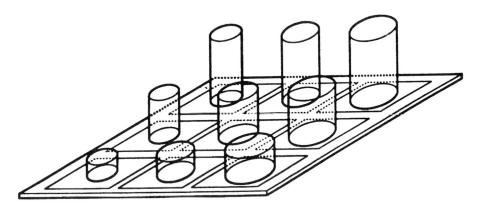

Figure 1.2 *Bruner's nine glasses problem*

language to call on, however, were only able to reproduce the pattern exactly as they had seen it.

It is now widely recognised that providing children with a relevant vocabulary and requiring them to formulate their ideas in discussion, is a vital element in helping children to develop flexibility in thinking and construct their own understandings about the world.

This has led to the recognition that a certain style of interaction between adults and children, and between pairs or small groups of children, can be enormously beneficial to learning. Paul Light (in Meadows 1983) has provided a useful review of research indicating that this style involves dialogue between adults and children in which there is 'co-construction' of meanings. Forman and Cazden (1985) have reviewed work demonstrating the help to learning provided by collaboration and dialogue between children.

Jerome Bruner's other major contribution to our understandings about young children as learners is encapsulated in his phrase 'the spiral curriculum'. This is his view that, in principle, anything can be taught to children of any age, provided it is presented in a way which is accessible to them. Thus, having encountered a set of ideas at a practical level when they are young, they will use this knowledge to help them understand the same ideas at a more symbolic or abstract level when they are older. So learning is viewed as a spiral in which the same point is returned to and revisited but each time at a higher or deeper level. He demonstrated this by, for example, successfully teaching eight-year-old children to understand quadratic equations. He achieved this by providing them with the practical example of working out the area of rectangles (see Wood 1988, chapter 7, for a review of this work).

Bruner's view about the constraints upon children's learning is very much in line with a whole range of contemporary research. Piaget's earlier notion that children are limited in what they can understand by certain kinds of logical deficiencies in their reasoning powers has been largely dismissed. As Margaret Donaldson (1978) argued, research shows that adults make the same kinds of logical errors as children, and have difficulties with the same kinds of reasoning problems. Children's learning is now seen as being limited much more simply by their lack of experience and of accumulated knowledge. This makes it more difficult for them to see what is relevant in any new situation, and to see what is the best way to proceed. When this is made clear by the context in which a task is presented, however, children's potential for learning is phenomenal and often way beyond our normal expectations, as Bruner ably demonstrated.

The current view of the child as learner, therefore, is one which recognises their considerable appetite and aptitude for learning. However, it is also important to recognise the nature of children's limitations and their particular needs if they are to flourish. These needs are both emotional and intellectual. As we shall see, research evidence suggests that to become effective learners young children need love and security, and they need intellectual challenge. In the remainder of this chapter I want to examine these needs and their implications for educational environments. The chapter concludes, lest we forget the importance of the enterprise upon which we are embarked, with a brief discussion of the evidence concerning the impact of quality early years education on children's later development.

The need for love and security

On the emotional side, in order to develop into effective learners within the school context it is clear that young children need love and security. An important element in the tradition of early years education has always been a recognition of the need to consider the whole child. Children's learning and intellectual development is inseparable from their emotional and social development. In their early years, as well as mastering fundamental skills and understandings, young children are also forming their basic attitudes to themselves as people and as learners. The basic attitudes they form at this stage have major implications for their future educational progress.

An enormous body of research evidence collected by developmental psychologists supports this view. High self-esteem and feelings of self-efficacy are strongly related to educational success, and low self-esteem and what has been termed 'learned helplessness' are equally related to educational difficulty. It is difficult to attribute cause and effect here, but there is clearly a positive cycle of mutual interaction between self-belief and achievement and, sadly, a negative downward spiral associated with self-doubt and failure. Rogers and Kutnick (1990) have provided a useful survey of work in this area and its important implications for teachers.

Essentially, there are three aspects to this. If they are to thrive emotionally and intellectually, young children need to feel **love and self-worth**, they need to feel **emotionally secure** and they need to feel **in control**.

Love and self-worth

Psychologists have investigated in considerable detail the ways in which the young child's sense of self develops in the first few years of life. From the earliest emergence within the first year of bodily awareness, and the recognition of the distinction between self and not-self, the young child's sense of self becomes rapidly differentiated. They develop a self-image of themselves as an individual, a self-identity of the sort of person they are and to which groups they belong (child, boy/girl, race, types of ability and so on), a distinction between their private and public selves (with an increasing number of roles within which they see themselves – son/daughter, sibling, friend, pupil), an ideal self to which they aspire, feelings of self-esteem and of self-worth.

In all this a crucial element is the ways in which they are viewed and treated by significant others in their lives. The metaphor has been developed by psychologists working in this area of the self as a mirror. Children's views about themselves develop as a reflection of the views transmitted to them by others in social interaction. This has also often been referred to as the Pygmalion effect, after the famous play by Shaw. In the play a flower girl is treated by everyone as a lady (after some grooming by Professor Higgins) and so she starts to view herself as a lady, and becomes one. All the evidence suggests that children who develop positive self-images and feelings of self-worth are those who have been surrounded in their earliest years by unconditional love and emotional warmth. Their parents or other carers have transmitted to them very powerfully that they are valued by others, and so they come to value themselves.

Emotional security

Alongside positive attitudes to themselves, young children need to develop feelings of trust in relation to their environment. The significance of feelings of emotional security was first highlighted by Harlow's famous experiments in the 1950s with baby monkeys. The initial experiments offered the babies a choice of two substitute but inanimate 'mothers', one which was soft and cuddly and another which was metal and hard but provided milk. The babies spent the vast majority of their time cuddling up to the soft model. Perhaps even more significantly, Harlow discovered that babies provided with a cuddly 'mother' of this kind became much more adventurous in exploring their environment than babies who were deprived of this obvious source of comfort.

In the 1950s the view was advanced by Bowlby that the emotional security needed by young children should ideally be provided by the biological mother or, failing that, by one constant adult figure in the child's life. In his excellent review of this and subsequent research, however, Rudolph Schaffer (1977) demonstrated that care did not need to be provided by one particular adult continuously. Rather, the quality and consistency of care emerged from research to be the crucial factors. The quality of care appears to be mostly a matter of how responsive the adult is to the child. The consistency of care is vital in giving the child a sense that their world is predictable. This has two elements, first that the same actions by the child produces the same response by the adult, and second that transitions between adult carers is handled carefully so that the child understands the programme of events.

Young children's almost obsessive concern for fairness (with rules applied consistently) and their strong preference for routine can be seen as clear outcomes of their need for emotional security. Their love of hearing familiar stories endlessly repeated is possibly a manifestation of the same phenomenon. This need for their experience to be predictable and to follow clear rules is very much linked to their need intellectually to make sense of their world, to which we return later. Emotionally, it is also strongly linked to their need to feel in control, to which we turn now.

Feeling in control

We have probably all played that game with young children of a certain age where the child performs an action, we respond in some way, and the child laughs (the 'dropping things out of the pram' game is a good example). Immediately the child does it again, we repeat our response and there is more laughter. And so it goes on, and on, and on. The adult always tires of this game before the child does because the child is in the process of discovering something really wonderful. They are in control of their world, they can make things happen.

This feeling of empowerment is fundamental to children developing positive attitudes to themselves, and particularly to themselves as learners. Within modern developmental psychology there has been a huge amount of research about this aspect of emotional development and its relation to motivation. This research has been concerned with examining what is called 'attribution theory' because it is concerned with the causes to which children attribute their successes and failures. Where children feel that their performance is determined by factors within their control (for example, how much effort they put into a particular task) they will respond positively to failure and try harder next time, believing all the time in their own ability to be successful on the task. Where they feel that their performance is determined by factors outside of their control (for example, their level of ability, or luck) they will respond negatively to failure and give up, believing that they will not succeed however much they try. It is clear that such 'learned helplessness' is extremely damaging to children's development as learners.

This model of 'attributions' explains well how poor self-esteem can result in lack of motivation, which in turn leads to lack of effort and consequent poor performance, confirming the child's view of themselves. The failing child thus becomes locked into a destructive self-fulfilling prophecy. In order to avoid this it is clearly vital that adults working with young children do everything in their power to give them the feeling of being in control.

Research on parenting styles is quite helpful here. Broadly speaking, researchers have found that it is possible to categorise parenting styles into three broad types. First, there is the 'autocratic' style, where rules are entirely constructed by the parent and enforced arbitrarily and inconsistently without explanation. At the opposite extreme there is the 'laissez-faire' style where there are no rules to which the child is expected to conform. Both these styles communicate low expectations to the child, a lack of responsiveness and consistency, and children suffering under these kinds of regimes typically have low self-esteem and little emotional security.

The third style is what might be termed 'authoritative' or 'democratic'. Here there are rules to which the child is expected to conform, they are applied consistently and they are discussed and negotiated with the child. Under this kind of regime children typically have high self-esteem and feel in control.

Implications for the early years teacher

- Create an atmosphere of emotional warmth, within which each child feels individually valued.
- Communicate high expectations to all children.
- Praise and recognise children's achievements, particularly when they are the result of a special effort.
- Run an orderly classroom which has regular classroom routines.
- Always explain to the children the programme of events for the day and prepare them for transitions.
- Put children in control of their own learning; allow them to make choices.
- Exercise democratic control; involve children in decisions about classroom rules and procedures and enforce rules fairly.
- Criticise a child's actions, but never the child.

The need for intellectual challenge

While it is clear that there is an intimate link between emotional and intellectual development, love and security on their own are not enough. Young children also need intellectual challenge. As we have reviewed, Piaget first argued, and it is now widely accepted, that children learn by a process of actively constructing their own understandings. All the evidence suggests that a learning environment which helps children to do this will, not surprisingly, be one which challenges them intellectually and stimulates them to be mentally active. It also turns out to be crucial, once again, that the children are put in control. Such an environment will provide **new experiences**, embedded in **meaningful contexts**, opportunities for **active styles of learning**, involving children in **problem solving, investigations** and opportunities for **self-expression**, and, perhaps most crucially of all, opportunities for learning through **play**.

Play

If we are to understand anything about the ways in which young children learn, we must understand first the central role of play. The distinction between work and play is entirely misleading in the context of young children's learning, for much of the evidence suggests that play is when children do their real learning (see Moyles 1989). Children's language development, for example, is commonly associated with playful approaches and activities – making up nonsense words, verbal jokes and puns, silly rhymes and so forth are all much enjoyed and of great benefit.

It was Bruner (1972), in a famous article entitled 'The nature and uses of immaturity', who first pointed out the relationship across different animal species between the capacity for learning and the length of immaturity, or dependence upon adults. He also pointed out that as the period of immaturity lengthens, so does the extent to which the young are playful. He argued that play is one of the key experiences through which young animals learn, and also the means by which their intellectual abilities themselves are developed. The human being, of course, has a much greater length of immaturity than any other animal, plays more and for longer, and is supreme, of course, in the ability to learn.

The crucial aspect of human intellectual ability which enables us to learn so effectively, Bruner argues, is our flexibility of thought. Play, he suggests, is all about developing flexibility of thought. It provides opportunities to try out possibilities, to put different elements of a situation together in various ways, to look at problems from different viewpoints. He demonstrated this in a series of experiments (e.g. see Sylva, Bruner and Genova 1984) where children were asked to solve practical problems. Typically in these experiments, one group of children was given the opportunity to play with the objects involved, while the other group was 'taught' how to use the objects in ways which would help solve the problem. Consistently, the 'play' group subsequently outperformed the 'taught' group when they were then left alone to tackle the problem. The children who had the experience of playing with the materials were more inventive in devising strategies to solve the problem, they persevered longer when their initial attempts did not work, and so were not surprisingly more successful in their attempts to solve the problem.

Observation of children at play gives some indication of why it might be such a powerful learning medium. During play children are usually totally engrossed in what they are doing. It is quite often repetitive and contains a strong element of practice. During play children set their own level of challenge, and so what they are doing is always developmentally appropriate (to a degree which tasks set by adults will never be). Play is spontaneous and initiated by the children themselves; in other words, during play children are in control of their own learning.

Mari Guha (1987) has argued that this last element is particularly significant. There are many examples in psychological research of tasks where being in control has turned out to be crucial for effective learning. Guha cites, for example, experiments concerned with visual learning in which subjects are required to wear 'goggles' which make everything look upside down. They are then required to sit in a wheelchair and learn to move safely through an environment. The results of such experiments show that subjects moving themselves around the environment (and having a lot of initial 'crashes') learn to do this much more quickly than those who are wheeled safely about by an adult helper.

The parallels here with Bruner's 'play' and 'taught' groups is striking and there are important implications for how we can most effectively help young children learn. A simple model which suggests that children learn what we teach them is clearly unsustainable. There is a role for the adult, however, in providing the right kind of learning environment, and this clearly needs to provide opportunities for play. Whenever a new material or process is introduced, for example, it is clear that children's learning will be enhanced if they are first allowed to play with them. When new information is being introduced, children need to be offered opportunities to incorporate this into their play also. As we discussed earlier, there is also a role for the adult in 'scaffolding' children's experiences within the learning environment, and various ways of participating and intervening in children's play can be enormously beneficial. Manning and Sharp (1977) have provided a very thorough and practical analysis of ways in which educators can, by these means, usefully structure and extend children's play in the classroom.

New experiences

Anyone who has spent any time at all with young children, and attempted to answer all the questions they keep asking, will be well aware of their apparently insatiable curiosity. I am reminded of the manic robot Johnny 5 in the film *Short Circuit* who continually and voraciously craves 'INPUT!'. Part of the notion of young children as active learners is a recognition of their compelling need for new experiences. Providing that they feel emotionally secure, as we have discussed, they will enthusiastically explore their environment and are highly motivated by novelty.

From the psychological perspective this is not surprising. It is one of the other distinguishing features of the human brain that it does, indeed, require a certain level of input. Unlike almost all other animals, we are very easily bored. If insufficient new information is being provided by the environment, furthermore, the human brain will provide its own amusement. Every day, we all daydream. In extreme circumstances (for example, in sensory deprivation experiments where the subject is kept motionless in a completely dark, soundproof booth) this can result in powerful hallucinations.

Within psychological research this kind of work has underpinned a well established relationship, known as the Yerkes-Dodson law, linking an individual's state of arousal and their performance on a task. Too little stimulation produces boredom and too much stimulation produces anxiety. Both are dysfunctional in terms of performance on a task, and of learning.

Thus, while we need to ensure that children feel in control of their classroom environment, we also need to ensure that they find it a stimulating, exciting and motivating place to be. We must never underestimate young children's abilities to absorb new information and to cope with new ideas. Young children, for example, love being introduced to new vocabulary, especially if the words are long and/or difficult (e.g. tyrannosaurus, equilateral, strato-cumulus etc). Further, there is an age-related factor here, whereby typically our optimum level of stimulation decreases as we get older. The chances are, therefore, that if you as an adult are feeling really comfortable with the pace of events in a classroom, some of the children will be bored!

Meaningful contexts

The dominant model in contemporary psychological research concerned with human learning is that of the child as an active information processor. As such, the child attempts to make sense of, and derive meaning from, experience by means of classifying, categorising and ordering new information and relating it to what is already known. This inductive style of learning involving the identification of patterns and regularities from the variety of our experience is a very dominant aspect of human functioning. The astonishing facility with which children learn their first language, by working out the rules for themselves (aided by a little 'motherese') is a good example of the power of inductive processes.

This search for patterns and regularities within the variety of experience has important implications for the ways in which young children make sense of new experiences. They expect to find pattern and regularity, and they expect new experiences to fit together in some way with what they already know. This was beautifully illustrated by an experiment in which young children were asked 'bizarre' questions, such as 'Is milk bigger than water?' and 'Is red heavier than yellow?' (see Hughes and Grieve in Donaldson *et al.* 1983). What happened was that the children answered the questions and did so in ways which illustrated their attempts to make sense of them in terms of the context in which they were asked and their own previous experience. Thus, they might reply that 'Milk is bigger than water because it's creamier' or 'Red is heavier than yellow because the yellow is a little plastic box and the red paint's got a big plastic box'.

As Hughes and Grieve point out, what the children were doing in response to these bizarre questions is what they do all the time when they are faced with new information or problems. It is for this reason that children's performance and understanding is always likely to be enhanced when tasks are presented in ways which help young children to make sense of them in the light of what they already know. In other words, tasks need to be placed in contexts which are meaningful to young children.

As we noted earlier, many of Piaget's tasks have been criticised precisely on the grounds that their meaning was not clear and children misinterpreted them in their attempts to make sense of them, based upon their previous experience. Donaldson (1978) reviewed a number of alternative versions of Piagetian tasks where an attempt had been made to place them in meaningful contexts and thus make their purpose more intelligible to young children.

For example, Piaget's famous number conservation task consisted of showing the child two equal rows of buttons (as shown in Figure 1.3, Part 1) and asking the child whether there were more white buttons or black buttons, or whether they were the same. One of the rows was then transformed by the experimenter (as shown in Figure 1.3, Part 2) and the

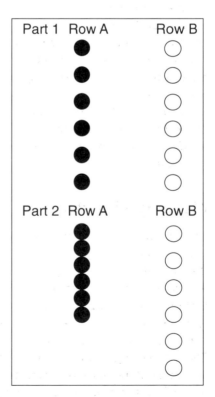

Figure 1.3 *Piaget's number conservation problem*

question was repeated. Piaget found that many young children could correctly recognise that the first two rows contained the same number, but said there were more white buttons in the second condition. He concluded that these young children were overwhelmed by their perceptions and that they lacked the logical understanding of the conservation of number.

When this task was repeated, however, by a colleague of Margaret Donaldson's, the transformation of one of the rows of buttons was effected by a 'naughty teddy' glove puppet. In these circumstances many more young children were able to say that the two rows still contained the same number.

Donaldson concludes that the introduction of the naughty teddy changes the meaning for the child of the second question. This question is made sense of by the children in relation to the social situation and their own previous experience. When the adult transforms the pattern and repeats the question, this means to some children that their first answer was wrong and the adult is helping them to see the correct answer. In the amended version, the second question is a cue to check that the naughty teddy hasn't lost or added any buttons during his mischief.

The lessons for the early years teacher are clear. Young children do not passively receive the information we provide for them. They are engaged continually in a process of active interpretation and transformation of new information. If we want to help them to make sense of their educational experiences we must ensure that we place new tasks in contexts which will enhance their meaning for young children. This often means actively making links with what the children already know and presenting the activity in the context of a story or game. As a consequence of children's limited symbolic understandings, it also means that hands-on experiences, where the children are gaining information directly through their senses, is always likely to be more effective. It is also a rationale for organising activities within the meaningful context of children's interests or a cross-curricular topic.

If children are to use their powerful inductive processes to find patterns and regularities in their experience it is also important to present the same ideas, concepts or processes in a variety of such meaningful contexts. Only in this way can children begin to disentangle what is relevant and what is irrelevant in relation to any particular idea. Children who are taught one way of carrying out a particular process are often left confused about the essential nature of the task. I have been told by young children that you cannot add together two numbers written side by side, you have to put one of them underneath the other. I also remember one of my own young daughters, on returning from a visit to the Science Museum, telling me excitedly about this machine she had seen (which sounded like an internal combustion engine from her description). When asked what she thought it was for, she replied that there was a lot of gravel all around it, so she thought it might be making that. Now she has seen lots of machines in different contexts, she has induced that the gravel around museum exhibits is usually purely cosmetic.

Mental activity

Related to the need for new experiences is the fact that we all find enjoyment in mental activity. As we have discussed, it was Piaget who first drew attention to the fundamental relationship between mental activity and learning. The kind of mental activity we need for learning can be stimulated in two main ways, through problem solving and self-expression. Both of these processes require us to restructure what we know and to make use of it in new ways. It is well established within modern developmental psychology that this kind of restructuring is required to integrate new information into our existing conceptual framework. In a very important sense, this is the essence of real learning.

Within a number of areas of research, the relationship between mental activity and learning has been clearly demonstrated. For example, within memory research, a range of research has confirmed what is known as the 'generation effect'. Information which has at least been partly generated or transformed in some way is always more memorable than that which has been simply received. It is for this reason that teaching spellings by providing anagrams from which the children have to generate the words is always more effective than simply giving a list of the words. Michael Howe (1984) usefully reviews a number of experiments which have demonstrated this point, and which suggest more active ways of presenting information to young children.

Problem solving is fundamental to human intellectual functioning. It is part of our need to make sense of our experience and gain control over our environment. Robert Fisher (1987, 1990), amongst others, has argued that as educators we can most effectively harness the power of young children's abilities to learn by presenting new ideas and information as problems to be solved, or areas to be investigated, for purposes which are meaningful and real to the children. He has also produced excellent reviews of the justification and practice of this kind of approach within primary education.

Within the purely cognitive sphere, however, it is also important because of the processes of cognitive restructuring involved. There is good evidence to suggest that the process of self-expression is important in helping children to become more able to make sense of their experiences. The Vygotskian notion of learning through the co-construction of meanings in social situations (as reviewed by Light, in Meadows 1983) and Bruner's notion of language as a 'tool of thought' are important here. In their explorations of young children's use of language in the home and school, Tizard and Hughes (1984) have presented evidence of children engaging in processes of intellectual search through talk. The kinds of meaningful dialogues with adults that are likely to stimulate this kind of mental activity, however, they found to be much more common in the home environment than in the school. They argue that as educators we must find means of developing quality conversations between ourselves and the children in our classrooms.

One way into this kind of activity which would appear to be well worth pursuing is that offered by the 'philosophy for children' approach originally developed by Matthew Lipman and reviewed by Fisher (1990). In essence, this approach consists of posing children with moral or ethical problems through the contexts of stories and then engaging them in philosophical debate about the issues raised. Children are encouraged to clarify their meanings, make explicit their assumptions, expose ambiguities and inconsistencies and so on. Exciting work has been done by using picture books with very young children (see, for example, Murris 1992). Young children reveal impressive abilities to reason, argue and use talk to communicate meaning through this kind of activity, and develop a range of vital intellectual skills in the process.

One of the clear disadvantages of the classroom environment relative to the home is, of course, to do with the adult–child ratio. For this reason, it is also important to stimulate challenging talk between the children. As a consequence, a range of educators have urged the more extensive use of collaborative groupwork in primary classrooms (see, for example, Dunne and Bennett 1990). As we reviewed earlier, research adopting a Vygotskian perspective (Forman and Cazden 1985) has demonstrated the various ways in which peer interaction during collaborative groupwork can enhance performance and stimulate learning. Requiring children to work in groups to solve problems, carry out investigations, or produce an imaginative response in the form of writing, drama, dance or whatever, is potentially of enormous benefit.

It is important to recognise that the value of self-expression is not limited to the medium of language. Requiring children to transform their experiences into various 'symbolic' modes of expression is likely to aid the processes of learning. When children draw, paint, dance, construct, model, make music and, indeed, play, they are engaged in the active process of making sense of their world in a way which is unique and individual to them, of which they are in control. The sheer vigour and enthusiasm with which young children engage in these kinds of activities is an important pointer to their significance.

Although I have attempted to separate out different elements in the psychological processes which relate to children's need for intellectual challenge, I must conclude by emphasising the powerful ways in which all these elements are of a piece. When children are playing, they are also nearly always problem solving, or investigating, or engaging in various forms of self-expression. Play often helps children to place new information in meaningful contexts.

It is also important to recognise the ways in which intellectual challenge contributes to emotional or affective elements of children's development. It is no accident that humans find activities of the type we have discussed here immensely enjoyable. Adults at play, for example, are often enjoying the mental challenge of solving problems (crosswords, jigsaws, puzzles, games) or of expressing themselves (music, art, drama). With enjoyment comes concentration, mental effort, motivation and achievement. Self-expression is important in its own right because it builds upon and enhances children's sense of individuality and self-worth. A child who has experienced the excitement of finding things out for themselves or of solving problems is learning to take risks, to persevere and to become an independent learner.

Implications for the early years teacher

- Provide opportunities for play of all kinds.
- Provide vivid, first-hand, new experiences.
- Place tasks in meaningful contexts: help children to make sense of new experiences by relating them to what they already know.
- Introduce the same idea in a variety of meaningful contexts.
- Organise tasks to stimulate mental activity: adopt problem-solving and investigational approaches wherever possible.
- Provide opportunities for self-expression: when children have learnt something new, give them a chance to make something of their own from it.
- Provide opportunities for meaningful conversations between groups of the children, and between the children and adults.

The impact of quality in early years education

It is now well established that a child's educational experience in the early years has both immediate effects upon their cognitive and social development and long-term effects upon their educational achievements and life prospects. Sylva and Wiltshire (1993) have reviewed a range of evidence which supports this position. This evidence includes studies of the Head Start programmes in the USA, the Child Health and Education Study (CHES) of a birth cohort in Britain and Swedish research on the effects of day care.

To begin with these various studies appear to produce inconsistent findings. Early studies of the Head Start programmes suggested immediate cognitive and social gains, but little lasting effect. The CHES study, on the other hand, found a clear association between pre-school attendance and educational achievements at age ten. Further analysis, however, reveals that lasting long-term effects are dependent upon the quality of the early educational experience. Sylva and Wiltshire note particularly the evidence of long-term impact achieved by High/Scope and other high quality, cognitively orientated pre-school programmes.

What emerges as significant about these particularly effective early educational environments is very much in line with the kinds of directions indicated in this chapter. These environments offered real intellectual challenge in the ways we have discussed, with the adult educators very much in the Vygotskian role of 'scaffolding' the child's experience. Within this framework, the child is put very much in control of their own learning.

In the High/Scope regime, for example, the central model of learning is the 'plan, do and review' cycle. Each child plans their activities for the session or the day in a small group with an adult educator. They then move off to carry out the planned activities, and later return to review progress again with their small group and the adult educator. This pattern builds in purposeful adult–child and child–child conversations which seem to Sylva and Wiltshire to be 'an embodiment of Vygotsky's notion of effective instruction within the zone of proximal development'(p. 36). (The High/Scope regime is examined in more detail in chapter 2.)

This way of working also places the responsibility very much on each child for their own learning. What all the high quality early years regimes identified by Sylva and Wiltshire did was to help children develop what they term a 'mastery' orientation to learning and to themselves. This relates very closely to the emotional issues we discussed earlier in the chapter. Children in high quality early years environments developed feelings of high self-esteem, with high aspirations and secure feelings of self-efficacy. Such children grew to believe that, through effort, they could solve problems, understand new ideas, develop skills and so on. They felt in control of their environments and confident in their abilities.

These are some of the themes which this chapter has attempted to illuminate, and which permeate all the other chapters of this book. If we wish to provide quality learning environments for our young children, these need to be informed by understandings about how young children learn and develop. The rest of the present volume is dedicated to indicating how these understandings can be translated, imaginatively and reflectively, into the everyday practice of the early years classroom.

References

Bruce, T. (1987) *Early Childhood Education*, London: Hodder & Stoughton.

Bruner, J.S. (1972) 'The nature and uses of immaturity', *American Psychologist*, 27, 1–28

Davis, A. (1991) 'Piaget, teachers and education: into the 1990's', in P. Light, S. Sheldon and M. Woodhead (eds) *Learning to Think*, London: Routledge.

Donaldson, M. (1978) *Children's Minds*, London: Fontana.

Donaldson, M., Grieve, R. and Pratt, C. (eds) (1983) *Early Childhood Development and Education*, Oxford: Basil Blackwell.

Dunne, E. and Bennett, N. (1990) *Talking and Learning in Groups*, London: Macmillan.

Fisher, R. (ed.) (1987) *Problem Solving in Primary Schools*, Oxford: Basil Blackwell.

—— (1990) *Teaching Children to Think*, Oxford: Basil Blackwell.

Forman, E.A. and Cazden, C.B. (1985) 'Exploring Vygotskian perspectives in education: the cognitive value of peer interaction', in J.V. Wertsch, (ed.) *Culture, Communication and Cognition*, Cambridge: Cambridge University Press.

Gelman, R. and Gallistel, C.R. (1978) *The Child's Understanding of Number*, Cambridge, Mass.: Harvard University Press.

Guha, M. (1987) 'Play in school', in G.M. Blenkin and A.V. Kelly (eds) *Early Childhood Education*, London: Paul Chapman.

Howe, M.J.A. (1984) *A Teacher's Guide to the Psychology of Learning*, Oxford: Basil Blackwell.

Manning, K. and Sharp, A. (1977) *Structuring Play in the Early Years at School*, Cardiff: Ward Lock Educational/ Drake Educational Associates.

Meadows, S. (ed.) (1983) *Developing Thinking*, London: Methuen.

Moll, L.C. (ed.) (1990) *Vygotsky and Education*, Cambridge: Cambridge University Press.

Moyles, J.R. (1989) *Just Playing? The Role and Status of Play in Early Childhood Education*, Milton Keynes: Open University Press.

Murris, K. (1992) *Teaching Philosophy with Picture Books*, London: Infonet Publications Ltd.

Rogers, C. and Kutnick, P. (eds) (1990) *The Social Psychology of the Primary School*, London: Routledge.

Schaffer, R. (1977) *Mothering*, London: Fontana.

Smith, P.K. and Cowie, H. (1991) *Understanding Children's Development*, 2nd Edn, Oxford: Basil Blackwell.

Sylva, K., Bruner, J.S. and Genova, P. (1984) 'The role of play in the problem-solving of children 3–5 years old', in P. Barnes, J. Oates, J. Chapman, V.

Lee and P. Czerniewska (eds) *Personality, Development and Learning*, Sevenoaks: Hodder & Stoughton.

Sylva, K. and Wiltshire, J. (1993) 'The impact of early learning on children's later development: a review prepared for the RSA inquiry "Start Right"', *European Early Childhood Education Research Journal*, 1, 17-40.

Tizard, B. and Hughes, M. (1984) *Young Children Learning: Talking and Thinking at Home and at School*, London: Fontana.

Wood, D. (1988) *How Children Think and Learn*, Oxford: Basil Blackwell.

Basic principles
and approaches

CHAPTER 2

Spinning the plates

ORGANISING THE EARLY YEARS CLASSROOM

Holly Anderson with Tandy Adlam, Penny Coltman, Emma
Cotton and Ros Daniels

Imagine being a juggler spinning plates. The act is a familiar one; it has been performed on stages up and down the country ever since music hall was popular entertainment. The plates spin round, the juggler runs from pole to pole twirling, maintaining momentum, sometimes increasing speed in the nick of time just as a plate begins to fall. For early years educators the management of a classroom can seem like this, juggling the needs and interests of all the children, making sure each one is gainfully occupied. Planning a motivating and purposeful activity for a small group takes an understanding of how children learn, and how teachers can affect that learning; whole class teaching, with all the children involved in the same activity, demands a range of complex skills too; but managing to organise groups of children and individuals so that each child is working at a suitable activity with the right amount of support seems to be the hardest to achieve.

It is easy to see the results of poor management. Children stand around in queues waiting for a small amount of attention from the teacher, frustration arises because children are overdependent on adult support and are unable to function without constant intervention, equipment is lost in the general chaos of a badly organised classroom; all these features cause problems for children and staff alike. However it seems as if the more talented the teacher, the more difficult it is to see the amount of thought and planning that goes on behind the scenes to facilitate the whole range of pupil–teacher interactions. Good teachers make the plate spinning seem easy, almost as if good management is by accident rather than design. The focus for this chapter therefore is to make explicit such skills, to explore how the organisation of the rooms and the management of children, resources and adults can support the education of the children within them.

Curriculum planning is easier to show than classroom management, and yet it is management which reflects the underlying philosophy of what is an appropriate learning environment and reveals our attitude to children as learners, as well as highlighting aspects of the curriculum and the way it is taught. To examine this, it is important to consider first what those of us working with young children feel we should be creating, and why.

Meeting children's needs and practical constraints

In chapter 1 in this book Whitebread refers to love and security, feeling in control, self expression and meaningful contexts as four basic needs young children have. Other early years educationalists would agree with this, supporting the notion that children should be involved in motivating, purposeful tasks and be encouraged to become independent learners. Links between home and school are seen as important to a child's educational success as well as providing security of continuity. Much value is placed on what the child brings to school. The work of the National Writing Project (1989), for example, has shown the amount of literacy knowledge children acquire from living in a print rich environment. This has complemented and reinforced the findings of researchers such as Tizard and Hughes (1984) and Gordon Wells (1987) who showed the subtle complexities of dialogue at home where there is a shared context and frame of reference.

However, in spite of this consensus, there are a number of constraints placed on teachers which make it difficult to put theory and belief into practice. Variables such as the age of the children, the number of children in each class (which at the time of writing is causing much concern with predictions that more and more primary children will be taught in classes of over 30, some over 35), the number of adults working with the children, the support offered by parents, the type of building, the size and shape of the room, the priorities identified by the school, even the type of school (nursery, infant or primary) all affect decisions about class management and organisation.

More recently, the statutory demands imposed by the national curriculum have begun to have an impact too, with studies showing that these do not fit easily into a developmental, holistic approach to teaching and learning (Blenkin and Kelly 1994, Cox and Sanders 1994). Neither does testing at seven, or six in many cases for the youngest Year 2 children, particularly when viewed alongside the importance attached to the results and the possibility of them being used in league tables. This can lead to pressures to implement a subject driven curriculum, and the reception class teacher can find herself at the beginning of the school year with a class of over 30 children, many of whom are under five. It is no wonder that concern is being expressed, not least from the teachers themselves (Pascal 1990, David 1991, Anning 1991, Bennett *et al.* 1992).

There is evidence that we need to share our educational beliefs with the parents of the children we teach, to counteract the growing trend in which parents are attaching more importance to formal acquisition of reading and writing in the early years (DES 1990, Cox and Sanders 1994). To quote from Angela Anning:

> In one sense, infant teachers are simply responding to the demands of society, or more specifically of parents, to get on with ' proper' schooling. On the whole parents favour the old elementary school tradition of instruction in the 3Rs – reading, writing and arithmetic. Froebel, Steiner, Montessori and discovery learning are seen by the majority of parents as the province of a minority of intellectuals and middle class romantic liberals who mostly have a shrewd knowledge of how to work the education system anyway. ' Normal' parents are suspicious of learning through play.
>
> (Anning 1991, p. 17)

It is clear that a partnership in which the school values what children bring from home and parents support the school's approach to education is something we must continue to work towards.

Educational principles and classroom practice

Just how are schools managing to balance the needs of the children they teach with these demands from outside and other constraints? What influence have pioneers such as Montessori and Froebel had on current practice? (see Anning 1991 for a description of ideologies). How are schools creating an environment in which the children have freedom of movement and opportunities to learn through play in the way Piaget (1962) and others have suggested is essential for cognitive development? If we believe in Bruner's (1977) notion of 'scaffolding' and Vygotsky's (1978) emphasis on working alongside children in their 'zone of proximal development', how do we find time to play with the children, supporting and extending their learning? How can those adults working in reception classes build on the good practice that is found in many nursery schools and classes? Bearing in mind that children in most other European countries do not start formal schooling until six, seven in Scandinavia, how do schools in the UK cater for the needs of children of this age? Is there a difference in the way classrooms are organised as the children move from reception into Years 1 and 2? What about those children in vertically grouped classes – is there a marked difference in the education of the four-, five-, six- and seven-year-olds?

In an attempt to answer some of these questions, this chapter looks at four early years teachers and how they manage their classes. Each one approaches her own situation from a different starting point, raising further questions to be considered. These have been put as a focus for discussion so that readers can reflect on some of the underlying issues which need to be explored. Inevitably there is variety in the ways classes are run, not least because of the different ages of the children and the type of school and environment. However, through each narrative a similar thread emerges – a commitment to the children and a determination that the curriculum should work for the children rather than against them.

A nursery class

The first account is from Tandy Adlam, a teacher in a city nursery school. She teaches the youngest of the children in this chapter, all the children being four and under, so for many it will be their first step away from home, the first time they compete for adult attention in a large group, the first time they play alongside other children. These factors have implications for the choices Tandy makes. The type of school also has a bearing; as a nursery school, the adult–pupil ratio is controlled by legislation, and most of the people working with the children are trained, either as nursery nurses or nursery teachers. This too will affect the way that adults are used, as will the fact that the school is organised on High/Scope lines (see Brown 1990). On reading the account, it is interesting to see how people as a resource are managed and how the classroom organisation helps the children adjust to being in a large group away from the familiar home setting.

Tandy's school

The nursery in which I work is purpose built with a large, accessible garden, catering for forty children at any one time. Sometimes activities can spill into an adjoining community room, but for the most part all activities take place in the main nursery room and garden.

There are two teachers, two nursery nurses and a full-time learning support assistant who work as a team, taking a High/Scope approach to classroom organisation. Although the staff plan the curriculum together and work with all the children in the nursery at certain times, each member of staff has particular responsibility for a certain group of children. This means that the children have the security of small group situations and the knowledge that particular adults are responsible for them, so they know who to go to if they are upset, for example. It also means that each member of staff can develop close relationships with the children in their group and monitor the children's progress very closely (see Figure 2.1).

Tandy's classroom

The room is divided into different areas to provide opportunity for the following activities to take place at the same time: painting, collage work and model making, drawing and writing, water play, wet and dry sand play, role-play, woodwork, puzzles and games, as well as construction and block play (see Figure 2.2).

Resources

There is low-level storage furniture in each area containing a selection of equipment, allowing children to choose items they need independently (see Figure 2.3). All equipment is stored in containers labelled with pictures and words, so that children can tell what is inside and replace things easily. The selection of equipment available in an area is changed weekly, to give the children varied experience in each area and to provide for progression in that area during the year.

Figure 2.1 *Tandy Adlam's nursery class: the children enjoy the security of working in a small group*

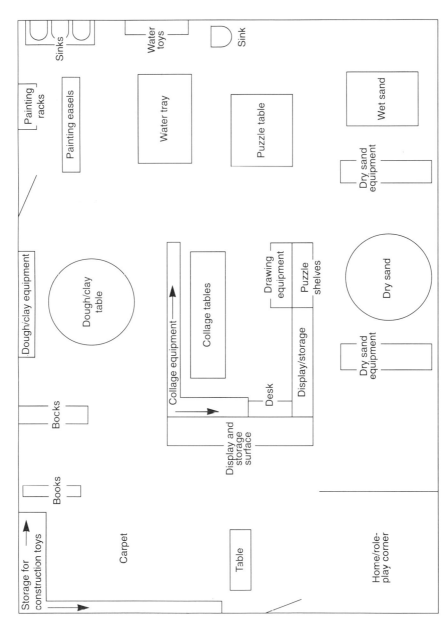

Figure 2.2 *Plan of Tandy Adlam's nursery classroom*

Figure 2.3 *Low-level storage of equipment to allow children independent access*

The pattern of the day

When the children arrive at the nursery they are welcomed by the adult in charge of their group, known as their 'key worker'. They then plan what they are going to do with their key worker, recording their choice pictorially, and setting about the task independently. In this way staff are free to support the children who need help or who are having trouble settling to an activity. At the end of this fifty-minute free choice session the children tidy the nursery and return to their key worker for 'recall time'. They talk about what they have been doing with the other children in their group, which encourages them to use descriptive language, consider the processes they have employed to complete certain activities and encourages them to listen to one another.

After a snack the children go out into the garden for about forty minutes, where again they can choose what they would like to play with. The staff prepare the garden before school each morning, ensuring that a variety of equipment is put out, including climbing apparatus, sand pit toys, wheeled toys, construction toys and role-play apparatus. Each type of equipment is also varied every few days, so for example the children might have funnels, sieves and pipes in the sand, followed by buckets, spades and moulds. Indoor activities are also extended in the garden, as children can engage in large-scale drawing and painting, or experiment with larger-scale water play equipment, for example.

The outdoor session is followed by 'small group time', when the children engage in an activity planned by their key worker. This might be a music or dance session, or a language, maths, art or science activity, giving the staff opportunity to extend children's learning and teach new skills. When planning small group activities, staff refer closely to the individual record sheets that they keep for each child. These records show progress in different High/Scope skill areas, such as language and literacy, movement, creative representation or initiative and social relations, allowing staff to pinpoint areas where children need most support and provide appropriate activities. At the end of group time the children have story time before going home.

Key points

So, in Tandy's school:

- the whole staff is involved in planning, supporting and recording children's learning;
- each member of staff is 'key worker' to a group of children, so that the children, whilst working with different adults, have the security of a central relationship;
- the children move freely between areas and are encouraged to manage their own time, making decisions about their own learning;
- language is seen as central to learning, with children describing both plans and activities to each other in small groups.

A reception class

Next is Emma Cotton, an experienced reception class teacher in an urban primary school. Her children are older, and in statutory school, but are still mainly under five in the autumn term when they all begin school. This means that at first they do not have to follow the National Curriculum, although, as in most nursery and reception classes, preparation for Key Stage 1 is seen as important. Pupil–teacher ratio is no longer controlled by legislation, and inevitably there are fewer adults per child than in Tandy's class. However Emma, like Tandy, does have a trained nursery nurse working with her (not uncommon, but by no means the norm in infant classrooms). The physical environment though is quite different from that of Tandy's class, being converted from a residential dwelling, so on reading this account it is interesting to see how the building has affected organisation. Access to the outside for one class is not easy, but open spaces and working areas have been created within the rooms to give flexibility and freedom of movement.

Emma's unit

It is important to state from the beginning that I am very fortunate to be working in a large building which has been converted specifically to cater for the needs of very young children and resourced both inside and outside with a range of high quality materials. Our early years base occupies a two-storey detached Victorian house with a large garden in which the school pond and wildlife area are also located. The rest of the classes are directly across the road (a leafy, suburban residential area of the city) in what was the original school building. Our unit is self-contained, and the two classes each have 34 reception children with a teacher and full-time nursery nurse; one class upstairs, the other (my class) downstairs.

Emma's classroom

Young children are extremely active individuals and require as much space as is possible in a classroom to work and play. Our room consists of two main spaces with a smaller room at one end, all open so that the children are free to comfortably move between each area. Having a large classroom means there are rarely large numbers of children in one area at any time, but more importantly, groups or individuals have the space in which to lay out the whole set of lego for the day, or to spread out and play the giant Snakes and Ladders game in the middle of the floor. This is not to suggest that the classroom is totally devoid of tables and chairs, but to remember that, as young children enjoy working on the floor and often naturally move their games or books down there, it is essential not to overfill the space (see Figure 2.4).

Our philosophy as teachers is explicit in the ways in which our classrooms are arranged, managed and constantly reviewed. My room is organised into main areas with the majority of resources located accordingly (see Figure 2.5). Broadly, these areas can be recognised as:

- a wet area incorporating sand, water, painting and chalking easels
- the workshop
- the office
- the block room
- the book corner
- the home corner

Figure 2.4 *Emma Cotton's class: reception children happily working on floor space*

- the computer
- the snack area

as well as a large working space in the main room with several tables.

Resources

Round these various areas are located shelves with puzzles, maths and language games and resources, labelled and stored in such a way that the children use them independently.

We believe the children in our unit are efficient, independent organisers of their own time and environment so have designed the classrooms to reflect and facilitate this belief. There is an explicit logic to the way resources are arranged with an expectation that children will understand this organisation and be helped to work and plan their own learning. Children make their own choices, plan their own work and organise their own working spaces. All the resources are visible and accessible to the children at all times, and we try to arrange them in an ordered and attractive way. If the children know where scissors and paper are found and can gather them without asking the teacher for support they become more independent and much time spent on managing the daily routine is released. In addition,

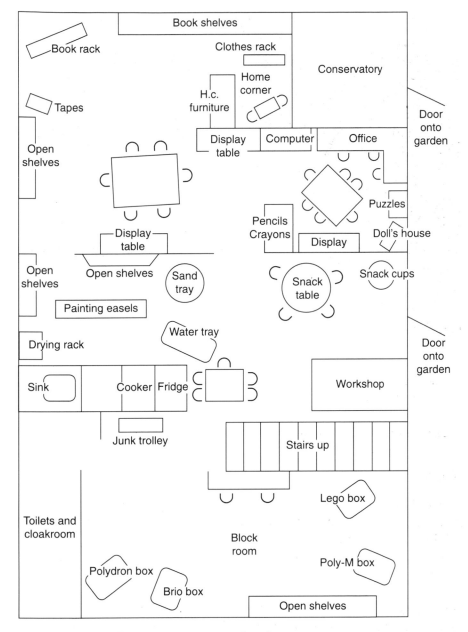

Figure 2.5 *Plan of Emma Cotton's reception classroom*

children know they have to return things and leave an area ready for the next child to use, thus being encouraged to take responsibility both for themselves and each other. This shared responsibility for resources is extended to include such things as changing the scrap materials in the workshop or the painting media used at the easels – we want the children to be aware of their environment and use these observations to enrich their work.

Classroom rules

I think the children feel a greater sense of security when they can understand the framework in which they work, also that they respond more positively when they have played a part in devising these rules. It makes sense to assume that children will want to follow a set of guidelines they can clearly understand and which they can relate to their classroom setting. We have relatively few rules in our class and have decided not to record them in any formal way. In most cases, we arrive at them through discussion with the children when a particular incident has occurred. It seems more effective to have a few meaningful rules than a long list of petty rules which make little sense to the children. Our rules are based around the ways in which we treat people around us, both children and adults; the way we use and respect our environment, and recognising behaviour which is clearly unacceptable and endangers the safety of others.

Planning the work of the adult educators

Once the adult's time is freed from routine management, it can be planned in the way other resources are, with thought given to adult input at all the different areas in the classroom. During the course of the week there will be times when an activity will rely heavily on adult intervention and require specific teaching input. To achieve this, such activities have to be balanced alongside ongoing activities which require less adult presence, and those which children can organise totally unaided. Young children are constantly questioning, discussing, arguing and commenting on what is happening around them and one of our roles is to facilitate this talk, extending and enriching it by sensitive intervention. Therefore we specifically plan for talk within the activities to make sure we are not missing vital opportunities to develop children's language skills. During a set period I will spend time in most areas of the classroom, playing with the children and talking with them. This has not only enabled me to scaffold their learning through play, but, when listening to the richness of conversation taking place in the home corner, the level of collaborative debate at the water tray, the wealth of imaginative language being used at the doll's house, I have a greater awareness of the linguistic skills children bring with them from home which in turn informs my planning and teaching.

Class routines

Whilst planning needs to be flexible, there also has to be a routine and structure, as children like to be able to predict what will happen next in the course of the day. I find it very amusing that, however implicit I consider our class routine to be, the children are incredibly quick to work it out for themselves and to question times when they see this routine being broken. When the school photographer came one morning and upset the routine, all of the children wanted to know when we would be having our PE session, and if I take the language session that the nursery nurse usually takes, most of the children notice and comment. They arrive with established routines from home but with expectations about how life in school will be. School life can be very fragmented but, having a separate unit, we are fortunate to be virtually free of the timetabling restrictions placed on the rest of the school, and apart from PE sessions and one sharing assembly we are able to devise our own pattern to the week.

The pattern of the day

We believe it is important to allow children to work virtually undisturbed and to have the opportunity to become engrossed in an activity without having to repeatedly stop for a television session or assembly. For this reason we do not have any formal registration times and the children have the choice to stay in the classroom during our two outside play sessions. We do feel it important to have some collective time together, so we gather as a class before lunchtime and hometime for stories, singing, sharing of work and class discussions, but for the rest of the time the children know they can come in and start work straightaway. Being familiar with, and feeling an ownership of, the classroom layout enables them to do this without constantly relying on adults. When the children know the pattern to the day and know they can spend as much time as they need on an activity of their choice they can work at their own pace and are more likely to dedicate themselves wholly to the task. We feel that stopping children constantly to fit in with an imposed timetable makes them reluctant to spend quality time on their work, that they see little point in refining, embellishing or simply enjoying an activity. The beauty of having a relatively undisturbed day is that the children are keen to return to activities, confident in the knowledge they can continue without interruption. Obviously there are patterns to the day we need to be aware of, but we have the freedom to extend an activity to the end of a session or to abandon our plans completely to follow an impromptu interest. It is important to have the confidence to do this without constantly looking at our watches, and not to feel we have to be restricted by either the curriculum or the timetable. This does not in any way mean I am suggesting that for the rest of the time the children are free to do whatever they want, rather that within a carefully organised, thoughtfully planned environment they are encouraged to become independent decision makers, familiar with the resources around them, confident in applying their own developing skills and supported by the adults in the class.

Records and assessments

As teachers we obviously have a duty to ensure an equal access to the curriculum for all children and we need to devise our own methods of monitoring not only this, but noting those children who may regularly be avoiding particular areas of the curriculum. We need to keep rigorous notes and observations about every child in the class – in practice often difficult to carry through! Other adults in the class can help here, either by freeing you to work with a particular child or group, or by monitoring the activity themselves.

Key points

Emma's account emphasises:

- ways in which she encourages children to take responsibility for themselves, for their behaviour, for the classroom environment and equipment. The layout of the room, the way in which equipment is stored and labelled, are all designed to this end;
- the involvement of the children in making decisions, which enables them to work independently and with confidence;
- that national curriculum subjects are covered, but there is no feeling that subject teaching dominates;
- that flexibility of working is important within a clear structure; this gives children a feeling of empowerment but also security;
- careful monitoring by the staff ensures that children have a balanced diet of experiences in all areas.

A Year 2 class

With the Rumbold report (DES 1990) stating the need to provide a child-centred curriculum for those under five, those working in reception classes are more able to justify the type of environment Emma has described than perhaps those working with older children. To see whether there is a marked change in organisation to ensure curriculum demands are met, Penny Coltman, who teaches a Year 2 class in a village church school, now describes her situation. These children, in a much smaller primary school than Emma's, are in the main school building and are firmly part of the establishment, old hands in the system with two years of full time education already behind them. This is the year in which they will take national tests in all three core subject areas, so specific aspects of the curriculum need to be taught. Will there be more emphasis on subjects rather than social and emotional needs? Will there be a marked separation between 'work' and 'play'? How does Penny cater for the needs of her six- and seven-year-olds?

Penny's classroom

For two years I shared a teaching post with a compulsive and highly expert furniture mover. Every possible permutation of space, table and storage unit was arranged, employed for about half a term or so and then rearranged. It was a remarkable learning experience. Through this process of regular experiment I discovered that the way to achieve the maximum floor area for children to use is to have as few tables as possible. Floor space is one of the most valuable commodities in the classroom. We sit together on the floor for stories, news times or for decision-making meetings. The children build imaginative layouts on the floor using roads and cars or sets such as Playmobil, and sometimes parts of the floor are covered with enormous PVC cloths , providing an extensive surface for painting or modelling. For these reasons the twenty-nine children in this class mostly work at three large tables positioned around a central space (see Figure 2.6). The 'teacher's desk' is merely a utilitarian piece of furniture in which personal equipment is stored. It is in no way central to the room and the ' teacher' is very rarely to be found anywhere near it. Its chair has long since been commandeered for the computer, providing an ideal height from which children can use a keyboard in comfort. Equipment is there to be used, and so storage is all at child height and clearly labelled. Children are encouraged to see for themselves when materials and apparatus are required, and to collect, use and return them independently. This principle would apply equally to glue pots, number lines or hand lenses.

Children's seating

At the beginning of each year the children are allocated places, after lengthy consultation with their previous teacher to ensure that friends are together

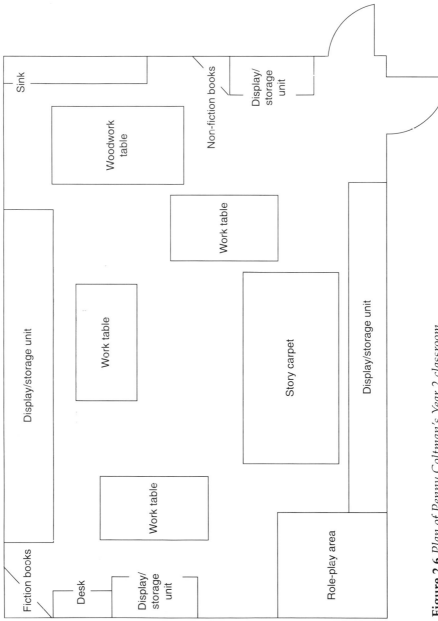

Figure 2.6 *Plan of Penny Coltman's Year 2 classroom*

where possible. This provides a touch of security for children entering a new room. There is a place ready, with a named pencil waiting, and no need to wander around the room looking for a friend or a spare seat. Over the ensuing weeks these placings will evolve rapidly as children ask to move. Such requests are a courtesy and are always granted unless there is simply not enough space on the desired table.

These places are used at the beginning of the day for registration, (knowing approximately where children should be helps to quickly identify absentees), and for a fair proportion of the day's work. Seating will be changed for maths, in which children work in differentiated groups, and on any occasion during the day when children are engaged in co-operative activities and may be working with other friends, either by their choice or mine.

Organisation of activities

Usually all the class will be working on similar tasks at any given time, which might be differentiated by complexity, recording method or outcome. Balance of curriculum is a constant consideration. Some areas are allotted fixed times, usually because of external factors. Maths is always at the same times partly because parents come in to help but also because all classes within Key Stage 1 have maths at the same times to enable fine tuning of differentiation by moving children between classes. Conversely, other areas of the curriculum are varied through the week, and there is no fixed daily or weekly routine. Activities are fitted in so as to provide the children with a varied diet. The result of this ranges from a quiet calm in which everyone is reading, drawing or writing, to a wonderful impression of organised chaos as we indulge 'en masse' in craft, art or technology. The moment at which a brilliant end product arises like a phoenix from this turmoil of activity is one of life's pleasures, and the grand clearing up operation is a lesson in itself. Being 'in charge of the bin bag' is seen as a highly prestigious position!

Role-play, fantasy and self-esteem

Developing a sense of cohesion within the class is one of the central aspects of my philosophy as a teacher and various techniques are used to promote this. One of the most important is the use of role-play and fantasy in the classroom, in which aspects of current topics are adopted and extended as classroom themes. A major project at the beginning of each term is the construction of a new topic-related role-play area in a sunny corner of the room. These areas are built for the children to play in, by the children themselves. They are large-scale and bold in design, providing a visual focus which has immediate impact when one enters the room. This collaborative construction not only acts as a topic stimulus but involves all the children in a practical and purposeful design and technology exercise which encourages the exploration and development of some imaginative and at times sophisticated engineering ideas. The proportionately large amount of space allocated to these areas, which have included teepees, tree houses, castles and hot air balloons, as well as more conventional shops and homes, is a reflection of the high status attributed to role-play in the classroom. Children in Year 2 are still very much in need of all the opportunities to explore concepts through enactment, benefiting from the associated linguistic activities and interactions.

Role-play will also become an integral part of the working day, permeating even the mundane and routine. An illustration of this approach was within a recent topic on sea travel. Every member of the class worked together to build role-play area in the form of a pirate ship, The Red Shark. In the interests of democracy the name of the ship was chosen by ballot. From this moment our classroom ceased to exist as we became crew members. Each child (and their teacher!) chose a suitably bloodthirsty pirate name by which they were addressed at all times, including registration. We adjourned to the ' main deck' for assemblies, and to 'the heads' when we needed the lavatory. Those of us who brought sandwiches for lunch had 'ship's biscuits', and the rest ate 'hot rations' in the 'galley'. We regularly 'cleaned the decks', were visited by either landlubbers, enemy crew or captains from other ships, and the biggest treat of all, for those who had achieved beyond the call of duty was to be forced to 'walk the plank!' At the end of the half term topic we celebrated with a Pirate Feast for which the crew prepared an amazing variety of theme related food.

Activities like this are not only great fun, but they also encourage a sense of pride and ownership as children develop a perception of their classroom as a place over which they have some influence and control. Similarly as collaborative skills develop, so does an awareness of collective responsibility, and caring, not only for the environment, but for each other. Courtesy within the classroom and empathy towards each other are qualities which are actively encouraged by example and request. The contributions made by children with learning difficulties to co-operative projects are just as valued as those made by the very able. Role-play in particular is an area in which children with special needs may shine. The consequent fillip to the self-esteem of these children, and the benefits of this to their progress is unquestionable.

Involving parents

A happy and open relationship with parents, based on confidence and trust, is crucial to the building of a successful relationship with their

Figure 2.7 *Penny Coltman's Year 2 class: the importance of role-play and fantasy*

children. Good communication is essential and parental visits to the class-room in the mornings as children are delivered are seen as valuable contact times, as are moments by the school gates at the end of the day. This is complimented by use of the usual reading record as an all purpose two-way news channel.

Parents are invited and indeed encouraged to be involved in many class-room activities. Several groups of children working on, for example, mathematics at the same time can be impossibly demanding on teacher input. Parents who have been suitably briefed provide a first point of reference to children playing a number game or solving a spatial problem. The regular contributions of volunteer parents working with me in listening to children read, result in every child in the class receiving uninterrupted hearing time at least three times a week, with more for those in difficulty. Sometimes the bonuses are unexpected. On countless occasions parents who have become involved as helpers have proved to be invaluable sources of both inspiration and practical support. In many ways parents are among the most valuable of available resources, and it is a great pity that this degree of voluntary support within the nation's classrooms is given so little formal recognition.

Key points

Penny, working with older children in a Year 2 class, displays some similarities of approach to those of Tandy and Emma:

- The children are given as much freedom of choice and independence in their learning as possible.
- With the older children there is still space for floor activities.
- A role play area is seen as enhancing learning across many curriculum areas.
- A concern is still clear to ensure that the children feel emotionally secure.

but also some differences:

- Alone with no other trained staff, she has to rely on parent volunteers for help so she includes this in her organisation, making it as easy as possible for those who can spare some time to work with her and the children.
- With older children, the range of needs widens, so support from parents and even across classes is considered enabling activities to be structured to best meet these needs. The timetable is planned with this in mind, as is the grouping of the children.
- Groups are flexible and designed for different purposes, but are often meant to reinforce collaboration. Whilst it is important to allow younger children opportunities to work together, it is as the children get older that more weight is given to collaborative learning.

A vertically grouped class

So all three teachers so far have very similar values. This is echoed in the final description by Ros Daniels who teaches a vertically grouped Key Stage 1 Class in a large town. In an infant school the whole staff can work together on designing a curriculum appropriate to the needs of the young children they teach. Ros and her colleagues have wanted to find ways in which to give the children in their care security and self-esteem, at the same time making learning both challenging and purposeful for all three year groups in each class.

Ros's infant school

During the last few years we, as a staff of a large infant school with a nursery class and hearing impaired unit, have developed a system which we feel meets the requirements of the national curriculum whilst at the same time being compatible with child-centred teaching and learning. Our policies are written by the whole staff and reflect the overall positive approach we have in our school towards all aspects of the children's learning and development. We have chosen to use developmental approaches in many areas of the curriculum; as a result no formal schemes are used in any subject areas and we encourage the children to take responsibility for their own learning during a daily timetabled session called 'planned activity time' (PAT). The children in the hearing impaired unit, taught a natural aural approach, integrate as fully as possible in the other classes, thus learning with the other children. As a staff we are constantly discussing the best ways to meet the needs of the children and we decided last year to restructure the classes so that we each now teach a vertically grouped class of Reception, Year 1 and Year 2 children.

The class rules

A key element in our philosophy is a positive behaviour policy based upon rights, rules and responsibilities, with the emphasis on the children taking control of their own behaviour within a highly structured environment (see Figure 2.8). Each class draws up its own set of rules which are then published so that the children know exactly what is expected of them. They can then enjoy their rights within this structured and clear framework and are consequently encouraged to take responsibility for themselves.

This independence and responsibility is achieved in a variety of ways. For example, the children go to the toilet without asking permission by placing their name card in a chart and they can have a drink in the classroom whenever they are thirsty. A sound chart is a visible reminder for the children to work within the agreed sound level.

THE FRAMEWORK OF OUR BEHAVIOUR POLICY

These 3 strands of discipline should work together to create a caring community atmosphere.

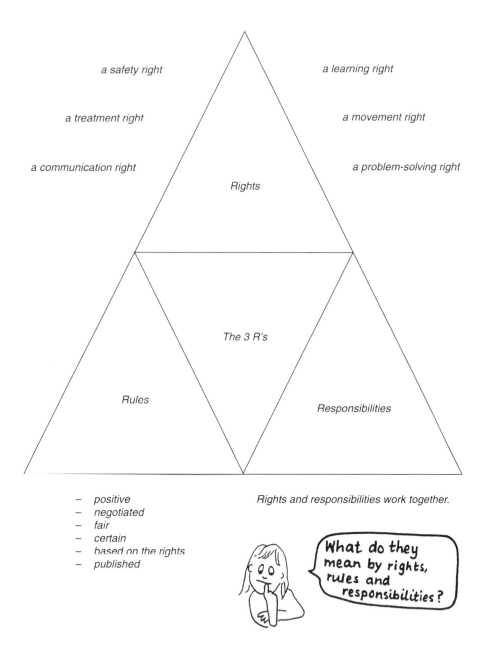

- positive
- negotiated
- fair
- certain
- based on the rights
- published

Figure 2.8 *The 3 Rs: rights, rules and responsibilities*

The pattern of the day

We feel the children need security as well as ownership. The way we negotiate the rules reflects both of these, as does the way we plan each day. This is a typical day in school:

Time	Activity
8.50	Children arrive at school and are individually welcomed. Books in book bags are changed ready to take home.
9.10	Register involving children (e.g. instead of saying their names or 'Yes, Miss', children are asked to complete a sentence started by the teacher. For example: 'I would like to . . . I like it when . . .')
9.20	Spelling activities, often with a partner (look, cover, write, check; multisensory sheets)
9.40	Maths activities (a variety on offer to meet different needs and abilities)
10.15	Playtime
10.35	Assembly
11.00	Planned activity time (PAT) Planning – verbal, storyboarding, design sheets, listing equipment, pictures Activity Recall/review in large group or with partners
12.00	Lunchtime
1.10	Register involving children (e.g. 'my favourite story is . . .) and friendship circles (self-esteem activities)
1.30	Writing workshop and sharing of writing
2.15	Reading session, apprenticeship approach (children read in a variety of ways in terms of groupings. Usually a collaborative partnership.)
2.45	Gathering together on the carpet in the reading area. Story: from the author of the week (e.g. Jan Ormerod)
3.00	Hometime

Whole class activities and groupwork

Each day has timetabled sessions which have a clearly defined beginning and end. In addition to this are curriculum input sessions which may be whole class activities or direct teaching of skills to a specific group of children. Examples of these are:

Writing workshops

These sessions vary in length and format. They involve the children in both collaborative and individualised writing activities. It is a designated writing time for children and adults. Many writing contexts are offered, from journal writing to writing in role, writing books and letters; giving a wide range of choices across a variety of genres.

A science input on air

The children are grouped according to their experience and provided with appropriate activities based upon the theme of air. Most of these sessions end with a sharing of all the activities engaged in by the class. These will include illustrative and investigative activities. These activities are recorded by an adult in each child's science diary with a diagnostic comment in shorthand.

Planned activity time

Alongside this teaching we operate PAT which encourages the children to take control of their own learning. This is a daily timetabled session in which children cannot be withdrawn by an adult for any reason. Although the children decide for themselves what they want to do, it is in no way a traditional 'choosing' time. Children are required to:

- initiate and plan their chosen activity;
- organise themselves;
- follow through their activity;
- review, recall and record their activity.

The children decide which of the classroom areas to work in and this is recorded and monitored by the teacher. They can spend between three and six sessions, by negotiation, in any one area and the children are encouraged to have autonomy over their work, the adult's role is that of facilitator and enabler.

The classroom environment

In order to work as we do, the classroom needs to be organised to give maximum space to the children and provide a range of starting points for their ideas. Interactive displays in the school, thematic collections of carefully selected resources, entice the children to explore a range of ideas. Simple stick puppets in a display, for example, encourage the children to re-enact the stories contained in surrounding books.

As another example, we used the story of 'Mrs Wishy Washy' (from the Story Chest books) to create a display which included fluffy slippers, a mop cap, an apron and a scrubbing brush, then provided a duck, a pig and a cow for the children to wash. Tabard costumes with animal headbands enabled the children to dress up as animals to enact the story and animal puppets invited a puppet show version to be created. A display such as this could also extend to a wider theme on farm animals, or keeping clean. We recently used this story to test out washing powders on muddy clothes! These displays provide a fundamental part of the children's learning, contributing to their independence.

Core areas in the classroom also give opportunities for children to create their own learning environment at whatever level is appropriate for them. The classroom (see Figure 2.9) therefore contains:

A reading area with:

- baskets of books
- baskets of props, puppets and toys to use with the books
- 2-D displays on pinboard
- tape recorder and tapes
- collections of stories
- author of the week
- wall diary etc.

A writing area with:

- hats (writing in role)
- pens, paper, felts
- paper: sizes, colours, shapes
- diaries
- telephones
- message pads
- menu layouts
- plans
- maps
- post box
- stamps
- sellotape etc.

A role-play area (changed half-termly), for example:

- castle
- museum
- art gallery

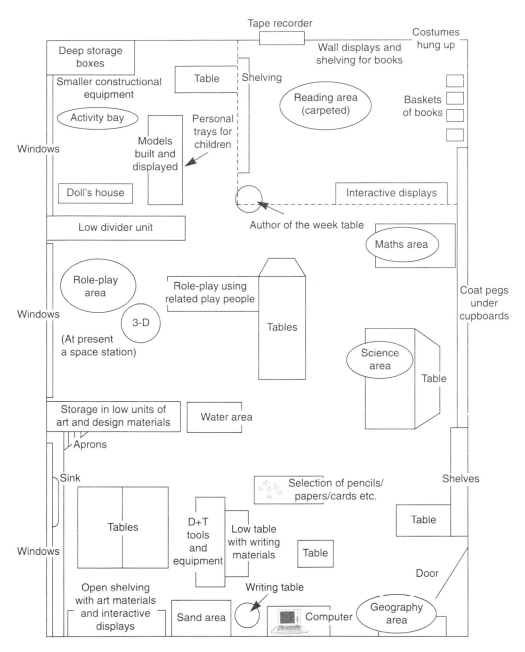

Figure 2.9 *Plan of Ros Daniel's vertically grouped classroom*

- rainforest
- cave
- jungle
- underwater
- world
- space
- North Pole
- pirate ship

A sand area with a range of equipment to encourage story making:

- animals
- dinosaurs
- wood
- string
- tools
- lollipop sticks
- playpeople
- trucks
- pulleys etc.

A water area with a range of equipment to encourage story making:

- water animals
- ice animals
- boats
- divers
- containers
- syringes
- shells
- pipes

An activity bay with:

- a range of small world role-play and constructional equipment (e.g. Playpeople contexts)

There are also art, design and making, science and maths areas all containing an interactive display plus a range of appropriate equipment and resources and we create a number of cross-curricular areas to link with the current topic or interests when the need arises.

These areas provide a stimulating and enticing environment which, supported by the way we organise the timetable, give the children control and motivation in their learning. We are fully committed to empowering the children and have adopted policies and practices which will allow this. By encouraging the children to take responsibility for their own learning we are enabling them to become both autonomous and confident learners – surely an essential aim at Key Stage 1.

Key points

Ros Daniels' approach again has similarities with the others:

- An emphasis on children developing autonomy and responsibility as learners: PAT time has similarities with the High/Scope organisation and she encourages her infant children to plan their work in the way that Tandy Adlam does with her nursery class.
- As with Penny's Year 2 class, specific curriculum areas are identified in the classroom organisation and there is a greater sense of the timetable including 'writing' and 'reading' activities. This appears to be a response to the more structured needs of the older children.
- An emphasis on children developing positive attitudes to themselves and to others.
- A concern to offer children as wide a range as possible of experiences and good quality resources.

The early years tradition and classroom organisation

What is striking is the extent to which all four teachers have, directly or indirectly, been influenced by a tradition of early years practice observed and described so eloquently by Susan Isaacs working in the early part of this century. Her philosophy is described thus:

> It is significant that Susan Isaacs saw the role of the teacher as not only supportive but interventionalist. The teacher must 'have the right answer ready for an intellectual problem' and is there to 'meet' the children's free enquiry and activity with careful structuring of learning experiences and situations. Though she valued observation of young children as highly as Maria Montessori and appreciated the values of the maternal nurturing role, she saw the role of the teacher as far more specialised, positive and active in promoting the child's learning.
>
> (Anning 1991, p. 15)

In the words of a teacher, Evelyn Lawrence, who worked at her school:

> the children do what appeals to them at the moment. The work of the educator is to select his material, and at times indirectly suggest activities, that the child will of his own accord do things which are useful for his work. Lately one or two of the children have drawn up rough outlines of their day's work . . . They are urged to answer their own questions, with the teachers to help them discover where the answers are to be found.
>
> (Drummond 1993, p. 18)

This child-centred, developmental pedagogy is not easy to maintain, as Drummond goes on to explore; there are tensions in balancing the needs of the individual with the needs of the group, especially when a statutory curriculum imposes its own restrictions. The teachers in this chapter show how much their organisation plays a part in supporting them, in partnership with a number of other adults, meet the children's needs in both affective and cognitive domains. The way the classrooms are managed enables the adults to have opportunities to be facilitators, enablers and instructors. Andrew Pollard and his co-writers (1993) see this teaching and learning process as a social construction of meaning, and suggest that there are three important conditions for this model of teaching to be put into effective practice:

- provision of a classroom context in which children are enabled to control and manage the construction of meaning and understanding;
- effective assessment and communication with the children so that relevant adult support and instruction is identified;
- provision of appropriate adult support and instruction for the subjects which form the curriculum.

(Pollard *et al.* 1993, p. 36)

There is no one way to organise a classroom, there are so many variables, so many factors to consider. However, by examining the practice of four early years specialists, a number of practical issues have been raised in the context of specific situations, which it is hoped will provide a framework through which the rest of the book can be viewed. Each of the teachers in this chapter manages to keep the plates spinning and puts the needs of the children at the centre of her plans, creating an environment in which all the children have some freedom to explore aspects of their world which fascinate, perplex and challenge them.

Pointers for organising the early years classroom

Points to take into account when considering how to use and organise the available resources in your classroom:

- Make the spaces in your classroom as flexible as possible; provide some usable floor space; be prepared to experiment with different arrangements.
- Provide children with opportunities to work in a variety of ways (alone, in groups, with an adult etc). The degree of structure and direction in tasks will depend upon the age range of the children.
- Provide flexibility and choice of activities.
- Give children responsibility and independence, including access to the resources they will need and opportunities to make decisions.
- Set and maintain clear rules and structures so that children have security.
- Make sure all adults are clear about their roles, and involve them in decision making.

References

Anning, A. (1991) *The First Years at School: Education 4 to 8*, Buckingham: Open University Press.

Bennett, S. and Kell, J. (1989) *A Good Start? Four Year Olds in Infant Schools*, Oxford: Basil Blackwell.

Bennett, S., Wragg, E., Carre, C., Carter, D. (1992) 'A longitudinal study of primary teachers' perceived competence in, and concerns about, National Curriculum implementation', *Research Papers in Education*, 7, pp. 53–78.

Blenkin, G. and Kelly, V. (eds) (1994) *The National Curriculum and Early Learning: An Evaluation*, London: Paul Chapman.

Brown, M. (1990) *An Introduction to High/Scope Approach to the National Curriculum*, Michigan: High/Scope Press.

Bruner J. (1977) *The Process of Education*, Cambridge, Mass.: Harvard University Press.

Cox, T. and Sanders, S. (1994) *The Impact of the National Curriculum on the Teaching of Five Year Olds*, London: Falmer Press.

David, T. (1991) *Under Five – Under Educated?*, Milton Keynes: Open University Press.

DES (1990) *Starting with Quality* (The Rumbold Report), London: HMSO.

Drummond, M.J. (1993) *Assessing Children's Learning*, London: David Fulton.

National Writing Project (1989) *Becoming a Writer*, Walton-on-Thames: Nelson

Pascal, C. (1990) *Under Fives in the Infant Classroom*, Stoke on Trent: Trentham Books.

Piaget, J. (1962) *Play, Dreams and Imitation in Childhood*, London: Routledge and Kegan Paul.

Pollard, A., Osborn, M., Abbott, D., Broadfoot, P. and Croll, P. (1993) 'Balancing priorities: children and the curriculum in the Nineties', in R.J. Campbell (ed.) *Breadth and Balance in the Primary Curriculum*, London: Falmer Press.

Tizard, B. and Hughes, M. (1984) *Young Children Learning: Talking and Thinking at Home and at School*, London: Fontana.

Vygotsky, L.S. (1978) *Mind in Society: The Development of Higher Psychological Processes* , Cambridge, Mass.: Harvard University Press.

Wells, G. (1987) *The Meaning Makers: Children Learning Language and Using Language to Learn*, Sevenoaks: Hodder & Stoughton.

CHAPTER 3

'My mum would pay anything for chocolate cake!'

ORGANISING THE WHOLE CURRICULUM: ENTERPRISE PROJECTS IN THE EARLY YEARS

Penny Coltman and David Whitebread

In the last few years, with the introduction of a statutory National Curriculum in maintained schools in England and Wales, there has inevitably been huge controversy about the curriculum. As regards its impact on the education of children in the four to eight years age range, some commentators have taken the extreme view that the National Curriculum is fundamentally at odds with early years education (e.g. Blenkin and Kelly 1994). Others have argued, however, that while there are dangers and difficulties, with imagination early years educators can be true to their principles, stay within the law, and provide the young children in their care with an appropriate, rich and stimulating curriculum (see, for example, the Early Years Curriculum Group 1989). This is the position taken within the present chapter. We want to discuss what the principles for such an early years curriculum might be, and then to demonstrate how these might be brought to life through one particular approach involving the use of enterprise projects.

The national curriculum and the early years curriculum

This chapter is not intended as a critique of the National Curriculum. However, its introduction in England and Wales has raised a number of issues which need to be addressed when we come to think about organising a curriculum for young children. These issues can be identified in terms of dangers or problems, on the one hand, and benefits, on the other hand, inherent in the National Curriculum approach.

Dangers and problems of the national curriculum

There are a number of dangers in the approach to the curriculum underlying the National Curriculum. We want to just mention three:

The early years and Key Stage 1

There has been a lack of clarity, and some consequent debate about precisely when young children should begin the national curriculum. As a result, in some schools children will be introduced to elements of the National Curriculum during their reception year (i.e. the year in which children become five years old), as they become 'ready', while in other schools the National Curriculum is not begun until Year 1 (i.e. the year which all children begin as five-year-olds). Whichever date is taken, however, there is a very real danger of 'downward' pressure on the early years curriculum. Early years educators working with three- to five-year-olds may be encouraged to view their work as a 'preparation' for the National Curriculum, and this can have a distorting influence. In particular, there is a danger that this kind of pressure can result in young children being hurried on to tasks for which they do not have the prerequisite skills and understandings. Particular concern has been expressed about the influence on four-year-olds in reception classes (e.g. see Cleave and Brown, 1991, whose book provides an excellent outline of an appropriate curriculum for four-year-olds). Here there is some evidence that children have been provided with a diet of seat-based, pencil and paper types of tasks at too early a stage. This kind of inappropriate provision can result in a loss of confidence amongst young children, and the development of entirely unhelpful anxieties about certain kinds of tasks (e.g. reading and writing, written numbers etc.). In the home context young children learn very effectively through various informal means when no one is deliberately attempting to 'teach' them anything. Continuity in terms of the ways in which young children are expected to learn is just one of the features of good links between the worlds of home and school which need to be in place if young children are to thrive in their first years in school.

We know from a range of research (e.g. Bennett *et al.* 1984) that it is enormously difficult to set tasks which are at precisely the appropriate level for each of the individual children in a primary school classroom. It is clearly vital that educators of young children make their judgements about appropriate tasks entirely on the basis of their understandings about young children's learning, and their knowledge of the particular children. Pressure to 'prepare' pre-school, nursery and reception children for Key Stage 1 can be entirely counter-productive.

A curriculum of separate subjects

A number of features of the ways in which the National Curriculum was established have been unhelpful in relation to the early years. From the outset the curriculum was conceived as consisting of a list of separate subjects. The curriculum for each of these subjects has been drawn up and revised by committees which have been dominated by subject specialists with higher education and secondary school backgrounds. It has been a major source of concern that separating out the curriculum into subjects in this way can lead to an 'artificiality' or lack of coherence in the educational experience offered to the young child. There is a strong tradition amongst early years educators that young children need an integrated curriculum, and this is a view supported by recent research (reviewed in chapter 1) emphasising the significance of 'meaningful contexts' for young children's learning. While the National Curriculum may have been presented as separate subjects, it is therefore vitally important that an integrated, topic-based approach is maintained within the early years. Palmer and Pettitt (1993), amongst others, have demonstrated very well how such an approach can be developed which is compatible with the National Curriculum. The enterprise projects described below (pages 61–71) within the present chapter are a particular example of a method of providing young children with a powerful, holistic experience which nevertheless covers a wide range of curriculum areas.

The 'delivery' model

The language of the National Curriculum documents has also reflected a bias towards an inappropriate model of teaching and learning in relation to the early years. These documents talk of the educator 'delivering' the curriculum to the children. Concerns about this model, and a perceived emphasis (particularly in earlier versions of the National Curriculum) on subject knowledge, have led to worries about the young child being placed in an unhelpfully passive learning role. As has also been reviewed in chapter 1, there is clear evidence from research that young children learn most effectively by means of 'active' styles of learning.

Allied to this concern has been the danger of a kind of 'tick list' approach to the curriculum. Once a particular aspect of the curriculum has been 'delivered' to the children, and some rudimentary assessment has been made that they have 'received' it, this aspect can be ticked off as having been covered, and we do not need to worry about it any more. In fact, of course, as anyone who has ever worked with young children is only too aware, the relationship between what we as educators attempt to 'teach' a child and what that child actually learns from the experience is often far more complex. Certainly, the development of skills and understandings by young children involves a highly active and complex set of processes which we are far from understanding. It is clear, also, that there are many and various ways and styles of learning, so that an activity or experience which might be highly effective for one child will be no help whatsoever to another. Effective teaching is, therefore, likely to involve constant revisiting of areas through a diversity of meaningful tasks which engage, in a variety of ways, the active involvement of young learners.

Benefits of the National Curriculum

On the other hand, the introduction has brought a number of direct and indirect benefits to early years education. Once again, we want to mention three:

Skills and understandings at Key Stage 1

The concerns about the overloading of the curriculum with subject content have not been nearly so great at Key Stage 1 as they have at later stages. On the whole, the curriculum at Key Stage 1 has been a helpful description of the skills and understandings which might reasonably be expected of young children. If anything, the main criticism would be that in some areas the abilities of young children have been under-estimated. Nevertheless, the statement of the curriculum contained in the Key Stage 1 statutory orders has largely given official recognition to a process of change in the early years curriculum from 'product' and towards 'process' which has been proceeding and gathering pace throughout the second part of this century. Fisher (1987) has neatly described this gradual but inexorable change in practice as one which:

> moves from simply teaching the children the facts of language, mathematics, history, geography, science and other 'disciplines', towards encouraging children to be scientists, historians, geographers, linguists and mathematicians, through the use of appropriate problem-solving skills and processes.
>
> (Introduction)

A broad and balanced curriculum

As well as giving official backing to modern early years practice in terms of styles of teaching and learning, the National Curriculum has confirmed the expansion of the curriculum for young children from the traditional 'three Rs' to a broader and more balanced diet. This, once again, is the culmination of a process which has been developing officially and unofficially for many years. The areas of learning and experience identified by HMI (DES 1985) in an earlier attempt to define the school curriculum (linguistic and literary, mathematical, aesthetic and creative, human and social, physical, scientific, technological, moral and spiritual) had already been widely accepted and used by early years educators (e.g. ILEA 1987; Drummond *et al.* 1989). While there may be concerns about the separation of the curriculum into distinct subjects, the requirement to introduce young children to skills and under-standings under such a wide range of subject headings does help to ensure, as Palmer and Pettitt (1993) have argued, that each child receives the broad and balanced curriculum to which they are entitled.

Re-evaluation of young children's learning

Some aspects of the introduction of the National Curriculum have obliged early years educators to re-evaluate their understandings about children's learning. The concomitant new arrangements for assessment, now co-ordi-nated by SCAA (School Curriculum and Assessment Authority), have obliged teachers to make assessments of children's skills and understand-ings in a much more analytical manner than hitherto. This has resulted in wide discussion amongst teachers and other early years educators concern-ing such matters as the validity and reliability of different kinds of evidence for children's learning, the sequence of children's learning in different areas, different levels of learning or understanding, and so on.

The new arrangements for school inspections, now organised by OFSTED (Office for Standards in Education), have obliged teachers to produce plans which more explicitly than before identify the intended 'learning outcomes' of the various activities and tasks for the children, and to think critically about the quality of learning taking place in their classrooms. As Anning (1991) has argued, there are a range of influences on early years educators' beliefs and understandings about young children's learning. They are influ-enced by the traditional beliefs and values of early years education as identified so helpfully, for example, by Bruce (1987). They are also influenced by their social and cultural surroundings, by the findings of developmental psychologists, by their own experiences as a learner, and by their experience of working on a daily basis with young children. What is clear, however, is that the quality of early years education can only be enhanced by these beliefs and understandings being made explicit, being articulated, and being con-stantly re-evaluated and examined in the light of new evidence.

There is no doubt that the last few years have been ones of considerable turmoil in education, and that teachers and other educators have been pulled in different directions, often as a consequence of muddle and lack of forethought amongst those in positions of power. However, now that the dust has settled to some extent, a clearer picture is emerging and it is not one which is entirely incompatible, in the present authors' view, with early years principles. One example of this might be the role afforded to play as a learning medium in early years classrooms. The important role of 'active', self-directed modes of learning, often in the form of one or other kind of play, has long been recognised by early years educators. There appears, however, possibly under the pressure referred to above to 'prepare' children for the National Curriculum, to have been a decline in the provision for play within early years classrooms. It is significant, if perhaps a little ironic, that in the recent OFSTED report on teaching in Reception classes (OFSTED 1993), which was generally very complimentary, the one area of concern expressed related to the lack of opportunities for children to learn through appropriately structured play. It is to be hoped that this new pressure from the inspection arrangements will counteract the earlier effect and give reception and other early years educators the strength to provide appropriately in this regard for their young children.

Principles for an early years curriculum

Through all this debate, in the view of the present authors, there are a number of important principles which should guide the content and organisation of the early years curriculum. These principles derive from the evidence about children's learning, and from the collective experiences and views of early years educators, as discussed in chapter 1. Despite the dangers, the National Curriculum is not necessarily incompatible with these principles, but they should guide the way it is taught and managed.

At this point it is worth reminding ourselves about the needs of young children identified in chapter 1. For the curriculum to be effective and appropriate, it needs to take into account these needs. As was argued there, to learn effectively young children need a curriculum and a style of teaching which provides them with emotional security and feelings of being in control. Young children need a curriculum which starts with what they understand and can do already, and helps them make sense of their world by providing them with meaningful tasks, which require their active engagement, and which give them opportunities to express their understandings in a variety of media, principally through imaginative play and talk. Young children's natural curiosity can be stimulated to help them learn effectively by providing novel first-hand experiences and opportunities to explore, investigate and solve problems.

From these understandings we have derived four principles which we believe should guide the organisation and management of the early years curriculum. These principles are as follows. Young children's learning will be enhanced when:

1 the content of the curriculum is **'meaningful'** to them and related to their existing knowledge and interests;

2 they are **active participants in their learning** rather than just passive recipients; they should have opportunities to make their own decisions about their learning;

3 they are encouraged to indulge their natural inclination to engage in **imaginative play** related to significant life experiences;

4 they are **emotionally secure** because there is continuity and good communication between the worlds of home and school.

Enterprise projects

These principles clearly support an integrated, topic-based approach, and this can be carried out in a whole variety of ways. In the remainder of this chapter, however, we want to demonstrate one kind of approach which seems to embody these principles in a particularly powerful way. This approach consists of what has been termed 'enterprise' projects (see DES 1990, for a general review of this kind of work in primary schools). In essence these consist of using some kind of adult 'enterprise' or place of work as a starting point, and enabling children to explore and investigate it, partly by carrying out a similar kind of enterprise themselves.

Over the last five years the authors have carried out an enterprise project each year with classes of young children ranging from Reception to Year 2. These have been focused on a bakery, puppet theatres, a newspaper, a museum, and a fashion show. The details of some of these projects have been reported elsewhere (Coltman and Whitebread 1992; Whitebread *et al.* 1993, 1994, 1995). What follows is a description of these projects and an analysis of the ways in which such projects provide a powerfully effective curriculum for children in the early years, particularly in relation to the four principles identified above.

All the projects involved the following basic elements:

- a visit to a local workplace to find out, by a variety of means, about the kinds of work carried out and the people who worked there;

- the children engaging in a related, small, real enterprise of their own, which involved research, planning, production, advertising, accounting etc.;
- opportunities for the children to represent their experiences for themselves in a variety of ways, through talk, play, drawing, modelling and writing;
- a fixed 'end point' in the form of an event towards which children could work and to which friends and families could be invited.

Learning through 'meaningful' work

The first principle is concerned with the extent to which the content of the curriculum is 'meaningful' to young children and related to their existing knowledge and interests. This also relates to the links between home-based styles of learning which are informal and for real purposes and school-based styles of learning which sometimes suffer by comparison by being formal and purposeless from the child's point of view. Research in relation to both language (Tizard and Hughes 1984) and mathematics (Hughes 1986) has demonstrated that most children find the informal, 'real' world of the home and the community a much more conducive environment for learning than the artificial and, from the child's point of view, 'meaningless' tasks of traditional schooling. This has led to a developing new pedagogy which emphasises the importance of children within school carrying out tasks for 'real' purposes within the context of real-world situations and problems (see, for example, Hall 1989, in relation to language and Atkinson 1992, in relation to maths).

This 'authenticity' was established within the enterprise projects which we carried out in a number of ways:

- **The localness of the workplaces** visited gave them a meaningfulness to the children through familiarity. The local newspaper was taken by many of the children's families, many had already visited the local museum and some of the children's friends and relations worked at the local bakery.

- **Projects related to the children's interests** e.g.: the bakery mainly made Christmas puddings; the puppet show gave them an opportunity to re-enact one of their favourite stories (Cinderella and Snow White were chosen, somewhat adapted to give everyone a part!); the contents of the newspaper they produced contained items of interest to them: reviews of latest children's films, a fashion page complete with photographs of six-to seven-year-old 'models' (an interest later developed in the fashion show project), Aunt Sherry's Problem Page (Dear Aunt Sherry, my brother is a pain in the neck!), and a page of Houses for Sale (the children's own houses, drawn and described by them – see Figure 3.1); the museum set up by the children exhibited artefacts provided by themselves, their families, village friends and the school and focused on the history of the school and the village.

House for sale. 5 bedrooms.
Dining room. Conservatory.
2 toilets. Kitchens. Large
pond in garden. Quiet area.
Good Price.
£80,000.

A lovely house with a large garden.
Close to the shops. Near to a school.
It has 1 main bedroom and a lounge.
1 roof garden and your own little
parking space next to the house.
Price £40,000.

This house has 2 bedrooms.
1 pool. Room under stairs.
Double glazing. Double bed.
A vase of flowers. It's a
bargain.
Price 70,000.

1 bed. home. Ballet room.
Disco room. 1 big bathroom
and a nice size kitchen.
Swimming pool and stable.
Come soon.
Price £100,000.

Figure 3.1 *The children advertise their own houses for sale*

- **A wide range of opportunities for learning through 'real' work including**:

writing for real purposes: the children wrote scripts, programmes, posters, price lists, guidebooks, official invitations to special guests, press releases, a whole newspaper, and, most excitingly as it turned out, a range of business letters. These included letters accompanying the donations to charities, but also letters to local businesses selling advertising space in the class newspaper, bids for an Arts Grant to support the puppet theatre companies, and for sponsorship for the class museums and the fashion show (see Figure 3.2). All these letters received formal and entirely business-like replies which were much treasured by the children.

real maths: a lot of book-keeping and accounting, of course, (see Figure 3.3) but also measuring ingredients for refreshments when parents and

Back to the Past Museum Company.
(a division of Class 4 enterprises).

27.1.94.

Dear Sir,

Please may you consider sponsoring our posters for our Back to the Past museum. We estimate the cost will be about 10 pounds. Your company logo will appear on all posters and we anticipate a large crowd of people attending.

Thankyou for your kind attention.

Yours Faithfully,

Matthew Paddick,

(Company Secretary.)

Figure 3.2 *Writing for real purposes: Matthew writes applying for sponsorship*

friends were invited in for the grand launch or opening; handling real money when children sold tickets, postcards, programmes etc.; setting out the seats in the 'auditorium' for the puppet shows, with tickets corresponding to numbered seats; measuring and making patterns and costumes to fit for the fashion show; making decisions about what to charge for various items in all the projects.

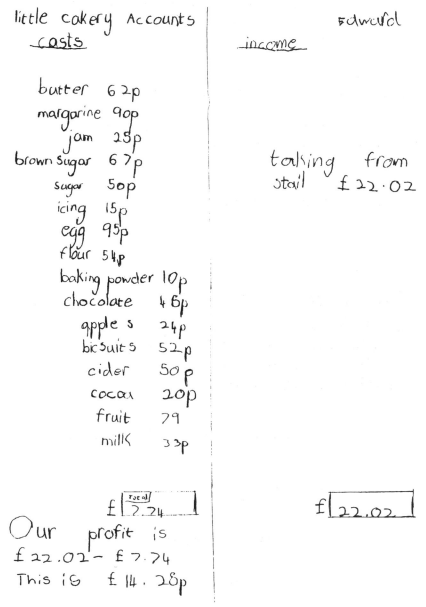

little cakery Accounts

Edward

costs

income

butter 62p
margarine 90p
jam 25p
brown sugar 67p
sugar 50p
icing 15p
egg 95p
flour 54p
baking powder 10p
chocolate 46p
apple s 24p
biscuits 52p
cider 50p
cocoa 20p
fruit 79
milk 33p

taking from
stall £22.02

£ | Total 7.24 |

£ | 22.02 |

Our profit is
£22.02 - £7.74
This is £14.28p

Figure 3.3 *Real maths: Edward's cake stall accounts*

genuine economic transactions: real money was used throughout; all costs were charged, but all the projects managed to make a good profit! The children were confronted with the simple realities of costs, prices, consumer preferences, profits and losses throughout the projects. Our records are full of fascinating discussions we held with children, particularly when they had to make decisions about pricing, for example. How much profit was it fair to make? What price would people pay for a newspaper? Children had to use their real-world knowledge to help them solve these problems. On one occasion a child volunteered that his mum would pay anything for chocolate cake!

work roles and processes emulated authentically: work roles were made explicit to the children. To help with this process, for example, badges for 'cook', 'market researcher', 'editor', 'museum guide', 'designer' and so on were often worn by the children when they carried out these roles. Processes seen by the children on visits were emulated in ways which made them as real as possible. Good examples of this would be the cataloguing procedures developed during the museums project, the computer booking system developed during the puppet theatre project, the operation of a real telephone by the children during the newspaper project on which they took calls to a 'tele-sales' service, and computer aided design for T-shirts in the fashion show (see Figure 3.4).

Figure 3.4 *Authentic work processes: Robert uses a computer graphics package to design his T-shirt*

Children being 'active' learners and empowered to make their own decisions

Our second principle concerns children being active participants in their learning rather than just passive recipients and having opportunities to make their own decisions about their learning. An 'active' style of learning is an intrinsic aspect of enterprise projects because the children are actually experiencing adult activities first-hand, and not simply being told about them. What goes along with this is that we must always be open to the children taking the initiative. A good example of this was a poster designed by one of the children. This was done in the evening at home inspired by a day of designing the role play area to accompany the fashion show project, and proudly brought into school the next morning. On another occasion, during the puppet theatre project, a child on her own initiative brought in to the class a large cardboard box which had contained her family's new washing machine. She explained that this was to be made into a puppet theatre. The provision of opportunities for imaginative play is also an important aspect of this 'active' involvement of children, and we will come on to this next.

What is significant here, however, are the opportunities enterprise projects offer, because of their intrinsically open-ended and problem-solving character, for children to take decisions and so develop feelings of empowerment. Tizard and Hughes (1984), among others, have pointed out how so much of what happens between adults and children in the home is child-initiated, whereas this is very much not the case often in the classroom. The consequent loss of feelings of control, self-efficacy and self-esteem for the young child can be very damaging. Research has consistently shown that self-esteem is whittled away by the difficulties many children face in relation to school learning. The strong relation between self-esteem and school achievement is well documented.

All the projects were set up in such a way as to allow the children considerable opportunities to make decisions and develop a real feeling of ownership and empowerment. The children made choices collectively about such matters as the name of the cake stall they set up and ran, which story to do as a puppet play, how to spend the profit made by their enterprise, and so on. Individually and in small groups they made a whole range of sophisticated decisions – about what to charge for postcards on sale in the museum 'shop', about the content and layout of their page in the class newspaper, about how many tickets to print for the puppet show, what information to include in the programmes, and so on. Many of these decisions involved considerable research and discussion. The mechanism of company board meetings was also used within some of the projects as a way of helping the children to review progress, and discuss and plan the work still to be done.

While, of course, they had their plans for the projects, the teachers involved always attempted, as a further way of empowering the children, to respond to and support initiatives coming from them. This is sometimes referred to as the 'dead bird' model of the curriculum, because children are inclined to bring in this kind of fascinating object, and the skilful early years educator has always made the most of such opportunities. But it is a feature of the curriculum which has been under threat from the pressures of the National Curriculum, and which it is desperately important that we preserve.

There are numerous examples of this from all the projects, but let us just mention two from the fashion show. Sometimes occasions arise because children, stimulated by their involvement in the project, bring in items with rich possibilities. During the fashion show project, a child arrived one day with a box full of Victorian hats, and the whole day was given over to examining them, finding out about how they were made, what they were made of, who wore them. Pictures were drawn, the children made their own Victorian hats, and so on.

Other occasions arise when an activity introduced by an adult is developed by the children in unexpected ways. An example of this arose when, as part of the fashion show project, an activity was introduced involving drawing a 2D scale drawing of the catwalk. This activity, which was planned to take about an hour, lasted for two days, as the children transformed it into a 3D modelling activity. Having completed the 2D drawing children began to add stand-up proscenium arches, which needed buttresses. Then they raised the catwalk plans onto box bases to show the height, added model pot plants, audiences on seats and delightfully accurate paper puppets of themselves in costume (initially on straws, but later on strings to facilitate twirling). With their models complete the children then gave miniature performances of the show to a tape of the music.

Opportunities for imaginative play

This last example leads us very well into our third curriculum principle. Once again, as was reviewed in chapter 1, there has been renewed interest in the ways that children's natural playfulness, usually given full rein in the home but very much curtailed within the school context, enhances the quality of their learning. Learning through play supports the strategies developed under the previous two headings. It helps children to derive meaning from their experiences. One of the main factors in the efficacy of play is also its self-directedness; play gives children control over their own learning.

The play corner in the classrooms during the projects was transformed into an imaginary cake shop, a practice puppet booth, a box office, a newspaper office, a museums office (see Figure 3.5) and a boutique. These were designed and largely built by the children, and played in to the point of destruction. During the puppet theatre project, for example, following the visit to the theatre, some of the children suggested that they turn part of the classroom into a box office. The teacher set about discussing with the class how they would go about rearranging the classroom to accommodate this. Tables were moved, chairs piled up, and carpets rearranged. A table was needed for the booking lady, a door for people to walk in, somewhere to display the puppets, a noticeboard for the posters, and so on. When the general environment of the box office had been created, discussion followed of what was needed to equip it. A telephone was installed, a computer, paper, pencils, pens, diary, tickets and a telephone book. From then on throughout the project there were always children in the box office busily taking telephone calls, writing messages, issuing tickets, taking money, making programmes and posters, putting up notices and signs and generally becoming thoroughly involved in the exciting new world of theatre management!

This kind of play was engaged in by the children throughout each of the projects with energy and enthusiasm. As the projects developed it was notable the extent to which new elements of the project, and new information which had been made available to the children, was incorporated in their play.

Figure 3.5 *Role play: the museum office*

Integrating the worlds of school and community

The final feature of the projects was the extent to which the divisions between the school and the outside adult community were broken down. As we have discussed, there is an important aspect of this to do with styles of learning, but continuity and good communication between the worlds of home and school is also a vital component in providing young children with emotional security in the classroom.

There were a number of aspects of this attempt at integrating the worlds of school and adult community within the projects:

- the children visited an adult place of work, and often one where adults they knew worked; our observations of the adults explaining their work to the children suggested this was an intense and satisfying experience for both parties;
- adults visited the classroom to explain their work to the children, and also to work alongside the children with their enterprises; this also, of course, supported the authenticity of the children's enterprises (see Figure 3.6);
- the children interacted with adults in the local community in a business-like manner (formal letters requesting sponsorship, selling advertising space, inviting local dignitaries to open the Grand Launch, giving interviews to the local press about the projects etc.);

Figure 3.6 *Adults working alongside the children: the local museum warden discusses one of the class's collection with Sam*

- the projects generated an enthusiasm which led to an enormous involvement of the parents and the wider community in all kinds of ways – lending resources (exhibits for the museum), helping with making (puppets, costumes, cakes), helping with research (important people being interviewed for the newspaper, and as a source of local history for the museum), attending the Grand Opening or Launch, providing expertise (photographs of the children as models for the fashion page, and the village policeman setting up a mock robbery, both for the newspaper), offering sponsorship, providing ideas and moral support.

The involvement and enthusiasm of the children and of the local communities for these enterprise projects has been particularly rewarding. An atmosphere of real teamwork was generated in which young children, parents, teachers and community shared the pleasure of co-operative purpose and achievement. The museum exhibitions, for example, were so popular that, when they were taken down in school, they had to be immediately remounted within the local museum which received large numbers of interested visitors, many of whom purchased some of the postcards designed and made by the children (see Figure 3.7). The video of the fashion show quickly sold out with copies being sent as far away as the Orkneys and northern Norway !

Figure 3.7 *Alexander's postcard: one of half a dozen which sold like hot cakes at the local museum*

Planning and assessment

Carrying out the kind of projects described in this chapter with young children can be an enormously rewarding and effective way of organising and developing the curriculum. As with any high quality teaching, however, it depends vitally upon detailed planning based upon careful assessments of the children's needs and abilities. We therefore need to conclude with some remarks about these crucially important aspects of the early years educator's work.

Progression

The topic-based approach to the curriculum has commonly been criticised because of the lack of progression in activities. One argument for teaching a more subject-based curriculum has been that it enables concepts and skills to be introduced and then built upon more systematically. It is, however, perfectly possible to build progression into the activities within a topic, given careful task analysis and planning. As part of the planning for the kind of enterprise projects described in this chapter, for example, it is important to analyse the planned activities in terms of different areas of the curriculum (see Figure 3.8). This ensures a good range and balance of skills is being addressed. It also leads on to an analysis of the nature of the skills and understandings to be taught. That the activities are placed in the meaningful context provided by the topic or project, however, enhances the children's understandings about their purpose and thus supports rather than detracts from the real progression in learning. Here are a couple of examples from the fashion show project:

Letter writing

introduced with letters to Father Christmas (not part of the project), which were chatty, informal, and concluded with 'love from . . .';

developed within the project with formal, thank you letters to some people from Marks & Spencer's children's clothes department who had been into school to talk to the children about the design process; these letters had a more formal layout with the school address, proper indentation, the date, began with 'Dear Sir' and concluded with 'Yours sincerely . . .', but the content was very straightforward;

concluded with formal letters with more complex content; these involved applying for sponsorship, inviting special guests to the fashion show, sending a charity donation (to Radio Cambridgeshire's Send-a-Cow

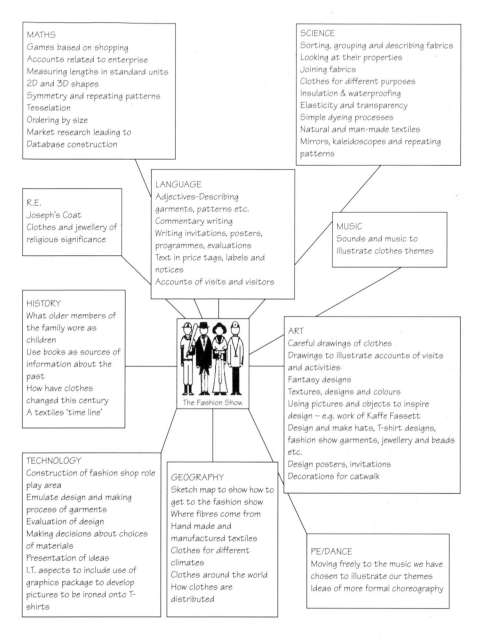

MATHS
Games based on shopping
Accounts related to enterprise
Measuring lengths in standard units
2D and 3D shapes
Symmetry and repeating patterns
Tesselation
Ordering by size
Market research leading to
Database construction

SCIENCE
Sorting, grouping and describing fabrics
Looking at their properties
Joining fabrics
Clothes for different purposes
Insulation & waterproofing
Elasticity and transparency
Simple dyeing processes
Natural and man-made textiles
Mirrors, kaleidoscopes and repeating
patterns

R.E.
Joseph's Coat
Clothes and jewellery of
religious significance

LANGUAGE
Adjectives-Describing
garments, patterns etc.
Commentary writing
Writing invitations, posters,
programmes, evaluations
Text in price tags, labels and
notices
Accounts of visits and visitors

MUSIC
Sounds and music to
illustrate clothes themes

HISTORY
What older members of
the family wore as
children
Use books as sources of
information about the
past
How have clothes
changed this century
A textiles 'time line'

The Fashion Show

ART
Careful drawings of clothes
Drawings to illustrate accounts of visits
and activities
Fantasy designs
Textures, designs and colours
Using pictures and objects to inspire
design – e.g. work of Kaffe Fassett
Design and make hats, T-shirt designs,
fashion show garments, jewellery and beads
etc.
Design posters, invitations
Decorations for catwalk

TECHNOLOGY
Construction of fashion shop role
play area
Emulate design and making
process of garments
Evaluation of design
Making decisions about choices
of materials
Presentation of ideas
I.T. aspects to include use of
graphics package to develop
pictures to be ironed onto T-
shirts

GEOGRAPHY
Sketch map to show how to
get to the fashion show
Where fibres come from
Hand made and
manufactured textiles
Clothes for different
climates
Clothes around the world
How clothes are
distributed

PE/DANCE
Moving freely to the music we have
chosen to illustrate our themes
Ideas of more formal choreography

Figure 3.8 *Analysis of planned activities for the fashion show project by subject*

appeal on this occasion!) and so forth (Figure 3.2 is a good example of this
stage); invariably replies were received to these letters, also written very
formally.

Tessellation

introduced by looking at patchwork patterns on fabrics and tessellating squares, rectangles and hexagons of different patterns; all these shapes tessellate with themselves in any orientation;

developed by looking at pattern cutting for various shapes which tessellate when the shape is rotated eg: T-shirt, sock, skirt (see Figure 3.9);

concluded by looking at real dressmaking patterns which did not tessellate and attempting to fit them onto rectangles of fabric in the most economical way (i.e. fitting in the most patterns with least waste, as we had seen at the clothes factory we visited).

Assessment

Early years educators have always placed great emphasis on making careful observations and assessments. In order to make assessments of an individual child's understanding or level of skill it is important to plan activities

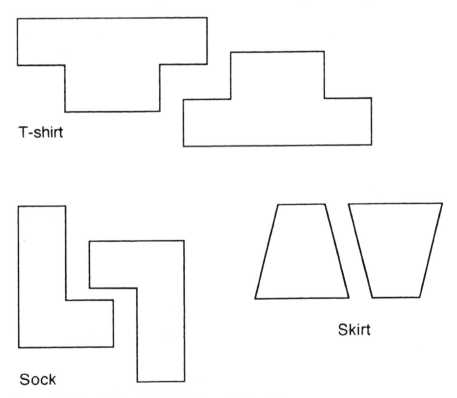

Figure 3.9 *Tessellating T-shirt, sock and skirt patterns*

which will enable the extent to which a child has made the new understanding or skill their own to be seen. This involves another kind of progression from *structured or closed activities* to introduce the new skills or concepts developing on to more *open-ended activities* which give the child opportunities to use what they have learnt in their own innovative ways.

It is entirely possible to build this kind of progression of activities into enterprise projects. The meaningful context, furthermore, provides a real purpose to the activities, and the child's real level of skill or understanding can be much more validly revealed than when they are carrying out an activity simply for its own sake, where the child's motivation and understanding of the requirements of the task are sometimes open to question. More open-ended activities reveal a child's thinking and abilities much more clearly than closed tasks, particularly of the 'Blue Peter' variety where all the child has to do is follow instructions. They also provide children with opportunities to express themselves, to gain feelings of ownership, and to have a more memorable, first-hand experience. This is, of course, often what is happening, as we have reviewed, when children engage in imaginative play related to significant new experiences, and their play can be an important source for observations and assessments for this reason.

Within the enterprise projects many of the activities were planned with this kind of assessment in mind. Here are two examples, both from the fashion show project:

Measuring materials for costumes

structured or closed activities in which the children were taught various techniques for measuring themselves, including the use of appropriate measuring units and instruments;

open-ended activities where the children were required to use their measurements of themselves to measure out materials so that their costumes would be the right size; choice of method of measurement left to the children.

Emergent writing

structured or closed activities in which the children were taught the names of different garments, how to write out sizes, amounts of money, addresses and so forth;

open-ended activities in the role-play area, the 'Clothes R Us' boutique, including, for example, the provision of an order book in which children, role-playing as shop assistants, could write out orders taken from other children role-playing as customers (see Figure 3.10).

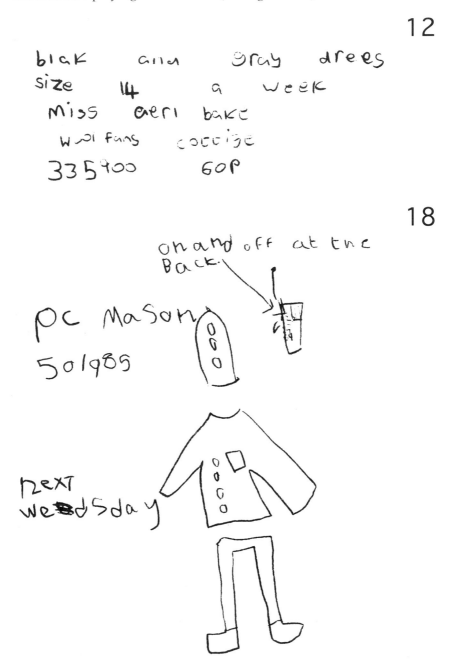

Figure 3.10 *Writing in the role-play area as a means of assessment: orders placed in the 'Clothes R Us' order book*

Differentiation

Having planned for a progression in the children's understandings and skills, and made assessments of their responses to the various activities, it is, of course, vital to differentiate the activities so that each child can succeed at an appropriate level. There are numerous ways in which this can be done, and once again this needs to be planned. Here are some suggested means of doing this and some examples from the enterprise projects:

- **Outcome:** perhaps the simplest form of differentiation is to set up an activity so that the requirements are the same for all the children, but it is so open-ended that they can respond at their own level; *examples*: designing a poster, making a model catwalk.

- **Support:** once again, the requirements can be the same, but the level of the outcome needs to be similar, so this common level of achievement is reached by means of variable levels of adult support; *examples*: making a costume, baking a cake.

- **Recording method:** the activity may be the same for everyone, but the children may be required to record what they have done in more or less sophisticated ways; *example*: a science activity on the qualities of different textiles recorded by sticking samples of the textiles on paper, by drawings, or by descriptive writing.

- **Complexity:** finally, the children may be given tasks to do which are all related to the same skill or concept, but which are at different stages in the progression of work planned; *example*: mapwork related to the destinations of different garments made at the clothes factory involving activities at three levels:
  – countries located on world map and drawings of garments attached
  – journey of garments to Hong Kong investigated and a list made of the continents they travel through
  – journey of garments through the UK to the port investigated; compass directions, road numbers and towns travelled through recorded.

Conclusion

Within education there is growing interest currently related to developing more experiential, problem-solving approaches to teaching and learning across the curriculum (Fisher 1987, provides a good review of work in primary schools). We have attempted to show that enterprise projects can provide an excellent basis for this kind of development. There was an intensity of 'real' learning for the children within these projects which was very special. The enthusiasm with which the children, their teachers, parents and other members of the local communities still recall the projects, in some cases now after several years have elapsed, is a testimony to their significance for all who participated in them. We have attempted to demonstrate in this chapter that such projects form an excellent basis for organising an appropriate and effective early years curriculum. Through this kind of project it is possible to meet the needs of young children. They arrive at school confident and expert learners in the informal context of their home environment. Through the kind of curriculum organisation proposed here they are enabled to make the transition to becoming equally effective and assured in the environment of the school.

Pointers for organising the early years curriculum

- With thought and imagination, it is possible to organise the early years curriculum in ways which are compatible with the demands of the National Curriculum, and with our understandings about how children learn.

- Young children's learning will be enhanced when:
  1 the content of the curriculum is **'meaningful'** to them and related to their existing knowledge and interests;
  2 they are **active participants in their learning** rather than just passive recipients; they should have opportunities to make their own decisions about their learning;
  3 they are encouraged to indulge their natural inclination to engage in **imaginative play** related to significant life experiences;
  4 they are **emotionally secure** because there is continuity and good communication between the worlds of home and school.

- These principles can be embodied powerfully within 'enterprise' projects.

- The success of this model of curriculum organisation depends upon:
  1 clearly identified **progressions** of related activities;
  2 **assessment** of children's level of understanding or skill using **open-ended activities**;
  3 **differentiation** of activities so that each child can succeed at an appropriate level.

References

Anning, A. (1991) *The First Years at School: Education 4 to 8*, Buckingham: Open University Press.

Atkinson, S. (ed.) (1992) *Mathematics with Reason*, London: Hodder & Stoughton.

Bennett, N., Desforges, C., Cockburn, A. and Wilkinson, B. (1984) *The Quality of Pupil Learning Experiences*, London: Lawrence Erlbaum.

Blenkin, G. and Kelly, V. (eds) (1994) *The National Curriculum and Early Learning: An Evaluation*, London: Paul Chapman.

Bruce, T. (1987) *Early Childhood Education*, London: Hodder & Stoughton.

Cleave, S. and Brown, S. (1991) *Early to School: 4 Year Olds in Infant Classes*, London: Routledge.

Coltman, P. and Whitebread, D. (1992) 'The Little Bakery: an Infant Class develops EIU', *Economic Awareness*, 5, 1, pp. 3–9.

DES (1985) *The Curriculum from 5 to 16*, Curriculum Matters 2, HMI Series, London: HMSO.

DES (1990) *Mini-Enterprise in schools: Some Aspects of Current Practice: A Report of HMI*, London: HMSO.

Drummond, M.J., Lally, M. and Pugh, G. (eds) (1989) *Working with Children: Developing a Curriculum for the Early Years*, Nottingham: National Children's Bureau / Nottingham Educational Supplies.

Early Years Curriculum Group (1989) *Early Childhood Education: The Early Years Curriculum and the National Curriculum*, Stoke-on-Trent: Trentham Books.

Fisher, R. (ed.) (1987) *Problem Solving in Primary Schools*, Oxford: Basil Blackwell.

Hall, N. (ed.) (1989) *Writing with Reason*, Sevenoaks: Hodder & Stoughton.

Hughes, M. (1986) *Children and Number*, Oxford: Basil Blackwell.

ILEA (1987) *The Early Years: A Curriculum for Young Children*, London: ILEA Centre for Learning Resources.

OFSTED (1993) *First Class: The Standards and Quality of Education in Reception Classes*, London: HMSO.

Palmer, J. and Pettitt, D. (1993) *Topic Work in the Early Years*, London: Routledge.

Tizard, B. and Hughes, M. (1984) *Young Children Learning: Talking and Thinking at Home and at School*, London: Fontana,

Whitebread, D., Coltman, P. and Farmery, J. (1993) 'Project file: a puppet theatre', *Child Education*, 70, 6, 31–8.

Whitebread, D., Coltman, P. and Bryant, P. (1994) 'Project file: a class museum', *Child Education*, 71, 12, 27–34.

Whitebread, D., Coltman, P. and Davison, S. (1995) 'Project file: infant newshounds', *Child Education*, 72, 1, 29–36.

CHAPTER 4

'Do you know what MY name is?'

ASSESSMENT IN THE EARLY YEARS: SOME EXAMPLES FROM SCIENCE

Rachel Sparks Linfield and Paul Warwick

The assessment process itself should not determine what is to be taught and learned. It should be the servant, not the master, of the curriculum. Yet it should not simply be a bolt on addition at the end. Rather it should be an integral part of the educational process, continually providing both 'feedback' and 'feedforward'. It therefore needs to be incorporated systematically into teaching strategies and practices at all levels.

(DES 1987, para. 4)

In recent years assessment has been the subject of much debate. Questions have been asked about what and how we should assess. Standard Assessment Tasks have been criticised for poorly worded questions and inappropriate content which does not allow children to demonstrate what they know. Educators have grown anxious over the problems of assessing thirty-plus children in a wide range of practical and conceptual areas. Yet early years educators have always monitored their pupils' development, to inform their day to day teaching and to allow them to report learners' achievements. They have used a combination of formative assessment, where the emphasis is on planning the next steps to be taken with a child, and summative assessment, providing a snapshot of the child's achievements and abilities at a particular stage, in building a picture of the whole child. They have, in fact, always seen assessment as an 'integral part' of the learning process. In doing this, they have made assessment all-embracing, and most would certainly agree with the thoughts of Hurst and Lally:

> Assessment of young children must cover all aspects of a child's devel-
> opment and must be concerned with attitudes, feelings, social and
> physical characteristics . . . Learning is not compartmentalised under
> subject headings for young children.
>
> (Hurst and Lally 1992, p. 55)

It may seem odd, therefore, that this chapter focuses on the assessment of
science. There are a number of reasons for taking this approach. First, it will
become clear that the methods/modes of formative, ongoing assessment to
be discussed can be used in relation to any curriculum area. Focusing, however, on just one helps to present a clear and coherent picture. Second,
though there are clear distinctions in their nature, many subjects within the
early years curriculum have a 'concept/process split' and science is a particularly good example of this. Third, the practical and investigative nature
of science corresponds closely with accepted procedures fundamental to
young children's attempts to make sense of the world (see chapter 13).
Lastly, whilst the early years curriculum does, and should, integrate facets of
different curriculum areas into a cohesive whole, it is clearly important to
analyse children's achievements in relation to specific areas of development.

This chapter reviews the assessment of science in the early years and the
various methods which early years educators have employed. In particular,
the different modes of formative assessment – those intended to inform day
by day, week by week teaching decisions – are considered in relation to the
science curriculum. Some of the key problems in making assessments of
young children's scientific knowledge and skills are discussed. It is hoped
that the suggestions made will prove helpful to early years educators who
wish to assess the children with whom they work. The central importance of
this to teaching and learning is perhaps best captured by Drummond:

> The process of assessing children's learning – by looking closely at it
> and striving to understand it is the only certain safeguard against
> children's failure, the only certain guarantee of children's progress
> and development.
>
> (Drummond 1993, p. 10)

So, first we shall consider what we should be assessing.

What to assess

When people think about understanding in science they are usually referring to the need to assimilate a body of knowledge. Within science, however,

the way in which knowledge is acquired, tested and changed is largely through practical experimentation and investigation. Here there is much in common with other subjects of the early years curriculum, though within science this experimental way of working is fundamental at all levels. It is important that the educator considers not only the development of science concepts but also the development of the procedural understanding – what Gott and Duggan (1995) term 'the thinking behind the doing' – essential to solving science problems. For example, when investigating what makes a 'good' sandcastle the educator might hope that the child would consider ideas such as: What is sand like? How is it changed by the addition of water? She might also hope that the child would observe purposefully, record appropriately and perhaps even consider some of the factors that would contribute towards a fair test for various sandcastles.

As children move through nursery and primary education they will thus be combining knowledge of basic facts and a simple understanding of science concepts, with knowledge and recall of basic skills and an understanding of basic procedures for practical experimentation. Gott and Duggan (1995) show that both the concepts and the understanding of procedures necessary for successful, practical experimentation develop alongside one another. This allows the child to tackle increasingly complex problems using their increasing conceptual and procedural understanding.

Assessment of science requires educators to gather appropriate evidence to enable them to make judgements about children's performance in relation to both conceptual and procedural understanding. The question is: what needs to be considered when planning for assessment within the early years? Educators understand the necessity of defining clear teaching objectives, ensuring that both teaching and assessment are focused. In formative assessment the educator will use various modes which seem to suit the task. Cavendish *et al.* (1990) identify these as:

- observation of children at work;
- the assessment of products; these might include written work, drawings, models etc.;
- discussion and questioning;
- reflection by the educator (without the child present).

The focus of this chapter is on the detail associated with some of these modes of assessment. Let us briefly consider each, whilst of course acknowledging that an educator is likely to combine assessment modes (perhaps discussing a piece of work with a child whilst observing their attempts to solve a problem). Following this initial discussion of the modes of assessment, case studies and examples of their use are provided.

Observation of children's work

Clayden and Peacock (1994) point to the importance of observing 'with a purpose' in the assessment of both conceptual and procedural understanding in science. The particular contribution of observation to the assessment of procedural understanding will immediately be apparent: how can we know whether an early years' child is, for example, using their understanding of what fair testing means within a particular activity, unless we are able to make focused observations as the child works? Whether related to procedural or conceptual understanding, the ability to recognise the significance of what is observed derives from an understanding not only of the child but also of the structure of science. Having a grasp of the development of conceptual and procedural understanding allows the educator to plan purposefully and to use observation as a genuine assessment tool. Knowing what to assess is as important as knowing how to assess.

Assessment of products

The products of children's scientific endeavours are widely used for assessment. The Primary SPACE Research Reports (e.g. Watt and Russell 1990) demonstrate how helpful children's drawings can be in presenting their understanding of science concepts. They also show how educators may use written work, completed artefacts, simple tables and graphs, the results of sorting or sequencing activities and concept maps to assess children in science. Ollerenshaw and Ritchie (1993) present some clear case studies in the use of all these forms of recording, but when it comes to assessment that uses such products some notes of caution must be sounded. As has been asserted, it is notoriously difficult to get any feel for a child's level of procedural understanding without observing them engaged in carrying out practical tasks. Particularly with young children there are limited opportunities for the products of science activities to convey this understanding. Even with conceptual understanding, however, the educator must be wary that what they are presented with genuinely conveys the child's interpretation of the area of science in question. The example of straw assessment found later in this chapter neatly illustrates this point.

Discussion and questioning

If products alone can be an unreliable guide for assessment, then the central importance of discussion and questioning becomes clear. Feasey and Thompson (1992) show how deliberate questioning strategies, sometimes focusing on practical activities and sometimes on products, can not only move children forward in their understanding but are also a powerful aid to assessment. Discussion can genuinely involve children in the assessment of their own work and this, perhaps, is one of the many steps towards the creation of autonomous learners.

Reflection by the educator

Finally, the role of reflection by the educator, not considered elsewhere in this chapter, deserves a few words. The keys to this are sound planning based upon an understanding of both children and science, together with frequently used opportunities for classroom assessment based upon a combination of the modes already discussed. In reviewing such evidence the educator can incorporate into her thinking the whole child – their performance in other areas, their special needs, whether English is their first language – and armed with such information, whether or not it is formalised in a recording structure, the educator has a good chance of making appropriate judgements about where to go next with her children.

Let us now consider in detail some examples and case studies that will hopefully give the flavour of using some of the modes of assessment introduced above for formative assessment. These examples start with two case studies which look at discussion as a mode of assessment, as the authors believe that discussion is fundamental for allowing children to develop their ideas and for the educator to access them.

The picture as stimulus for discussion

A four- to five-year-old class was working on a project entitled 'All Around Me'. Children had been on walks and collected items for their 'interest table'. They had looked at the local countryside and had made drawings of all that they had seen. The teacher became aware that children talked about living things but was uncertain that all her class used the phrase 'living thing' to mean the same thing. During an afternoon of 'All Around Me' activities she showed the picture reproduced in Figure 4.1 and asked children to pick out living and non-living things. Transcripts of three of the conversations are given. The children had all been in the reception class for two terms.

Figure 4.1 *A picture containing living and non-living things*

Conversation 1 between teacher (*T*) and girl aged 5 (*G*).

T   What in the picture is living?
G   Nothing, it's only a picture.
T   Pretend it isn't a picture but it's outside.
G   It's all living. The hedgehog, the sun, the tree, the apple, the mummy, the smoke- it's moving.
T   Is the car living?
G   Yes, it's all real. Not pretend. It's real.

This conversation indicates that this child believed 'living' to mean 'real'.
  Conversation 2 between teacher (*T*) and girl aged 5 years 3 months (*G*).

T   What can you see in the picture that is living?
G   The people.
T   Anything else?
G   The butterfly. The hedgehog, I think it's living but it looks funny. Is it supposed to be real?
T   I think it's supposed to be like the hedgehogs we find outside. Not like the toy one in our book corner.
G   Hedgehogs outside aren't always living. I saw one 'deaded' in the road. A car had 'runned' over it.
T   Are the apples living?
G   No. The tree is.
T   Why do you say that?
G   The tree can grow until it gets cut down. The apples just fall off.

Here the child had a concept of living to do with growth. She readily recognised animals as living but was confused about apples.

Conversation 3 between teacher (*T*) and boy aged 4 years 7 months (*B*).

T Can you see two things in this picture that are living?
B Mmm. The butterfly?
T And?
B The children.
T Can you see anything that is not living?
B The hedgehog might be dead. The car might have gone over it.
T Is –
B But I don't think so. I think it's happy.
T Is the house living?
B People might live in it.
T Is the tree living?
B No.
T Why not?
B It just grows. It's not 'alive'.
T How do you mean, 'it's not alive'?
B It can't walk.

In this conversation the boy readily identified humans and animals as living. Trees, however, were not viewed as alive.

As a result of these, and similar conversations, the teacher realised that within her reception class the word 'living' held many different meanings. The majority saw animals and humans as living but did not view plants in the same way. For some 'living' was synonymous with 'can move'. The teacher followed up the conversations with more experiences of 'living things'. The discussions provided clear evidence of understanding and mis-understanding of a concept. They demonstrate the importance of listening to children and the use of a picture for assessing understanding.

Fiction as stimulus for discussion

The second example of formative assessment through discussion occurred with a six- to seven-year-old class which had been following a topic on 'Our Bodies'. Their teacher had read *Funnybones* by Janet and Alan Ahlberg to the class. Later in the week, whilst dissecting owl pellets one child was dis-tressed to find individual bones coming out of his pellet.

B The bones are broken.
T If you handle them carefully they won't be.
B No, look. They're all broken.
T No. That's a rib. And this one is like one in your leg.

B It's broken.
T No. Bring it to our poster of the human skeleton.
B See it's broken.
T No – it's like this bone here [Teacher points to lower leg bone].
B But it's not joined on.
T Joined on?
B No. These pellet bones wouldn't work.

The conversation revealed that the child did not see a skeleton as being composed of individual bones. Further discussion showed that the boy believed that skeletons such as those depicted in *Funnybones* could be self-supporting and walk independently. This informal assessment again can be seen as providing important information about concept development.

Definitions

Here the way much scientific language has different connotations in everyday use is considered. The following definitions were given by six- to seven-year-old children when their teacher asked them to help her make a scientific dictionary.

force
- an army
- being made to do something
- something big
- a push or a pull

fair test
- everyone gets a go at doing it
- you do it lots of times and things are the same, like we all grew cress in pots; put one pot in the cupboard and one by the window
- all the same
- a dead heat

sound
- you can hear it
- something nice – not like noise
- you hear them but not bangs
- it's exciting

electricity
- it lights bulbs
- it's in batteries
- it's like crosses and minuses, the minuses are blue.
- you mustn't put knitting needles in plug holes because electricity might come out.

table
- you put results in it
- we do experiments on tables
- they've got four legs.

The comments came from children who had been through nursery school together, entered school as reception infants and had similar experiences within science. Yet, their understanding of scientific concepts varied. The definitions show the importance of taking children on from where they are and ensuring that the educator and pupils have shared meanings.

Children's drawings

A five- to six-year-old class was asked to observe a straw in a glass of water and to draw what they had observed. The teacher hoped that the children would notice that the straw appeared to bend. The teacher intended to let four children at a time observe and draw and to use the drawings as evidence of observing the bent straw. The following conversations, however, again show the importance of talking to children and watching them at work. These observations were to surprise the teacher.

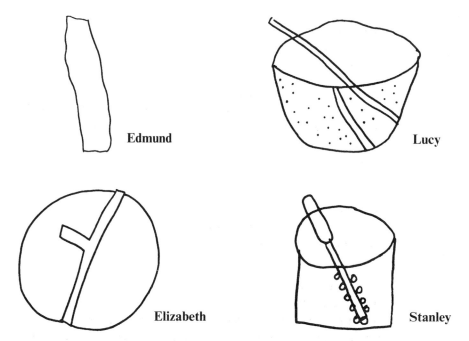

Figure 4.2 *Four children's drawings of a straw in a glass of water*

In the four examples of the children's drawings (Figure 4.2), those of Lucy and Elizabeth seem to reflect knowledge that the straw appears to bend. Edmund, though, seems to have only seen a straight straw. Observation of the infants at work, and discussion with them, however, showed otherwise.

While watching the children the teacher realised that Stanley was not drawing what he had observed. Instead, he tried to copy Lucy's drawing and then decided to draw the pipette he had used in a previous experiment! The teacher was most impressed by Lucy when she saw the elliptical bowl. They discussed her finished picture:

T   What have you drawn?
L   The straw.
T   What's under the straw? [She pointed at what she imagined was the straw's reflection.]
L   It's that mark on the table. I did it when I was colouring.
T   And the dots? [She thought they were bubbles.]
L   That's pen on the table. Shall I get a cloth to wipe it off?

This conversation showed that what the teacher was seeing in the picture was not what Lucy had intended.

The final surprise came through talking to Edmund.

T   Can you see the straw in the glass?
E   Yes.
T   Does it look like the one out of the water?
E   No, the one in the water's bent.
T   Why haven't you drawn it bent?
E   'Cos it's only pretend. Really the straw is straight.

Edmund had not only observed the bent straw but also knew this was just an optical effect. Without discussion this knowledge would not have been evident.

The experience of watching the infants at work and of discussing their drawings, raises the question of how often through looking at 'written' evidence we make the assumption that children have understood a concept when discussion would prove otherwise. Equally, how often do we think children have not understood when actually they do? Frequently children perceive things differently from adults. Many children use drawings to record what they 'know' rather than what they 'see' (see chapter 12). Clearly discussion has much to offer here to valid assessment.

Concept maps

Many educators will already be familiar with concept maps as a means of assessing children's knowledge prior to an activity. As envisaged by Novak and Gowin (1984) they are a method of constructing hierarchies of concepts with 'propositional links' showing how those concepts are related. With young children, however, it is more sensible to simplify concept mapping, making it a method of showing links between concepts but ignoring the hierarchical structure of those concepts. To give an example, consider the words 'tree' and 'water'; how are these related? Using an arrow to show the nature and direction of the relationship, the simple map illustrated in Figure 4.3 might be produced:

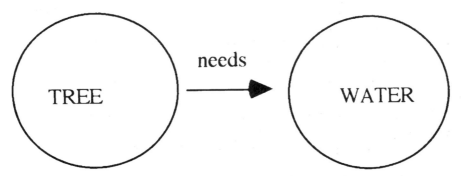

Figure 4.3 *A concept map showing the relationship between 'tree' and 'water'*

This simple idea can be extended by the educator to establish the initial understanding that children have of key ideas they will encounter in a lesson or through a topic. The concept maps in Figures 4.4 and 4.5 were drawn by two six-year-old children prior to carrying out some work with plants. They were based upon the following words provided by the teacher – seed, flower, bulb, water, light, bud, stalk:

The understanding expressed by the children in the two maps is substantially different. This suggests that even if similar activities were carried out by these children the educator would have different expectations of them and would be likely to question them in a manner more focused to their level of understanding. This technique is an important one for any educator with a broadly constructivist view of learning, where the notion of children constructing their own sense of the world is central (see chapter 1). For the constructivist 'what is already in the learner's mind matters' (Ollerenshaw and Ritchie 1993), since it will provide a basis for subsequent teaching and for the conceptual change that results. Harlen (1993) points out how easy even very young children find the technique, and in assessing pre-

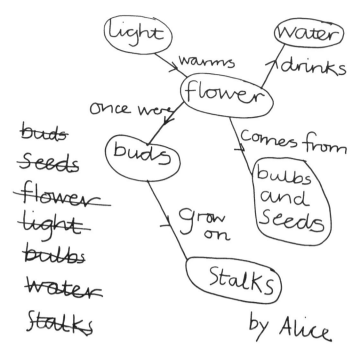

Figure 4.4 *A concept map by Alice, aged 6*

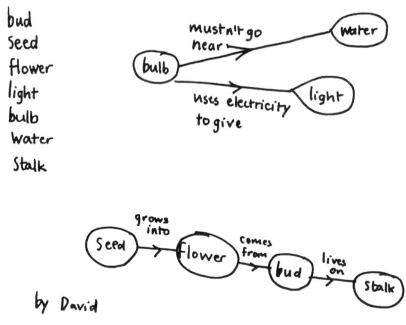

Figure 4.5 *A concept map by David, aged 6*

and post-teaching maps the educator is able not only to see how the child's concepts have developed, but also to assess the effectiveness of the work that has been carried out.

It will be apparent that children need to be taught this technique and need to understand particularly how important the 'joining words' are in making the whole thing have meaning. As with all methods used for recording children's thoughts it should not be used too frequently. This is not just to prevent fatigue on the part of the children; concept maps are time-consuming for the educator to analyse and should be seen as only one tool in the assessment armoury.

In the early years in particular there are benefits to modifying the technique still further. The creation of group or class concept maps is a beneficial way of encouraging discussion and can provide a basis in itself for the children to challenge one another's ideas. In some respects this is rather like the use of floor books, but instead of recording ideas in a list the educator has specific concepts that form the basis of creating the map and the children are encouraged to discuss possible linkages. Carrying out this exercise both before and after a lesson or longer topic can be, as suggested above, most revealing. A further refinement with younger children is to create 'picture concept maps'. Moving around pictures rather than words and articulating relationships between them can help some children, and not only those who might be bilingual or who might have problems with reading, to express properly the extent of their understanding.

Using story and drama

Stories and drama can provide an excellent medium for the assessment of scientific concepts. Fairy tales such as 'Goldilocks and the Three Bears' can set a problem for children to solve through science. Goldilocks for example had problems when deciding which porridge to eat and which bed to sleep in. Questions can be asked as to how Goldilocks knew which bowl was too hot and why was one bowl cold? How can we keep things warm? Are metal, china or wooden bowls better for keeping things warm? In the classroom work might have taken place on the properties of materials. In drama, children could take on a role of Goldilocks, a bear, shopkeeper selling bowls, parent of Goldilocks etc. Through acting out the story and making choices children's application of concepts may be assessed. Educators may choose to be in role and to guide conversations or to be observers. The drama provides children with an opportunity to discuss and to draw on knowledge acquired through science.

A five- to six-year-old class had been doing a topic on magnets. They had used magnets to pick up steel and iron objects, to sort materials and to make games. A few weeks after the project had finished the teacher decided to use the story *Magnet Boy* (Hendy and Sparks Linfield 1995) to assess children's concepts of magnets. The story tells of a boy who receives a very strong magnetic badge for his birthday and uses it in school to find his teacher's key. By using the story in drama the teacher discovered a wide range of magnetic concepts. She found that children who in the classroom had successfully completed a range of experiments had little idea of magnetic strength or of the fact that magnets will not attract all metals. Others who had shown limited interest in magnets whilst conducting the experiments enthusiastically discussed the Magnet Boy, wanted to make 'strong magnetic badges' and demonstrated good understanding of the concepts of magnetism. When asked how useful she had found the story for assessing her class in science she replied:

> Very useful. Although I've often carried out assessments of science I've always done them as part of classroom activities. The story and drama has put the science in the real world. It's shown me who understands, who doesn't know what a metal is and who needs to have a lot more practical experience of magnets.

Assessment for summative purposes

In assessing children for formative purposes the teacher is slowly able to build a picture of the child in relation to a particular curriculum area. From time to time, however, it may be necessary to assess for summative purposes some aspects of concept, or particularly process, development. This may result from the educator's desire to 'run a check' on the appropriateness of their own formative assessments, or it may be built into a school's assessment procedures. Whatever the reasons for embarking upon what might be seen as more formal assessments, there are a number of principles and procedures that the authors feel should be adopted.

The first of these is that, for these summative assessments, the focus should be limited. The activity that the children are carrying out is likely to allow them to use a range of skills and concepts; yet for assessment purposes the educator should focus on just two to three assessment objectives, which may or may not relate to National Curriculum programme of study statements. For example, in an activity on changing materials, the teacher may have an assessment objective related to science processes:

Assessment objective: To recognise when a test or comparison is unfair.

Having established what is to be assessed it is now possible to sort out some precise evidence, related to the specific activity, that will give a guide to whether the child is achieving the objective. In relation to our example it may be:

Evidence: Child is able to articulate why items selected for melting must be the same size.

Having planned two to four assessment objectives in this way, the educator will then give the task to the children and, working with them, will assess their performance. It would be useful for her to have criteria which allow her to differentiate the performance of individuals in relation to each objective. The following may provide a basis for such differentiation:

Criteria:
a)	can carry out the objective competently and independently;
b)	can carry out the objective independently at a simple basic level but with no guarantee that could reliably do so on another occasion;
c)	can reliably carry out the objective with adult support.

It may be that such a structure for formal assessment tasks could help early years educators in their assessments, but such tasks should never be used as a substitute for ongoing formative assessments using the range of modes already discussed.

Attitudes

No one observing young children involved in scientific investigations will fail to notice the enthusiasm and interest of the majority of children. Yet likes and dislikes for certain activities can cause problems if educators are not aware of them. Whilst simply talking to children can provide evidence of attitudes, many children enjoy assessing their own performance and completing their own records of development and interest. The example in Figure 4. 6 shows one completed by a six-year-old boy. Self-assessment such as this can help children to take responsibility for their own learning and to develop their autonomy. Children who are unable to complete such sheets unaided enjoy working with an adult or older child to scribe for them. Sheets with smiley faces and pictures also may be used.

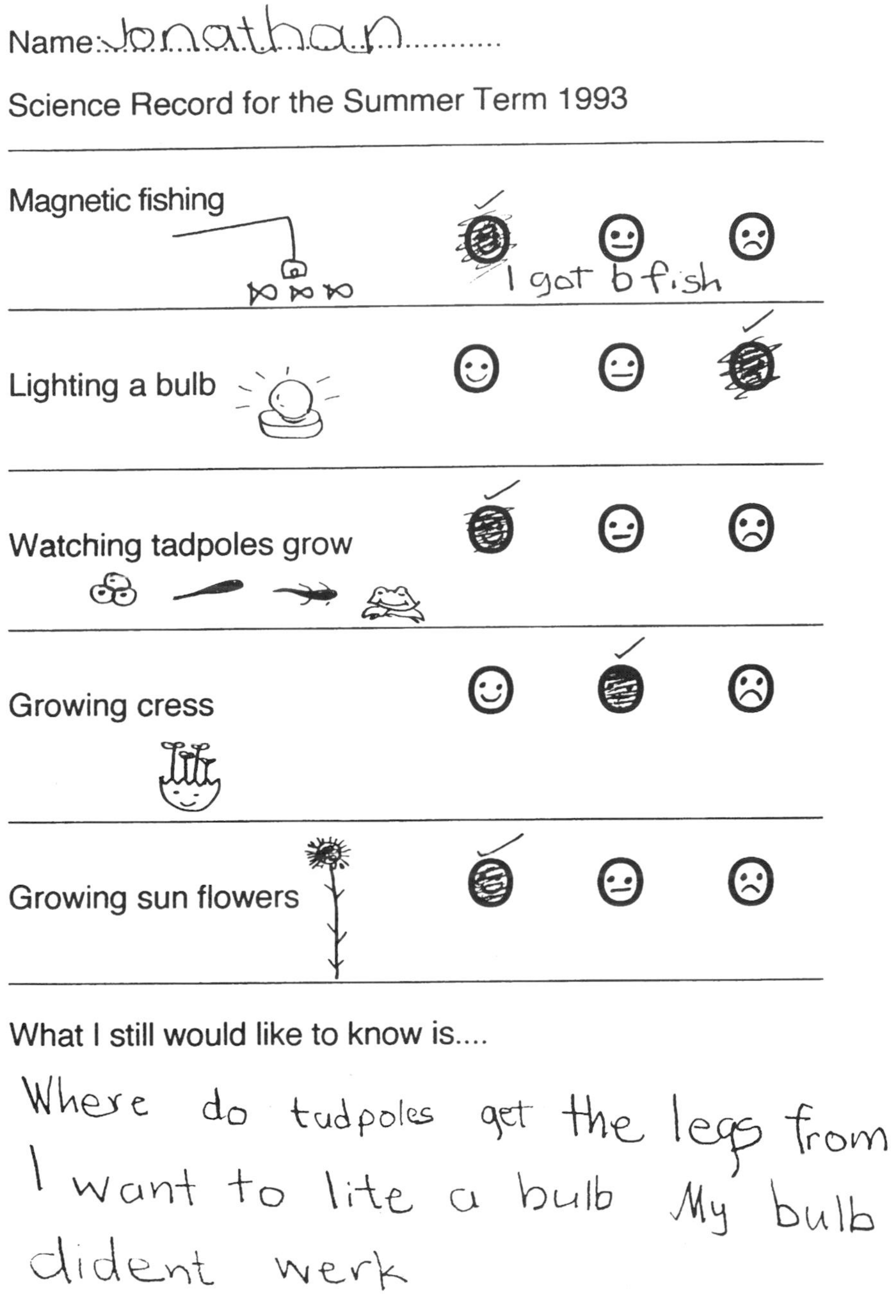
Name: Jonathan

Science Record for the Summer Term 1993

Magnetic fishing — I got 6 fish

Lighting a bulb

Watching tadpoles grow

Growing cress

Growing sun flowers

What I still would like to know is....

Where do tadpoles get the legs from I want to lite a bulb My bulb dident werk

Figure 4.6 *Self-assessment by Jonathan, aged 6*

Pointers for assessing early years

The following points are, we believe, central to effective formative assessment in the early years:

- Be aware of the wide variety of opportunities for formative assessment.
- Plan for and take time to listen to and to observe children.
- Appreciate that discussion holds the key to much effective assessment.
- Ensure language holds a common meaning. Many scientific words have other meanings in common usage.
- Keep a notebook with a page for each child for formative assessment. Jot down useful observations and discussion points, dating each entry.

References

Cavendish, S., Galton, M., Hargreaves, L. and Harlen, W. (1990) *Assessing Science in the Primary Classroom 1. Observing Activities*, London: Paul Chapman.

Clayden, E. and Peacock, A. (1994) *Science for Curriculum Leaders*, London: Routledge.

DES (1987) *National Curriculum: Task Group on Assessment and Testing – a Report*, London: HMSO.

Drummond, M. (1993) *Assessing Children's Learning*, London: David Fulton.

Feasey, R. and Thompson, L. (1992) *Effective Questioning in Science*, Durham: Durham School of Education.

Gott, R. and Duggan, S. (1995) *Investigative Work in the Science Curriculum*, Buckingham, Philadelphia: Open University Press.

Harlen, W. (1993) *Teaching and Learning Primary Science*, London: Paul Chapman.

Hendy, L. and Sparks Linfield, R. (1995) *KS1 Science Through Stories*, Cambridge: Pearson Publishing.

Hurst, V. and Lally, M. (1992) 'Assessment and the nursery curriculum' in G. Blenkin and A. Kelly (eds) *Assessment in Early Childhood Education*, London: Paul Chapman.

Novak, J. and Gowin, D. (1984) *Learning How to Learn*, Cambridge: Cambridge University Press.

Ollerenshaw, C. and Ritchie, R. (1993) *Primary Science: Making It Work*, London: David Fulton.

Sparks Linfield, R. (1994) 'Straw assessment', *Primary Science Review*, 35, 17.

Watt, D. and Russell T. (1990) *Sound: Primary SPACE Project Research Reports*, Liverpool: Liverpool University Press.

Play and language

CHAPTER 5

'It is only a story, isn't it?'

DRAMA IN THE FORM OF INTERACTIVE STORY-MAKING IN THE EARLY YEARS CLASSROOM

Lesley Hendy

Mention of the word 'drama' to gatherings of student or practising teachers creates a perceptible *frisson* which travels through the group. 'I hope she isn't going to make us get up and do something' or 'I'm not making a fool of myself' are common comments heard at the beginning of drama courses. Generally speaking there is a great misconception amongst adults about the nature of drama in education. For many the memory of reading Shakespeare around the class or the participation in performance, requiring the learning and delivering of lines, has caused their adult misgivings. However, drama in education concerns the making of meaning rather than the making of plays. Why is it that something in which we engaged so willingly as small children and was a natural part of our play can give us such a sense of fear and apprehension as adults?

The answer may lie in the lack of play and especially role-play as an integral part of the curriculum in the later years of our education, and in many instances, the over-emphasis on text and text delivery. As our schooling progresses, it becomes dominated by objective truths and ideas. Personal response through play and role-play is often regarded as unreliable and self-indulgent. By adulthood the wonderful spontaneity and creativity found in small children has been replaced by feelings of inadequacy and social foolishness. I would argue that teaching is a form of role-play; if we as teachers cannot engage in it, then we will not be able to encourage our children's creativity and sense of self-worth.

Interestingly, business and industry have rediscovered the use of role-play as an important constituent of management training. There are now few courses in which there is not an element of role-play used to build team-spirit, to explore difficulties in groups or as a means of engaging in problem solving and decision making. These are precisely the things that the good early years specialist wants to encourage in her children's learning and development.

In this chapter I shall outline some ways in which drama, in the form of interactive story-making, can be used as an effective learning medium in the early years classroom, from adult intervention of play in the 'home corner' to making stories with children. I shall also discuss the use of 'drama strategies' as a way of providing time for reflection and widening experience within story-making. In doing so I hope to allay apprehensions about drama and provide early years educators with a strong rationale for including drama as a teaching tool within the planning of the curriculum.

Why drama is important in the early years

Role-play is a stage of progression within the natural development of children's play. It offers us as educators a ready-made medium in which we can engage with our children. Through the 'as if . . .' i.e. the ability to pretend and to leave the real world for that of fiction, it gives a different viewing point from which to consider, discover and make meaning of the world.

Within the Dearing revision of the National Curriculum, drama has been recognised as an important aspect of schooling and has been given a higher profile. The English speaking and listening programmes of study at Key Stage 1 section d, specify:

'Pupils should be encouraged to participate in *drama activities*, improvisation and performances of varying kinds, using language appropriate to a role or situation.'

(p. 4)

The inclusion of dramatic activity in the new National Curriculum English orders would appear to be for the encouragement of purposeful language. Some significant research has shown the importance of role-play in the development of early language (Sylva, Bruner and Genova 1976, Hutt 1989, Kitson 1994) and a recent OFSTED report 'First Class' (OFSTED 1994) indicated that where 'drama and role-play were used effectively' there appeared to be 'better overall standards in literacy' (p 8).

Nonetheless, the use of drama should not be seen as exclusive to the development of language but should be extended across the curriculum and used in any circumstances that require children to describe and communicate their findings and observations (science, maths, geography, history, design and technology). All aspects of the curriculum can be enhanced when children are given a fictional, 'as if' context in which to discuss and communicate what they know.

Drama work, as well as giving opportunities to explore the curriculum in different ways, can also provide the teacher with the opportunity for a group activity which involves social interaction and the exchange of ideas. Through such an activity children can pose and solve problems, make group decisions and use their knowledge and skills in a different environment. By bringing into the classroom the dimension of action, drama enhances learning through the use of PEOPLE – SPACE – TIME. Through the creation of a fictional world, children are given the opportunity of being who they like, where they like and when they like. For example, they could enter a fictional world, as themselves, trying to find solutions to such matters as how to clean up their village as part of a project on the environment. They might be mice trying to reach the moon in order to see whether it is really made of cheese as part of a topic on the sun and moon. They could be a group of servants worried about the disappearance of Snow White or alternatively farmers trying to work out how you can remove milk from a broken down milk tanker.

The use of fictional contexts puts children in control by utilising their existing language, experience, motivations and interests; at the same time the teacher can intervene to bring new shape and fresh ways of looking at things from the children's existing experience. These opportunities provide the teacher with a wide range of potential contexts otherwise unavailable.

The overall purpose of drama as a way of learning should be to affect change which may occur in a number of dimensions. It may, for example, bring about change in:

- the level of knowledge and understanding;
- ways of thinking;
- attitude;
- the expectation of what role-play can offer;
- existing language;
- awareness and the needs of others.

When using drama as a method of learning, there will also be a change in the relationship that exists between language use and the control of knowledge, through the opportunities provided for children to set the agenda and to learn about things that interest them. This can be achieved even within the constraints of an over-full curriculum.

The general characteristics of drama as a learning medium could be described as:

- a method of teaching that helps present information and ideas within a different form of communication (sometimes children are the experts, the teacher the one who needs to be taught);
- a means of giving children some control over their learning, thereby giving them greater access to knowledge and ideas (children are given opportunities to choose the problems that have to be solved and the decisions to be made);
- a method of giving children a fictional situation in which they can respond outside the structure of the ordinary classroom (the shy child is given a context in which to act as someone else);
- an alternative means of describing and communicating which allows pupils to bring their own knowledge about the world into the classroom (children with specialised knowledge such as fishing or horse-riding are able to make a fuller contribution);
- a method of learning that allows pupils and teachers to function as equals;
- a method of providing a 'need to know' which can heighten the learning that has taken place or will take place back in the classroom (children often want to research into something that has arisen within a story).

If drama activity is about anything, it is about the learning and turning-points in life. Such moments can cause the participants to reflect on their actions and to re-think some of their ideas from within a safe environment. To sustain the action the players have to use their knowledge, both factual and subjective, and they will be introduced to new material, both factual and objective, which they must use to help them solve problems and take decisions. This is where the teacher plays such a crucial role. As Readman and Lamont (1994) reflect:

> It is the responsibility of the teacher to:
> - resist any assumptions about the kind of role(s) children might adopt;
> - select content areas which reflect genuine cultural diversity;
> - enable children to adopt roles which challenge any stereotypes;
> - offer children opportunities to work collaboratively.
>
> (p. 16)

Out of the home corner

In the early years classroom the most obvious place to begin is with the 'home corner'. 'Home corners' in the classroom are usually the province of children only and sometimes it is important to allow the children to play alone. But there are other times when an adult could enter into the fantasy situation and play with them.

Knowing when and how to intervene constructively, without the children feeling the teacher is intruding, takes sensitivity and watchfulness. Initially just passing by and engaging in short conversations in role will help build trust. On a recent visit to an infant classroom where the teacher had set up a seaside cafe in her 'home corner', I was encouraged to buy chips and join a complaint about the lack of salt and vinegar!

When you gauge that the children are ready to accept you, an adult, into their 'make-believe' world, more time can be spent with them in their 'home corners'. By renaming it 'role-play' area, many more possibilities become available. A 'home corner' can confine the activities to domestic situations, but by providing different types of environment the children are enabled to explore different kinds of activity. 'Role-play' corners should be seen by the children as more than just places for dressing up and pushing the doll's pram. The creation of a 'role-play' area could involve the class in making things to go in it and might require use of maths, design and technology or information technology. By allowing children to be part of the setting up, we can encourage them to play their part in a variety of constructive ways.

Intervention by adults

Having joined the children at play and adopted a role within their make-believe, we can both initiate or respond in order to facilitate learning. Each intervention by the teacher varies the learning opportunities and the possible learning outcomes (Baldwin and Hendy 1994). It is particularly effective if the teacher identifies and utilises learning opportunities which arise naturally and are offered by the children themselves. It is important for children to feel some ownership of the story and that their contributions to the dramatic play are valued. The teacher may enter the story as the patient or the customer but they must treat the 'doctor' or 'dentist', 'travel agent' or 'greengrocer' with the same respect as if it were real life. This will help to develop the shared fiction in a more open way, and as other children hear the conversation they can be encouraged to join in. The teacher's intervention will also help the child in role to become more committed to their part in the fiction. By using this approach we are able to indicate to the children that their dramatic play is valued and highly regarded. We communicate that it is important to us and is a respected form of activity.

Types of role-play area

'Role-play' areas do not always have to represent familiar locations: any place and any time is possible. Some examples might be:

- places that take children back in time, such as castles, sailing ships, pirate ships, old houses, to begin to give small children a sense of the past;
- time travel settings, such as a space ship or a time machine ;
- fairy story places, such as the Three Little Pigs' brick house, Little Red Riding Hood's cottage, Cinderella's kitchen or the Seven Dwarfs' house;
- places of the imagination, such as the all-green room, the upside-down room, the room of dreams.

All these possibilities for role-play corners could develop children's speaking and listening and allow exploration of other areas of the curriculum. What we choose to provide for our children will determine the learning opportunities we can exploit.

By entering children's dramatic play in this way, we are able to build up trust and commitment. We are able to add dimensions which children are usually unable to sustain for themselves. This can be extended later when bigger group or whole-class drama is undertaken. Our interventions can add the dimension of persistence and consequence; what children do and say can be challenged, questioned and analysed, not just by the adult but by the children themselves.

The Greek word for drama means 'living through' and the action of the drama needs to be lived through by players using 'make-believe' to create the setting for their pretend existence. Within this fantasy world it is important that all agree to take part and share the same action. Adults must be careful never to begin in role without telling the children that they are doing so. By saying 'Can I play?', informs children of our intentions. All the players must employ knowledge they have brought with them from their real lives to help them in the pretend world. Life experience and factual knowledge are applied in an active way, frequently providing a genuine 'need to know'. It is important that children and adults are always aware that they are playing. They must be able to 'hold two worlds in their head at the same time' (Readman and Lamont 1994, p. 27). All should be aware that at any time the 'make-believe' can cease which paradoxically creates the safety. Vygotsky described this ability to live in these two worlds as the 'dual affect'. Aristotle also described this phenomenon as 'metaxis' – the real world and the fantasy world of the drama coming together in the mind of the player.

By having to express their feelings, their thinking and their actions to each other, drama causes children to communicate in a meaningful way and to think more deeply about the consequences of their actions. The random 'play' shooting of the playground, for instance, can be challenged – shooting hurts people and this can be explored. Also, by needing to interpret the action of others, often in unfamiliar ways, and by having the opportunity to replay, change and reflect upon different parts of the action, drama allows children to have new experiences and to test out their reactions in a 'safe' environment.

Using improvisation as the medium for dramatic activity

The national curriculum uses the term *improvisation* as the medium for dramatic activity. This perhaps needs some definition. Within most groups, either students or early years educators, there is some common understanding as to what this term means but less understanding of how it works. It could best be defined as an active method of working which requires both children and teachers to enter a fictional world in which they will be able to:

- explore human relationships and behaviour;
- have a first-hand experience of events and ideas;
- have a genuine need to talk and listen;
- solve problems and make decisions;

sometimes as themselves or sometimes as other people.

In this fictional world, both dialogue and non-verbal action between participants is made up as the situation proceeds, as with ordinary conversations and actions in real life. The group does not have a pre-written script which is learnt and spoken and acted. Through the fictional context, the dialogue and non-verbal action can be steered to include anything the teacher or the children want to discuss or explore. This activity is known as continuous improvisation; it carries on as long as all participants are able to sustain it. Drama in the classroom uses elements that are also to be found in theatrical action: human relationships and situations driven by tension and suspense caused by complications in the plot linked through place and time, using movement and language

It is very difficult to sustain continuous improvisation for long periods of time, as young children can quickly become disengaged from the group activity either because they feel their contribution is not being heard or as they become absorbed in their own story-making. Maintaining improvisation with very large groups may not be easy and, with ever increasing class size, drama needs to be carefully planned and organised.

Drama strategies as a tool for planning

Over recent years the use of drama strategies has become an important aspect of drama planning and structuring. A drama strategy is a structuring device that helps the teacher focus the children on certain aspects of the drama being created. With their use a teacher can interrupt the story to:

- help build a shared environment – Are we all in the same wood? What common understanding do we have about circuses? As we look at the island what do we all see?
- move the plot on if the story is not going anywhere or has become rather circular in its development;
- look at something that has happened to help build group identity about the dilemma – this stops children's insatiable desire for 'what happens next'.

In some instances the group can go back and re-run a section which might be leading the children somewhere they do not want to go. 'Unlike real life' as one student observed 'you can re-wind and change what has just been done.'

Some useful drama strategies that work with early years

Most good books on educational drama contain descriptions and uses for drama strategies (eg: Baldwin and Hendy 1994, Readman and Lamont 1994, Woolland 1993, Neelands 1990). The ones I have included are those I personally have found most suitable for work with early years children.

Teacher-in-Role is possibly the drama strategy most familiar to educators. This is a very powerful one as it allows the teacher to enter the fictional world alongside the children and to structure the story from within. When first introduced to this strategy, teachers-in-training can find the prospect of entering into the context with the children rather daunting; organising the action from the outside seems a much safer option. Those who are willing to undertake teacher-in-role and participate fully in the drama-making find that this is one of the most effective and adaptable strategies they can employ.

Other strategies include:

- *still-image*: the group or smaller groups take up a pose to construct a picture to describe what they want to say;
- *circle time*: the whole group gathers in a seated circle to discuss events and make group decisions. A useful device for calming and controlling the group;
- *what can you see?* each child describes an environment, an event, a person to build a group image;
- *thought-tracking*: individuals say aloud what they think and feel about an event , character or idea;
- *collective role-play*: several children take on the role of one character and support each other in what they say;
- *small-group work*: a small group of children are asked to create a small scene, with or without dialogue, to show what might have happened during an event or what might happen if an idea is carried out.

Planning dramatic activity

By using the elements of theatrical action, improvisation and drama strategies teachers have the tools to plan and structure story-making. The dramatic activity is based on creating a context for improvised situations to take place which can be enhanced by the use of other strategies. As has already been suggested, using drama as education is about making meaning for children rather than making plays.

The structuring of the drama must provide a strong **dilemma** (tension and suspense) from which the children can build belief; in other words something must happen to engage their interest. The children need to be able to enter the role behaving 'as if' it were so. To work, the activity must provide enough stimulation for the children to have a common willingness to 'suspend disbelief'.

Young children possess an innate ability to understand the structuring of stories. They instinctively know that once the story of the drama has started something is going to happen (Hendy 1995). They know that the protagonists in the story will come across complications and dilemmas that have to be solved – Red Riding Hood meets a wolf who wants to eat her, the Three Little Pigs are chased by a wolf intend on destroying their homes and eating them. These dilemmas are strong and life threatening. This does not mean to say that all drama must be about life and death situations but something must be happening which creates a powerful tension that will hold the interest and create contexts in which new knowledge and understandings can take place.

Choosing the context

Choosing the context is an important factor in the planning for early years. Well-known children's stories are a good basis for starting as they often have interesting settings that capture the imagination of small children, for example, a story with a strong narrative or one with interesting characters or ideas. Having selected the context it is worth identifying some of the learning areas which might be explored as the story develops. Stories set in woods or the outdoors might lead to environmental issues or aspects of geography, stories set indoors might provide a background for work in science or maths whereas stories set long ago might produce some interesting insight into history and things of the past.

After the theme has been selected key learning areas should be identified: These can be universal ideas such as

- How do we find out about what people are like?
- How do we deal with people who are different?
- How do we deal with the things that frighten us?

or more curriculum-based learning such as:

- How do we describe similarities and differences between materials? (science)
- How do we design something which will carry us on the wind? (technology)
- Can we recount a story from our past? (history)
- How might we describe something that is 3D in shape? (maths)

To answer some of these questions the story can be structured, through the use of improvisation and drama strategies to explore the key learning areas. Using 'The Three Little Pigs' as an example, (see detailed plan in Figure 5.1) the universal question from this story might be:

How do we cope with bullies and people who seem more powerful than us?

The curriculum-based questions might be focused on design and technology, maths, science and English (see Figure 5.2).

Stories undertaken by young children do not have to be exclusively fantasy based. Stories which involve children pretending to be in familiar surroundings can be effective vehicles to introduce information or test children's knowledge in maths, science, design and technology and other areas of the curriculum. Such stories could be termed 'home' stories as they are

Learning intentions	Planning	Making the story
To encourage listening skills To provide information about the building of homes To develop geographical vocabulary	Circle time Teacher-in-role Whole group-in-role Continuous improvisation	Gather the children into sitting circle time. Tell the children you are going to start the story as the mother of the Three Little Pigs. Leave the group and return looking very worried. Greet the children as if they were friends of your three sons. Tell them how worried you are because you had to send your sons away. You were too poor to look after them any more and they had to make their own way in the world. They have been gone some time and none of them has written to you to tell you about what has happened to them. Ask the friends if they could help you find out what has happened. Pack a basket with some food, lock your house and start on your journey. Tell the children you are nervous because you've not travelled outside your village before. Allow children to chose the way. As you walk along ask the children to identify the different geographical features that you pass like slopes, hills, roads, bridges, rivers etc. Arrive near the sea where the soil is very sandy. Mention the softness of the soil. Freeze the action. Tell the children that when you return, pushing an imaginary wheelbarrow, you are the man who sold the pigs the straw.
To develop imaginative response To provide information about buildings and materials To provide opportunity for mathematical language	Teacher-in-role Whole group-in-role Continuous improvisation	Enter as the man with the straw and greet the children by saying 'Hello, I haven't seen you around these parts. The old lady pig looks tired. What might you be doing here?' Encourage them to tell you about Mother Pig's problem and get them to ask you whether you have seen the Three Little Pigs. Tell the children you sold them some straw and you left them just here building a house out of it. There is no sign of them but notice there is straw blowing about. Ask the children to collect it up so it won't go to waste. Make the straw into bundles and put them in your wheelbarrow. You could use the opportunity to do some counting exercises. You sold them ten bundles but you've only picked up enough for eight, how many are missing? etc. Discuss with them whether sand is a very good place to build a house and whether straw is really a good material especially in a high wind. Take your leave of them and go out. Freeze the action.
To provide opportunity to recall information	Teacher-in-role Whole group-in-role Continuous improvisation	Tell the children you are going back to be the mother. Restart the action by coming to the children and asking who they were talking to and what he had said to them. Try to steer the conversation onto the building of houses in the wrong place with the wrong materials. Continue along the road, moving from the sea into some woods where you will meet the wood-cutter. Tell the children you can see a man through the trees. You are too tired to run. Could they go on ahead and speak to him for you? Freeze the action.
To provide opportunity to ask questions, examine information and respond	Teacher-in-role Whole group-in-role Continuous improvisation	Move in front of the children and restart the action by miming wood cutting. Wait to see if they start to talk to you. If not turn and notice them saying something like, 'You startled me. I didn't hear you coming. Can I do something for you?' Engage them in talk about house building with sticks and how you sold the pigs some sticks and they were going to build a house in the clearing over there. Take them to the clearing but find nothing but broken sticks scattered all around. Tell them you're sorry but you have no idea where the pigs have gone but you told them it was a silly idea to build a house from thin sticks. Make your excuses about having to get back to work and leave them. Freeze the action.
To develop understanding of other people's feelings	Circle time Simple thought-tracking	Gather them into circle time. Ask them to become the tired and worried mother. Go round the group touching each child gently on the shoulder. As you do so ask them to say aloud what the mother pig is thinking as she watches the friends coming back without her children.

Figure 5.1 *Interactive story-making plan for 'The Three Little Pigs' to be used in a topic about homes and buildings*

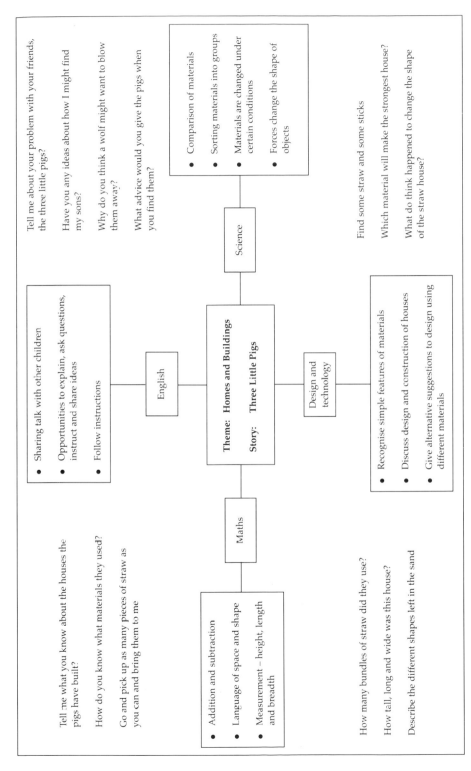

Figure 5.2 *Developing the core curriculum through questioning*

based in reality and all the activities are controlled by natural laws, in other words there is *no magic*. Such active stories are a useful way of helping young children learn more about their world. *Fantasy stories*, on the other hand, have a different feel and are rooted in the imagination. This kind of drama work can extend children's imaginative powers, allowing the possibility of all worlds and ideas, however bizarre and extraordinary.

Planning must take into consideration the children's willingness to:

- adopt a role;
- make-believe with regard to actions and situations;
- make-believe with regard to objects;
- maintain the make-believe verbally;
- maintain the make-believe through movement;
- interact with the rest of the group;
- keep to the structure and the rules of playing.

Teachers must also plan with a commitment to their own participation in mind. Children are not able to engage in effective learning through drama unless the adult has:

- a genuine desire to work in this medium;
- an eagerness to enter the child's world, believe in what they are doing and to take their work seriously;
- an understanding of how improvisation and drama strategies function and can be used;
- knowledge of the learning potential of any particular story together with ability to keep this to the fore;
- techniques to introduce problems for the group to solve;
- the willingness to take risks;
- the willingness to work beside the children and allow the group to make decisions.

Making the contract

It is important that before engaging in interactive story-making both children and adults enter into a contract which makes clear the plan of action, the expectations and the responsibilities of how to proceed when the story-making has begun. As has already been advised, never begin a story until all participants know what they are expected to do.

Some examples of interactive story-making

Working with a modern children's story

A teacher-in-training recently decided to use Nick Butterworth's *After the Storm* as the basis for her drama. This story has the setting of a wood in which a storm has taken place and the animals have been left homeless. This story provided a richness of learning possibilities she could explore with her reception class. The class topic was 'animals' so this story fitted well into the overall curriculum planning.

She began to examine her areas of learning. The wood setting would allow her to test out the children's knowledge of trees and animal habitats, work that they had already undertaken in the classroom. She wanted to discover how much knowledge the children had of the science attainment target 2 'Living Processes and Living Things' Level 1 and 2. She wanted to see whether she could introduce some information about shape and space as the children in their role as animals started to think about the design of their new homes. Design and making would be a strong feature of the story. Geography could be covered as the children made observations about their damaged habitat. By asking the children to remember what it had been like before the storm and sequence events before they heard the great wind, she hoped to increase their sense of the past. Gradually, through careful planning, she was able to build up the learning potential inherent in the story.

Throughout she was keen to let the 'animals' tell their own story but by participating herself in the role of a water rat she was able to question, pose problems and stretch their understanding. **Tension** was created by the children who introduced the idea of the wolves. These animals were never seen but were always present throughout, driving the 'animals' to find a new home quickly before they were eaten. Not having the right tools or materials also became a major problem and slowed up progress on the new homes. Rescue came in the role of 'Wise Owl', a character again introduced by a child, who invited all the animals to his home in the tree and gave them tea.

Most of the story was done through continuous **improvisation** but she introduced some other strategies to increase reflection and commitment. At the very beginning the children were asked to stand quietly in a circle and look at the tree. She went round to each child in their role as an 'animal' and asked them what could they see. Gradually they built up a group picture of the tree fallen in the wood. She then asked each of them to go and rescue something from their home. They returned to the circle and showed the others what they had rescued and what it meant to them. Many of these items were then used in the story. At the end of the story each child was asked to pretend to be a photograph (**still-image**) of their animal standing outside their new home. She subsequently read them the story and it became a big favourite with the class.

Working from children's ideas

When working from children's ideas the teacher has to be able to 'think on her feet' and to seize learning opportunities as they arise. Such work is ideal for building group co-operation and extending children's ability to solve problems and to take decisions. This does not mean that there is no previous planning involved but the planning will be of a more fluid nature, predicting beforehand what learning could be achieved if certain situations arise. With experience, teachers can engineer situations whatever line the story is taking. The following example comes from a story developed by a vertically grouped class who had been working on the theme of castles.

The session commenced with a **discussion circle**. The children sat together with the adults and decided where they were, who they were and what they were doing. They wanted to be servants to a King and they were to be preparing a grand banquet. To start the action in a controlled manner each child was asked to enter the story space and take up a pose of the job they are doing (**still-image**) as if someone had painted a picture of them. When all the children were assembled the action began.

The story began slowly with all the children 'acting out' mixing and peeling and roasting etc. In my role as a new servant I asked for jobs to do and was told where everything was. I created **problems** by not doing my work well and was helped by the other servants. From this I learnt a great deal about the children. Their knowledge of food preparation was very good and we had a long discussion about the best way to cook the potatoes. I asked **questions** about what I thought I knew about cooking and checked whether I was correct. In this instance the children were the 'experts' and I was the novice.

Before long the first major complication, the one that changes the course of the story line, occurred. A child shouted 'Fire!' and before long we were running about trying to put out the flames. This was an opportunity to talk about the dangers of fire: How did it start? What happens when you get too near the flames? How do you deal with burns? etc. Having dealt with this complication another arose. A second child told us that it was not the servants' carelessness which started the fire but a dragon the King had locked in the dungeon for burning people. The dragon was now crying and its tears had put out the flames.

As we sat down amongst the ruins of the King's banquet we discussed how we could help the sad dragon. Could we trust it not to burn us? How do you learn to trust people who have done you harm? Was the dragon really fierce or was she just afraid? Why might she have been burning villages and people before she was captured? After the discussion each 'servant' was asked to say aloud what they thought and felt about the dragon (**thought-tracking**) and the bravest were dispatched to release her from her prison. **Questions** in such stories are endless and can lead to many learning opportunities of a kind that are difficult to discuss in normal classroom situations as they do not necessarily arise.

To describe all the events in this story would take too long here but suffice to say some ninety minutes later the dragon had been taken home to her babies and the 'servants' complete with cooked banquet returned to the castle to feed the King. Many areas of the curriculum were covered including:

Maths	– how big will we need to make our magic carpet to hold all the servants and the dragon? How can we measure the length of the dragon without a tape measure?
Science	– do dragons eat the same things as people? How fast did we need to run to get our magic carpet to fly?
Geography	where in the world do dragons live? What sort of terrain will we be walking through if we land in the mountains?
Music	– let's make up a quiet song to sing to the dragon's baby to make her sleep.

The stories made up in this way are very special to children. I always make the point at the end to tell children that no one has ever heard this story before, it is new and it belongs to them. By writing these stories into book-form they can make a popular addition to the book corner.

Making use of a fairy story

Through the employment of **teacher-in-role**, the mother of the Three Pigs asked the children, in role as the pigs' friends, to help her search for them. By placing the context (the who, where, what and when) outside the events in the story the teacher gave herself more scope for exploration. The children's knowledge of the original story helped them create a sequence of events, but more as detectives piecing together evidence on their journey than participants acting out the story as it happened.

The story began with a **discussion circle** where the teacher told the children who she was going to be. She said when she returned to the circle she would be in role as the mother of the Three Little Pigs and that they, the children, would be some of the pigs' friends. She asked them to close their eyes while she went out of the circle.

On returning she began to tell them about her children and how worried she was as they had been away for a very long time and she had received only one letter since they had left home. She reached into her pocket for a letter (which she had prepared earlier). She read it to the children. The letter said 'Hello Mum, we are fine. We have built a house made of straw and we are very proud of it. We have heard there is a wolf about so we will take care.' She asked the children **questions** about wolves and what they are like – should she be worried? Should she go and look for them? Would the children like to join her?

In **small groups** they draw maps of the landscape around the pigs' home using pictures and symbols to represent different places. These maps were used on the journey. **Questions** were asked about the locality – which way did they go? Did they go north, south, east or west? Did they go over the hills or through the woods? The path through the woods was chosen. As it grew dark they thought about a shelter for the night. Where will be the best place? How will they protect themselves from the wolf? Where will they find something to eat?

As the session progressed the children's interest was sustained by the teacher in her role as mother. By introducing **challenges** and **problems** through effective questioning and leading discussion and by allowing children to direct the story and make it their own, she was able to exploit much of its learning potential. Through skilful use of drama strategies she created moments of reflection on events, people or ideas when and where they are needed.

The session ended where it had begun, in a **discussion circle**. The pigs had been found, the wolf vanquished and all the participants were ready for bed.

Drama as a time saver

Contrary to popular thinking, teaching through drama is not a drain on precious classroom time. Through working in this active way teachers are given a powerful method of teaching and learning which is not always available in other forms of classroom organisation. Learning by doing through the use of this interactive method encourages the retention of information. Recently a seven-year-old was able to tell me, in great detail, the events of an interactive story she had made two years previously in her reception class. Through the different modes of talking story-making promotes, children are able to articulate what they know. With careful planning and structuring, drama, in the form of interactive story-making, provides a time-saving method of introducing children to new learning , challenging their assumptions and ideas and testing their existing knowledge within different contexts. This type of activity makes a significant contribution to children's social, emotional and cognitive development in their early years.

Pointers for early years drama

Some points to remember when using drama in the early years classroom:

- Story-making is a natural activity in early childhood.
- Drama as education is about making meaning rather than making plays.
- Drama is a useful teaching tool across the curriculum and not exclusive to language development.
- The teacher as well as the children must be willing to 'suspend disbelief' and participate in the 'as if'.
- Planning for drama is strengthened by effective use of drama strategies.
- The context for the story must contain interesting complications and dilemmas.
- By its active nature drama is an efficient and time-saving method of introducing new learning or testing old knowledge.

References

Baldwin, P. and Hendy, L. (1994) *The Drama Box*, London: HarperCollins.

Hendy, L. (1995) 'Playing, role-playing and dramatic activity', *Early Years*, 15, 2, pp. 13–22.

Hutt, C. (1989) 'Fantasy play', in S. J. Hutt *et al.* (eds) *Play, Exploration and Learning*, London: Routledge.

Kitson, N. (1994) 'Fantasy play: a case for adult intervention', in J. Moyles (ed.) *The Excellence of Play*, Buckingham: Open University Press.

Neelands, J. (1990) *Structuring Drama Work*, Cambridge: Cambridge University Press.

OFSTED (1993) *First Class*, London: HMSO.

Readman, G. and Lamont, G. (1994) *Drama: A Handbook for Teachers*, London: BBC Education.

Sylva, K., Bruner, J. and Genova P. (1976) 'The role of play in the problem-solving of children 3–5 years old' in J. Bruner *et al.* (eds) *Play: its Role in Development and Evolution*, Harmondsworth: Penguin.

Woolland, B. (1993) *The Teaching of Drama in the Primary School*, London: Longmans.

CHAPTER 6

'You be de and I'll be de . . .'

LANGUAGE, NARRATIVE AND IMAGINATIVE PLAY

Jenny Daniels

Carol Fox (1993) has shown how young children can tell imaginative fantasy stories playing themselves into the discourses of literature and literacy. They make maximal use of written stories heard from books, long before they can read and write themselves. This chapter looks at another context for language learning – the point at which the child becomes a pupil and has to 'read' the discourses of the classroom. Margaret Meek (1989) has used the term, 'what goes here?' to describe the way in which children are encultured into different social contexts, in this case the classroom culture. As part of these learning processes, I want to argue for the importance of creative play in the infant classroom, and emphasise the benefits of children using narrative play with the encouragement and support of an actively involved educator.

Stories heard in the infant classroom

Sixty or so faces looked intently at the brightly striped puppet theatre standing in the corner of the classroom. The afternoon was hot and sticky, the children wriggled and shuffled to make themselves cooler and more comfortable. A teacher looked on indulgently from the doorway. There was no need for her intervention, they were all absorbed in the puppet play. She went off to join her colleagues, preparing for the school fete at the weekend.

A typical event in the life of an infant school. Nothing remarkable, the children enjoying the entertainment provided by the puppet plays. I was there with a group of nursery nurses from the local college, helping them to organise the event and act as host for the different stories they had written. The context was not the best for learning. The children were packed into a small space on an unbelievably hot day, the traffic just outside roared by incessantly on the ring road. It was the kind of situation which invites frayed tempers and results in tears. Yet here they sat, lost in the worlds of Max the monkey and Supergran. As I watched their faces, the registering of emotion and their total involvement in the story, it was clear that the event was deeply significant for them.

Margaret Meek (1989) has shown how important story is for children, how it opens up possible worlds and encourages engagement at a deep and profound level. We use it frequently in the infant school, drawing on the vast range of traditional and cultural stories available to us. But what do the children do with all this information? How do they process and internalise the complex structures which stories contain? What is the nature of the experience involved in listening to stories? These were some of my thoughts as I waited for the next play – and it is the starting point for the ideas in this chapter.

I wanted to investigate some of these questions in relation to children's learning and language. If a dramatic story (the puppet play) could have such a powerful effect on young children, how could we as educators harness this phenomenon and incorporate it into good classroom practice? Stories are sometimes used as the testing ground for understanding, the narrative reduced to a comprehension exercise. It would have been tragic to merely ask questions such as 'What happened?' in the puppet plays which the children had seen. I wanted them to recreate the excitement and involvement which the original stories had so obviously stimulated.

During the following week I went back to the school and took the puppets with me. Working with small groups of children who had seen the plays, I asked them to help the puppets to remember what they had to say. This was not an invitation to repeat the script verbatim, rather an opportunity to play in a context framed by the previous experience of the performance. I wanted to see what they had taken from the puppet plays and what role 'play' had in the learning process. How did children as young as five use their linguistic ability in order to engage in complex language structures and interactions?

It is interesting to note that within the National Curriculum the importance of story is emphasised, both telling stories and listening to them. Children are encouraged to use their oracy skills to explore, develop and clarify ideas, predicting outcomes and discussing possibilities. The varied language resources which young children bring to their early schooling are acknowledged. There is strong emphasis on language as performance, the importance of clarity and using language with a sense of audience. The response to drama which they have watched or participated in is to be encouraged.

In some respects, however, the requirements at Key Stage 1 seem to sadly underestimate the abilities of young children. It only asks children to 'consider what has been heard and to remember specific points' when they are clearly capable of much richer and more purposeful responses, as I quickly discovered when I invited these particular four- and five-year-olds to play with the puppets.

The invitation to play with the puppet characters allowed considerable freedom of choice and made limited demands on straight memory skills. Given the intensity with which the children engaged with the puppet plays, there would be no difficulty in asking for their participation in a play response.

Stories and re-telling

Children hear stories from a wide range of sources: books, radio and television, stories shared from everyday living and family events. All these stories, despite the apparent informality of some, do in fact carry formal, complex structures. Carol Fox (1993) has shown how children, when given the opportunity, can themselves take control and construct stories which draw on a huge range of linguistic devices and skills. Her careful deconstruction of their oral storying has provided valuable insight into the rich granary of pre-school narratives of different kinds from different sources. Margaret Meek (Foreword in Fox 1993, p. viii) makes the point succinctly: 'The most dramatic evidence is that, in storying, children understand the potentiality of the complexity of language long before they have a fully conscious grasp of its nature.'

The children studied by Fox were pre-school, and all of the data collected was from the home context. I was curious to see what happened to children when they went to school. If young children can be so skilled in their narrative knowledge, how do they use it in a schooled situation? What can teachers do to enhance and develop this impressive ability?

Play and learning

Early years educators recognise the tremendous value of fantasy or pretend play. In play, children can reach depths of understanding and complexity which the busy 'doing' activities of the infant classroom do not allow for. Lesley Hendy (1995) has eloquently expressed the plea for taking children's play seriously. She argues for teachers to use this valuable resource for learning and development by engaging in the children's story making in an active and participatory manner. An early years educator can benefit enormously by adopting a role in the children's fantasy play. However, it still seems to be a very special educator who is prepared to join in the play activity on the children's terms.

Perhaps a way of developing this idea is to acknowledge that children are more than capable of structuring and developing their own play. Vygotsky has shown how children can work in the zone of proximal development, 'with the help of more able peers'. Narrative play is the perfect situation for such activity for the following reasons:

- the children have to collaborate;
- the enterprise carries shared outcomes;
- the children trawl the depths of their language resources;
- the 'knowledge of audience' frames the language interaction.

I now want to describe children's responses to two of the puppet plays and, in the transcriptions, show the complexity of language use being employed. An analysis of the language and explanations of some of the references reveal how hard children work in order to play.

The original puppet story: 'Max the Naughty Monkey'

The puppet plays were an assignment for nursery nurse training. Much of these courses centres on child care and health, but all students have to complete a communication module, largely to improve literacy skills. The opportunity to work creatively with puppets for a specific audience was a valued contribution. Students were invited to write their own scripts with a minimum number of characters (the puppet theatre has limited space). Interestingly, all the plays produced had a moral theme, usually incorporating exhortations to 'keep clean', ' be good' and generally 'do as you are told.' Such cautionary tales were the direct result of the training the students themselves were experiencing.

The story of Max the Naughty Monkey is typical. Max is the one who never quite 'gets it right', so that when asked by his mother to help bake a cake, the ingredients are spilled, the cake is burnt and Max is banished from the kitchen. Mum regrets her harsh words and bakes another cake to make amends. Slippery Sam the snake almost steals it but Max saves the cake, Slippery Sam is taken to the police station and Mum and Max are reconciled. The narrative is accompanied by many chases and requests to the audience for help. The burlesque nature of puppetry lends itself to such performances. The children were fascinated by the play, identifying their own frustrated attempts to do things properly with Max's mistakes. The level of audience participation was understandably high.

What follows is the transcript of Kate (5.2) and Samantha (4.11). They had been in the reception class from January of that year. The puppet shows went to schools at the beginning of July.

I returned to the school the following week and asked for small groups of children, (preferably friends but certainly mixed ability groups). We then went to a small room off the staff room which had taping equipment and the puppets used by the nursery nurses the previous week. Sam and Kate had just completed some work, so were allowed to be the first story tellers.

Transcript of 'Max the Naughty Monkey' – the retelling

R = Researcher
K = Kate (5 years, 2 months)
S = Sam (4 years, 11 months)

Puppet Play Characters
(M) = Mother : played by Kate
(Max) = Max : played by Sam

R   You remember you saw quite a few different plays didn't you? Yes. Now I've got a bit of a problem today because those puppets have to do another show for some other children this afternoon and they've forgotten what it is they have to say. They've forgotten their story. Could you tell it to them, do you think?
K and S   Yes.

(Both girls were keen to help but a little unsure about the nature of the request.)

R   Shall we look at the first one? Because . . .

[I take one of the puppets out of the bag.]

R   Who is this?
K   It were . . .
R   Do you remember about the monkey?

[I put on the monkey puppet, but, understandably, they want to play with the puppets themselves. I hand the two puppets over to them.]

R   OK, would you like to be Mrs Monkey and you be Max the monkey and you try and tell them what it is they have got to do this afternoon, for the other children. What happens first?

K   Mm . . . His mother said he could make some cakes.

(Kate stays in the third person when telling me. Her voice is low and hesitant, her body language indicating what she wants to do but 'reading' that the situation is not appropriate in her understanding of school/classroom behaviour.)

R   You get him to do it then.

K (M)   Max, please can you make some cakes for me? . . . I'll get you a bowl.

[Sam starts action for baking cakes]

R   Shall we get a pretend bowl?

K   Yeah.

R   There's a pretend bowl.

K   Thank you.

[Girls act out the kitchen scene.]

K (M)   Here you are Max. Oh no! Look now Max, look what you've done! It's all gone over the new carpet! Tch! Go out and get your boots on – I know there's nothing on the telly . . . Why don't you go and pick some cherries?

(The spilling of food was in the original play, but Kate elaborates the script using language and incidents from home. She is able to draw on other scripts and incorporate them into the puppet story.)

S (*Max*)   It's raining.

K (M)   Well get your hood up then!

[Sam moves Max as if going outside.]

S (*Max*)   I can't, I haven't got one.

K   He . . .

[Both girls giggle self-consciously]

(Sam mentions the rain and introduces a new idea to the story. Perhaps in order to maintain the narrative, she is aware that the action needs to move outside. There is considerable collaboration needed in order to keep the story going. Kate predicts the difficulty of the situation. After introducing the idea of going outside, she realises that the puppet is not suitably dressed! Again both girls are recreating their own context, finding the original one unsatisfactory.)

Kate very quickly 'imagines' the home situation and uses her known scripts to extend the action. Watching TV was not mentioned in the original script, but Kate incorporates it. Sam enters the discourse in a similar way. She imaginatively projects her puppet into the events with the comment, 'It's raining'. Kate cannot resist mimicking her mother. Both girls are operating in a shared, imagined context. Sam chooses to slip back to reality – the puppet does not have a hood. Sam and Kate giggle as they register the movement in and out of the real world and their world of imaginative play. Fortunately, it does not embarrass them enough to curtail the storying. They went on to develop the story and elaborate with further adventures of Max. The girls regarded each story as a performance and were keen to rehearse each episode once they had negotiated the structure. In one case they repeated the play four times, not giving identical performances, but certainly maintaining high levels of concentration and motivation in order to reach a standard they themselves were happy with.

Commentary on the transcript: children 'making sense' of their experiences

At the time of collecting the data I was very much 'feeling my way through'. Quite by chance, the children stumbled on the idea of wearing the puppets themselves, and this then 'released' them to show skill and understanding which I would not have thought possible. As this was the first attempt at asking the children to use the puppets, my role in the retelling was more evident. Certainly in the beginning stages I am 'scaffolding' (albeit unconsciously at this point) and helping the children to construct the framework and discourse in which I wanted them to play. After only six months of schooling, Kate has learned that certain types of play are part of playground and home culture and not welcome in the classroom. When permission is granted, she can talk fluently and imaginatively.

What was interesting, and proved to be true on subsequent retellings, was that the children always tried to tell the story in the third person. Kate includes the puppets in some of her statements (e.g. 'He's got to throw the flour on the floor') but largely they are directed towards me. She is looking to the power base for some clues as to what is wanted. Yet the seeds of intention are already there in as much as the puppet is included by her body movement in her statement. She is searching for a sign which will make legitimate the type of play she feels she would like to do, but at the same time is aware of a 'school-type' situation which usually demands a different response.

I find the way in which the girls adopt the character of the puppets fascinating. Having told Kate that it is permissible to wear the puppets, I then reinforce it by telling her directly, 'You get him to do it then'. Even so, there is considerable reluctance. 'To do it' for Kate means entering a type of play and language which she feels is unacceptable or unwelcome in school or in front of an adult. When I actually join in the fantasy play by getting the pretend bowl, both girls relax and are able to move the story along on their own terms.

Kate uses a discourse which draws upon her experience of arguments with mum on a wet day. She makes reference to flour being spilt on a new carpet. This was not mentioned in the original play, but it was a new item in Kate's home which her mother was, quite rightly, anxious to preserve! The frequent reminders from home can easily be drawn on in this play situation. A script of warnings forms the basis for any young child's early attempts at language, and Kate is able to use it to her own advantage here.

Another part of the transcript which puzzled me was Kate's reference to Max the Monkey going for a walk and picking cherries for dinner. Again, no mention of cherries was made in the original and I could not understand the connection. It was only when I watched the video of the play that sense dawned! The students had designed a backdrop with a cherry tree for Slippery Sam to hide in. Kate was merely making sense of what was available – that is – using all the clues given, in the same way that she would use pictures to help understand a text. The contextual clues given by the backdrops and the few props used took on a new significance after this. It was a salutary lesson to me that Margaret Donaldson (1978) was right – children do go to extraordinary lengths to make sense of their world even if in this case it left the teacher somewhat confused.

In this particular retelling my presence was very much 'there', working with the children and giving them the support necessary to scaffold their storytelling. On a second retelling the scaffolding was not necessary, both girls could produce a confident and articulate performance – and I was relegated to the audience!

'Supergran to the Rescue'

The second puppet play we chose to play with was 'Supergran to the Rescue'. It had been very popular at the first performance, partly because of the re-showing of the *Supergran* series on television at the time, and also because the student performance was dramatic and the narrative highly moralistic. The story centres on two children shopping at the supermarket with their mother. She tells them to wait by the sweet shelves while she goes to buy some cheese. Tired and bored, the children disobey and go to look at the toys. They get lost in the large supermarket and after searching in vain for mum, are rescued by Supergran. It made riveting viewing for five-year-olds!

The two children invited to play with the puppets this time were Rachel and Ruth. They were more confident in school than Kate and Sam, and very keen to take part in the puppetry. There is an element of competition in their verbal play, but it is used in an interesting manner.

Transcript of 'Supergran to the Rescue' – the re-telling

T = Teacher
Ra = Rachel (6 Years)
R = Ruth (6 years)

Puppet Play Characters
(*R*) = Rachel, (*M*) = Mummy : mostly played by Rachel
(*S*) = Sam, (*SG*) = Supergran : played by Ruth

R   You be d' mummy and I'll be d' . . . Hello. My name is . . .?   W h a t ' s my name?

[Ruth 'thinks' herself into role. Trips up on name.]

Ra   We've got to do Supergran first.
R (*SG*)   I'm Supergran. And this is Rachel.

(Ruth keeps the action by choosing 'Rachel' as the name. The original puppets were James and Lucy.)

Ra   And this is Sam.

(Sam is Rachel's younger brother.)

R   And this is Mummy. This story is about when Sam and Rachel, when they get lost at the supermarket. They are a bit silly in this story! So do you want to know what the story is all about?
Ra   One day they all went to the shops and Sam and Rachel said that . . .

[She adopts the puppet voice of Sam.]

(*S*)   . . .This isn't nice! I don't like shopping. I want to go and get the Shreddies first.
R (*R*)   I want some sweets.
Ra (*M*)   No, you've had sweets. [An argument ensues.] No. You've had sweets today.
R (*R*)   Ooooh. Why not?

Ra (M)   Have them tomorrow. Now wait there while I go and get . . . some cheese.

[Mummy puppet leaves.]

Ra (S)   Let's go and look at the toys.
R (R)   No, we'd better not. We might lose Mummy.
Ra   Come on.
R   Oh, OK.

[The two puppets move away from the stage to go and look at the toys. The conversation continues in the imagined toy department of the supermarket.]

Ra   Look. That's easy!
R   Look . . .
R (S)   Where's Mummy? [Sam starts to cry.]
Ra (SG)   What's the matter with you two?
R (S)   We've lost our Mummy. Who are you?
Ra (SG)   I'm Supergran. I'll find her for you.
R (as Rachel!)   We've lost our Mummy somewhere. She's gone to get the . . . cheese for Daddy's supper and we can't find her anywhere.
R (SG)   Is that her?
R (R and S)   Where? There she is, there . . .

[A chase sequence follows.]

Ra (M)   Oh children. I've been looking for you all over the place. Where have you been?
R and Ra (R and S)   We went to see the toys and we got lost.
Ra (M)   Why didn't you stay where I told you to?

[Rachel then gets the Mummy puppet to smack the children. She does not verbalise the morality and the action is one which parodies the original, with its heavy moral theme.]

Commentary on the transcript: children using 'scripts'

Two things are striking about the retelling. One is the children's sophisticated 'sense of audience'. They go to considerable lengths to make the narrative as clear as possible and have an acute sense of performance – of 'getting it right', not just in terms of straight comprehension skills and recall, but in the more subtle way in which their own experience is included in order to keep the sense of the story. It is what Kathleen Nelson (1982) refers to as 'script'. The script is a general event representation derived from and applied to social contexts. It is basically an ordered sequence of actions appropriate to a particular spatial–temporal context, organised around a goal.

Both children are using language in a very sophisticated way. As well as the performative quality to their play, they also deal with:

a) a puppet on each hand (after initial negotiation, roles and names are ascribed);
b) the original story which was seen over a week before;
c) the narrative action and sequence of events.

In order to bring the elements together, Ruth and Rachel use script knowledge from their home context, and at the same time respond to each other in the real world (as opposed to their play world). The ease and familiarity of such discourses are impressive.

Rachel's 'script' for going shopping is one which in her real life experience includes buying Shreddies – obviously invested with particular meaning as a sought after and enjoyed item. Working consciously with her known script she incorporates it into the retelling of the puppet play. The flavour of the story is kept, although the text changes in the retelling. A similar incident happens with reference to the puppets going to look at the toys. Rachel's own experience of such a situation is to look specifically at 'games' – although they are not mentioned in the original – and she introduces the comment, 'Look. That's easy'. 'That' refers to a puzzle which she has obviously mastered before. Rachel is using her own known script in order to move the story along. This results in:

1   A puzzle which Rachel has experience of and has found easy.
2   The same puzzle seen by Rachel in a supermarket at some time.
3   The fantasy of the puppet play and the characters being moved to a specific area in the supermarket.
4   The introduction of (2) using (1) as a motive for action within the framework of the imaginative play.

Interestingly, both children have difficulty attributing motives unless there is an affective element of their remembering – such as Shreddies or the toys. In other words, the affective sphere is important as a means to cognition and certainly to memory. Without it having some personal meaning – the motive is more likely to 'float away'. Hence Rachel's difficulty in remembering what mummy goes off to buy. Had it been sweets she might have had the recall easily, but cheese is possibly of minor importance to a six-year-old.

In writing the play, the initial impetus for the nursery nurses was to encourage the children not to stray away from mum when they went shopping. Both Mum and Supergran enforce the moral to the children, but Ruth and Rachel do not repeat it. They accept it as a necessary part of the action, but are actually more excited by the fear of being lost and the heightened tension they can demonstrate to the audience. Again the affective has more power than the intended morality.

Rachel and Ruth react differently to the story. On an intra-personal level they draw on past experience and individual concerns. Ruth takes the initiative by suggesting 'Rachel' as the name for one puppet, and Rachel quickly responds by giving the other puppet the name of her younger brother. There may be a jostling of egos, but once the metaphor of the play is called up by both children, they concentrate on making it work for them. Valerie Walkerdine (1982) has demonstrated the way in which children position themselves in a discourse, how they need to negotiate the metaphor called up in order to engage in imaginative play. On an interpersonal level Rachel and Ruth skilfully negotiate, through language, a shared social context. This is made more difficult by being a performance, that is, they have to mediate their understanding, in role, to a defined audience. There is little evidence of egocentrism here. Meanings are achieved by way of carefully managed social interaction with, interestingly, no teacher intervention. Rachel and Ruth are successfully operating in the 'zone of proximal development' (Vygotsky 1978, p. 84).

The original play was imbued with a heavy moral message, the nursery nurses wanted the narrative to teach children the importance of staying close to the parent/carer. The children recognised the tone and content of such a cautionary tale, but it did not have the desired effect. At six, they were already familiar with genre and genre knowledge. Rather than accept the moral message the children actively subvert it by getting the mummy puppet to smack the disobedient children. The nursery nurses would have been mortified – such a reaction was certainly not part of their intention in writing the play! Rachel and Ruth demonstrate that they not only understand the genre of puppetry (that physical violence is part of the burlesque), but also the intended morality which they choose to parody. In effect, imaginative play allows them a degree of freedom on an issue to which the real world is peculiarly sensitive.

What young children know about being language users

It seems, then, that children in the early years have the ability to co-operate and maintain a high level of self-regulation. The transcripts reflect the sophistication and understanding of each other's needs, with an awareness that language has a variety of functions which they can draw upon. There is corroboration, explication, hypothesising and prediction. All these are spun around the web of moving the story along and being aware of what the other child (puppet) is doing. In every case, a child could successfully manipulate two puppets.

The key to these discourses was the encouragement and legitimation of play, especially narrative play. Plowden (1962) recognised that play is vital to children's learning and should be central to good practice in infant classrooms. Since then, play has been associated with material objects for play (sand, water, tactile objects, toys etc.), all provided for 'doing' activities. I am concerned that fantasy (or language) play has not been central to our ideas of what constitutes play. Concrete experience represents safe and neutral ground for the educator who can monitor a child's activity and experience. National Curriculum requirements reflect this model of behaviour in the early years. However, the transcripts reveal how central imaginative play is, how the model which children are working with is highly sophisticated and extending their language skills in a complex and enjoyable manner.

The children in this study showed that they were competent in all these skills, and capable of so much more. They clearly trawled their linguistic ability in order to play with the puppet narratives – but 'choosing words with precision', as the National Curriculum puts it, is hardly the right description! What emerges is a simplistic model of language in the National Curriculum, one which does not take into account the rich variety and fine tuning of young children's language interactions.

Imaginative play is the key to children drawing on all their abilities in order to enhance their learning. In every case in the retellings, children thought an adult question invited a regurgitation of the original story. Perhaps this is not surprising when for much of the time at school, they are being asked to verify their observations – to 'get it right'. The success of the puppet plays was not just the power of performance, but the recognition of 'play' and its central role in good early years practice.

The children described in this chapter clearly enjoyed their play with the puppets and wanted to repeat the experience. The class teacher subsequently encouraged all the children to make puppets and perform plays for each other. She commented on the high level of engagement and the degree of collaboration which even the most difficult children could deal with. Their ability to self-regulate and organise co-operatively was impressive. The children who had actually played with the nursery nurse puppets asked if they could use free time on Friday afternoons to do some drama. They worked in the library, unsupervised, for some six to eight weeks. I then received a request from the class teacher to visit and see their performance. Fortunately,

I was able to video their version of Cinderella. It was detailed and organised, each child having an appropriate role and drawing on a range of dramatic conventions (including a highly satirical parody of teaching staff!) It was remarkable in its originality, delivery and sense of performance, all achieved without adult intervention.

Puppets can be an ideal way to encourage imaginative play in the infant classroom. The spontaneous role-play which all children engage in can be refined when they use creative play. Perhaps we need to take more seriously the drama games (play) they produce, recognising the cognitive and emotional benefits to be gained from such activities. I would like to think that no child in our nursery and infant classes would ever again have to look to the early years educator for permission to engage in imaginative play in the classroom. It is time to recognise its value as an integral part of learning, bringing play from the playground 'in from the cold'. When children ask us to join in a play situation we should recognise the importance of such activity and respond with sensitivity and understanding. Too often children are sent to play when so called 'real work' is completed. The invitation, 'you be d' ' is one we will ignore at our peril!

Pointers for the use of narrative play

- Narrative play allows children to trawl their language resources, making use of literary knowledge from books and stories.
- Children exercise considerable self-regulation in their wish to organise and express ideas.
- Narrative play encourages sophisticated collaboration.
- Early years educators need to be able to initiate, encourage, support and be actively involved in narrative play.
- Intervention in the play process must be sensitively manoeuvred. Sometimes we need the confidence to 'stand back' and let the children continue uninterrupted.
- Narrative play can form the basis for many other activities in the early years classroom – not least a growing confidence in all forms of language use and function.

References

Donaldson, M. (1978) *Children's Minds*, London: Fontana.
Fox, C. (1993) *At the Very Edge of the Forest*, London: Cassell.

Hendy, L. (1995) 'Playing, role-playing and dramatic activity', *Early Years*, 15, 2, pp. 13–22.

Meek, M. (1989) *How Texts Teach What Readers Learn*, Stroud: Thimble Press.

Nelson, K. (1982) 'Social Cognition in a Script Framework', in J.H. Flavell and L. Ross (eds) *Social Cognitive Development*, Cambridge: Cambridge University Press.

Plowden Report (1962) *Children and their Primary Schools*, London: HMSO.

Vygotsky, L.S. (1978) *Mind in Society: the Development of Higher Psychological Processes*, Cambridge, Mass: Harvard University Press.

Walkerdine, V. (1982) 'From context to text', in M. Beveridge (ed.) *Children Thinking Through Language*, London: Arnold.

CHAPTER 7

'Is there a seven in your name?'
WRITING IN THE EARLY YEARS

Sally Wilkinson

The aim of this chapter is to look at ways in which we as educators can provide opportunities which will nurture children as writers. Young children are constantly exposed to print in the environment in which they live, whether at home, play group, in the street or at school. They see adults and older children writing notes to each other, lists for a shopping trip and letters both formal and informal. They begin to realise that these marks on paper are regarded as important by those around them and can have many uses. Just as they learn to talk by experimenting with spoken language and imitating those around them, children will often experiment with marks on paper. They will try out patterns and attempt to communicate through this medium themselves.

These independent marks, are often referred to as 'emergent writing'. This term encompasses the vast number of ways in which young children use marks and letters to make meaning. As Yetta Goodman (1986) described, from a young age children engage in writing tasks for a wide variety of reasons and by the age of two most children have begun to use symbols to represent real things. Therefore, by the time children enter a nursery or reception class they may already be very experienced emergent writers. They may be mark makers or they may be aware of the alphabetic nature of print. It is our job, as educators, to build on these skills, and the knowledge and understanding of writing which the children have. This involves adopting a developmental approach to writing whereby the children's emergent writing is acknowledged and they are encouraged to 'have a go' rather than copy from an adult model. The implications this has for how writing is approached in school, the contexts in which it happens and ways of encouraging children as independent writers will form the basis for this chapter.

Understanding children writing

Ann Browne, in her book *Helping Children to Write* (1993), correctly says that before we undertake the planning of a writing curriculum for young children we should have some understanding of what writing is for, how it is used and how it looks from the child's point of view. In his nursery class Josh has been looking at snails. Part of his response to this experience (see Figure 7.1) is to make sweeping circular marks across his paper which he says, as he does so, are the snails, and to make dots under this which he says is his writing. Josh is clearly showing, even in this early stage of his hand co-ordination development, that he knows that drawing and writing are formed by different sorts of marks.

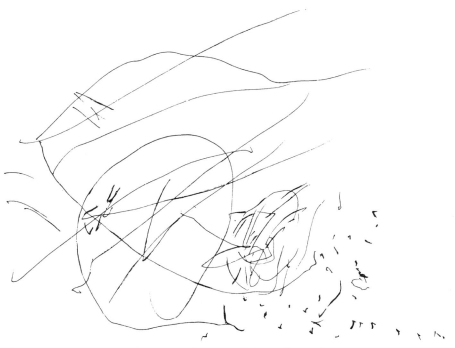

Figure 7.1 *Drawing and writing about snails by Josh, aged 3*

Other children of a similar age might respond with:

- marks mostly horizontal
- zig-zags
- single or linked round shapes
- straight and round marks imitating letter shapes
- large circular shapes

- one letter from their name repeated
- assorted letters from their name.

How children respond in these early stages varies greatly and is not part of a rigid hierarchy of stages. As the many examples of children's writing collected by teachers involved in the National Writing Project (1989) showed, some children experiment with all of the above, others with only one or two.

It does seem to be true however that the appearance of the marks in general reflects the children's cultural background, with marks being formed in the direction and following the orientation used by adults around them. Therefore, a child used to seeing adults using a Chinese script may well emphasise vertical marks in their writing. It is also often the case that children who prefer writing with their left hand, or who have not yet shown a preference, may start much of their mark making from the right-hand side of the paper.

Children whose mother tongue is not English may also include characters from their home language in their writing. In the piece of writing shown in Figure 7.2 Fatima is experimenting with a wonderful array of letter and character shapes based on written forms found in English and Bengali.

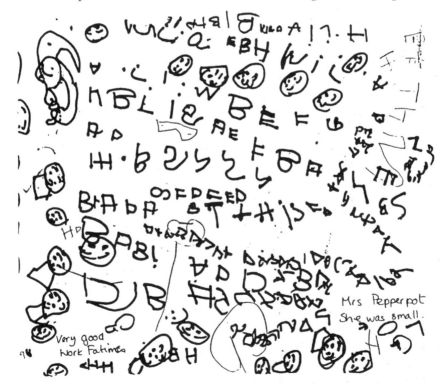

Figure 7.2 *Letter shapes drawn by Fatima showing the influence of English and Bengali written forms*

The way that writing is approached and organised in her class has meant that she is confident about herself as a writer and is willing to take risks with her writing. This piece of writing was in response to a story read by the class teacher who then wrote down what Fatima told her the writing said. She praised Fatima for using so many different letters and characters and they talked about the ones Fatima liked the best.

The role of the educator

As can be seen from the way Fatima's teacher responded to her writing, by encouraging children to write independently from the start, the role of the educator is altered significantly. Instead of spending time writing sentences for children to copy or answering requests for help with spelling, the educator has a more active role. Time can be spent talking with the children about their writing, observing the skills and knowledge they are using and joining with them as a fellow writer. As can be seen from Figure 7.3, the ways in which an educator can support and interact with children engaged in the writing process are many and varied.

What is certain is that the educator is at the centre of what happens in the classroom. We make decisions all the time which influence not only the opportunities children have for writing in our classrooms, but how they perceive the task of writing and themselves as writers. Writing needs to be presented as part of the whole language environment, a way of initiating or responding to communication and as something which can give pleasure for its own sake. The ways that activities are set up in the classroom should recognise that, '... reading, writing, talking about writing and talking in order to write must be continual possibilities; they overlap and interlock' (F. Smith 1982, p. 202).

Talking about writing

Making time for talk at various stages of the writing process is one way of improving the quality of the content of the writing that the children produce. Encouraging children to tell their stories to a friend who would:

- say which parts they liked;
- ask questions to clarify their understanding;
- make suggestions of additions or parts to alter;

means that a story is well established in a child's mind before a pen or pencil has been picked up. There is therefore less chance of the writer

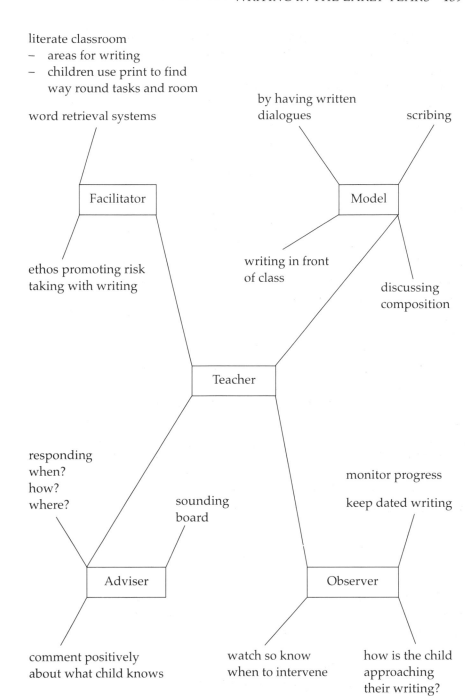

literate classroom
- areas for writing
- children use print to find
  way round tasks and room

word retrieval systems

by having written
dialogues

scribing

Facilitator

Model

ethos promoting risk
taking with writing

writing in front
of class

discussing
composition

Teacher

responding
when?
how?
where?

sounding
board

monitor progress

keep dated writing

Adviser

Observer

comment positively
about what child knows

watch so know
when to intervene

how is the child
approaching
their writing?

Figure 7.3 _Modes of interaction of the educator with children engaged in the
writing process_

coming to the mental block of what to write next as they have already rehearsed it orally. Using talk in this way asks the children to draft their writing orally. This is an important stage on the way to them being able, when they are more experienced writers, to alter and improve their work on paper and respond to written comments given by peers. The latter idea, which involves partners responding to each other's work, is perhaps usually thought of as only being appropriate for older children. However, as was demonstrated during the National Writing Project (1989), with the support of an educator, young children are able to use talk and writing to comment on a partner's work in a way that extends that child's ideas or encourages them to develop their writing further.

Known texts and writing

As well as recognising the importance of talk to writing we also need to encourage children to draw on the stories, poems and factual texts that they have heard or have read for themselves. This knowledge, coupled with real life experiences, forms the nucleus of the store of ideas which they tap when involved in writing. Adult writers constantly use ideas which have their basis in something they have once read. So we should value examples in children's writing (such as that by Dale in Figure 7.4) which show through the language used or the ideas expressed that they have drawn on known texts or forms of writing.

```
One day Sylvester was resting. Some
beans rolled to Sylvester's basket.
He was a cat.
The beans grew and grew and grew
into a Giant beanstalk. Sylvester
woke up and suckering suckertash and
he climbed the beanstalk . He
climbed  and climbed  and climbed
and climbded  to the giants castle
and when he went down he got knocked
into China.
```

Figure 7.4 *Sylvester the Cat by Dale: writing showing the influence of known texts*

Writing areas

Careful thought needs to be given to the balance between the children writing in response to a stimulus initiated by the educator and providing opportunities for them to decide on the reason for writing. By setting up a writing or graphics area in the classroom we are providing time and space for children to experiment with a variety of writing materials. They will also be able to make decisions about what they would like to write and how it will be organised. Setting up an area does not require a large space or a major cash outlay. A table against a wall with a notice board for children to display their writing if they wish is fine. A plan of a typical area is shown in Figure 7.5. If the demand is great the children can always spill over on to neighbouring tables. Equipping the area with a variety of writing implements is more important than having large quantities all the same. The same is true of the materials that are provided for the children to write on; old envelopes, a pad of forms, different shapes, sizes and colours of paper can all be gathered through requests to businesses, shops and parents. The writing area can also reflect topics going on in the class. For instance a topic on giants could mean that the writing area had giant size envelopes, paper and markers. A Year 1 class was helping to plan the planting for a flowerbed in their school grounds, so the materials in their writing area included forms from seed catalogues, labels and diagrams of the school grounds for them to annotate.

The writing area provides a low-risk environment in which children can rehearse favourite ways of writing, try new ideas and have control over the whole process from deciding on the purpose of their writing, to whether they will make a final neat copy. Sayarun, a Year 2 whose first language was Sylheti, often spent her time in the writing area writing letters to other children in the class. She would choose as her recipients those whom she thought needed cheering up, someone she wanted to congratulate, or someone who had not had a letter from the class postbox for a while. As her letter to her teacher shows (Figure 7.6), she understood many of the functions which letters could fulfil.

The postbox was an important feature of the writing area as it provided an authentic opportunity for writing to others, something which definitely motivated the children to write and influenced the quality of the writing that they produced.

Another child in the same class wrote his first truly independent piece of writing in the writing area. He had joined the Year 2 class from another school and was convinced that he could only write by copying an adult's model. At first much of his time in the writing area was spent drawing or on the phone to his grandmother. After a few weeks he posted his first letter and sent it to his teacher (Figure 7.7).

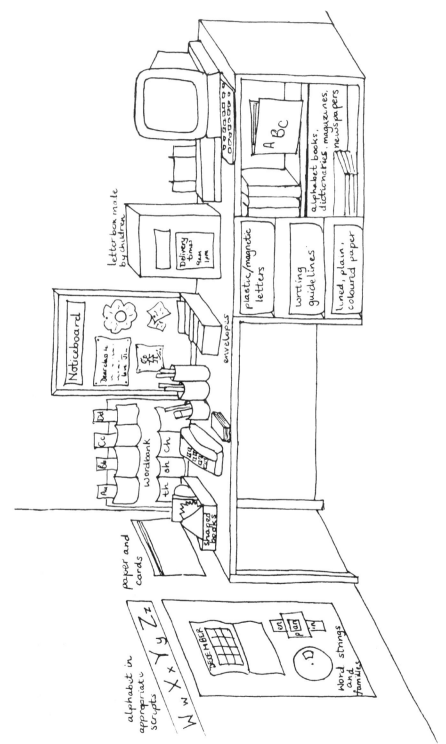

Figure 7.5 *Plan of a classroom writing area*

Notes

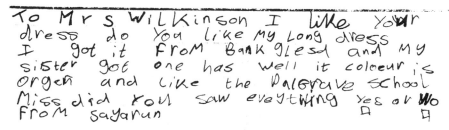

To Mr s WilKinson I like your
dress do you like my Long dress
I got it FroM BanK glesd and My
sister got one has well it coloeur is
orgen and Like the PalGrave school
Miss did you saw eveytwing Yes or No
FroM Sayarun

Figure 7.6 *Sayarun's letter to her teacher*

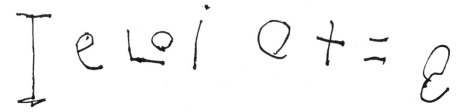

Figure 7.7 *Lee's first letter*

She was overjoyed to receive it and was also able to see from it what Lee understood about print. He had used letters from his name and had included mathematical signs as well. His drawing also began to include examples of environmental print such as car registrations, street signs and shop names. Lee spent time at weekends out with his father on his ice-cream van and was very interested in and knowledgeable about cars. It was not surprising, therefore, that these examples of environmental print were an important part of his first independent writing attempts.

Writing and role-play

Letters and postboxes also became an important focus for a Year 1 class who had been watching videos and listening to and reading stories about Postman Pat. An area of their classroom became Greendale Post Office and letters from the writing area and home corner were brought from the letter-box to the post office for sorting. The children also took on the roles of post master or mistress and customers, providing opportunities for form filling, marking of parcels and list making. Since the post office also sold cards, envelopes, writing paper and pens these could be purchased and used in the writing area or home corner to generate more post for Greendale staff to collect, sort and deliver.

In role-play situations it is important that the children have some under-standing of the context in which their writing takes place and the forms of writing which might be expected to take place there. Therefore, setting up some types of role-play area might involve the children being taken on a visit to see what sort of things are needed in the area and what people do who work in, for instance, a vet's surgery. Prior to setting up a travel agent's office in their classroom, one reception class visited a local travel agency and saw all the brochures, forms and computers which were used when people came to book a holiday. They asked the staff what they said to the cus-tomers and watched whilst information was filled in on the computer and forms. Back in the classroom they equipped their travel agency with the fol-lowing:

telephone	booking forms	pens
computer	tickets	pencils
diaries	timetables	ruler
note pads	labels	stapler
fax machine	posters	envelopes
(cardboard box		
with slits in)		

When the children were playing in the travel agent's office an adult some-times joined in with them, taking on the role of a customer or one of the staff of the travel agency. The way in which the children were able to use writing in their play was expanded both by their visit to the travel agent's and by an adult modelling the ways in which writing could occur. The children acting as customers would fill in forms on brochures and write notes in the home corner to remind them of what they wanted to ask the travel agents. Those being staff in the travel agent's office would type details into the computer, make notes, complete forms and fill in information in their diaries.

Providing authentic writing experiences, such as those above, in role-play means that the children are more likely to base their writing on realistic models of writing. The example in Figure 7.8 is from a nursery class and shows Chloe making the choice of an appropriate piece of paper for writing a shopping list from a selection of paper of various sizes available to her. She then wrote her list in the home corner (notice how many of her chosen let-ters are from her name) and took it with her when she went shopping in the class shop.

Figure 7.8 *Chloe's shopping list*

Purposes and audiences for writing

The importance of children having real reasons for writing in a range of forms and for a range of audiences is something which has been a major topic of discussion in recent years. The new English National Curriculum gives it a high priority by placing 'range' as the heading for its first set of statements of children's entitlement in writing.

When considering who the audience is for a piece of writing, it may be that for children writing in the writing area the answer could be a friend in the class who will receive their card or letter, someone at home or them-selves. The value of the latter should not be underestimated, as providing an opportunity for a child to write without any obligation for them to show their writing to anyone else, can contribute immensely to their writing development. The relaxing environment of the writing area can free some children to write in ways which they are not able to do when an educator has expectations of their achievement. Daniel was in Year 2 and his teacher felt that even though he had mastered the technical side of writing, she did not often succeed in motivating him to want to write. For Daniel the free-dom to write for himself and about whatever he wanted was essential. His story (Figure 7.9) began from a blank flap book that was part of the stock of the writing area and represents his greatest writing achievement during his first term in the class.

The examples of children writing during role-play showed how impor-tant it is for children to write in authentic situations, so that their play echoes the purposes for which writing is used in the real world. They can also gain much from writing to created audiences such as when a reception class received a letter from Roger the robot whom they had made from junk materials. They corresponded with 'Roger', in fact their class teacher, for several weeks, with the children asking Roger many questions about himself and responding to enquiries from him about themselves. The way in which children respond to their audience in this situation can vary. Some are happy to believe that Roger can write whilst others may be more sceptical. Even if the latter is true, the children are usually still willing to enter into corre-spondence if they know their letters will receive a reply.

Another way of providing opportunities for children to experiment with forms of writing which they do not usually have the opportunity of using is through writing in role to an imagined audience. Excellent stimuli for this are picture books such as *The Jolly Postman* and *Each Peach Pear Plum*, both by Janet and Allan Ahlberg. The former contains many examples of different reasons for writing which can lead the children to develop their own letters, catalogues and postcards. In the example in Figure 7.10 Darren's letter to BB Wolf draws directly on one in *The Jolly Postman* from Red Riding Hood's solicitors. Simon's, on the other hand, shows him devising the whole of the scenario for himself. He was invited to write something which could have been posted to one of the characters in *Each Peach Pear Plum* and he chose to write a postcard to Bo-Peep from her lost sheep. The way that he manages to express succinctly all that is necessary is just right for a postcard and the explanation of where the sheep have gone is so appropriate!

Making books

Book making gives children an excellent reason for writing. Seeing their book published, either within the class or for a wider school audience, is tremendous for developing children's self-esteem and their image of them-selves as writers. Often the books made by themselves and their peers are the ones which are the most popular in the book corner and are returned to over and over again. The actual recording of the text of a book can be done in several ways and does not have to be completed by the children. The role

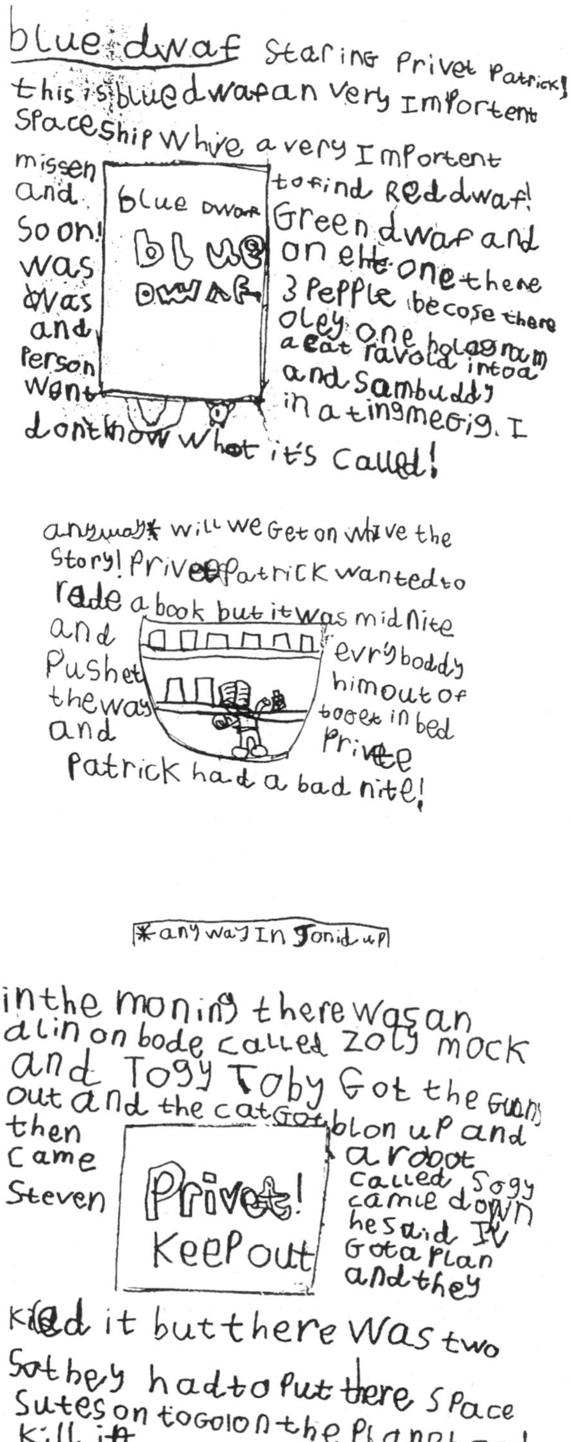

blue dwaf staring Privet Patrick!
this is blue dwaf an very Important
spaceship whive a very Important
missen and to find Red dwaf!
and Green dwaf and
so on! on eht one there
was 3 pepple becose there
bivas oley one holagram
and a cat ravold intoa
person and sambuddy
wont in a tingmeoig. I
dont know what it's called!

anyways will we Get on whive the
story! Privet Patrick wanted to
rade a book but it was midnite
and evryboddy
Pushet him out of
the way tooget in bed
and Privet
Patrick had a bad nite!

anyway In Jonid up

inthe moning there was an
alin on bode called Zoly Mock
and Togy Toby Got the Guns
out and the cat Got blon up and
then a roobt
came called sogy
Steven camie down
he said I
Got a Plan
and they

kild it butthere was two
So they had to Put there space
Sutes on tocoloin the Planet and
kill it.

Figure 7.9
*Daniel's story on a
self-chosen theme*

Figure 7.10 *Letters to BB Wolf and Bo-Peep by Darren and Simon*

of the educator may be to act as a scribe for a group of children, re-reading for them what they have composed so far and encouraging contributions from the whole group.

Collaborative writing

Sometimes being alone with a piece of paper is a daunting experience. Young children can feel that they don't have any ideas or are unsure of committing them to paper. Collaborating with other children means they can build on each other's ideas, discuss possible options and make adjustments together. It is another way in which talk becomes central to the writing process. The actual recording of the writing could be carried out by:

- the educator acting as scribe for the group;
- all the children in the group jointly;
- one or two children decided on by the group;
- a child nominated as scribe by the educator;
- an older child working with a younger child.

Children in a nursery class took turns to put their hands in a feely bag containing fruit and vegetables such as a pineapple, fennel and broccoli. As they told the educator about the contents of the bag he encouraged them to build on each other's comments. John began by describing the leaves of the pineapple as being like monster nails, so the educator encouraged the next child to extend from this by posing the question: 'Which part of the monster can you feel?' As a picture of the 'monster' was built up by the group, the educator showed how he had recorded their ideas and read them back to them. They then drew the monster working in pairs on large sheets of paper.

In this nursery class, the educator modelled not only how ideas could be recorded in writing but also how to combine ideas from several people. This modelling is appropriate with all age groups of young children and is one way in which educators can support the children's learning. Another way in which this support can be given by educators is through 'scaffolding' writing situations so as to reduce the scope for failure within them. A Year 2 class, in self-chosen groups of three, embarked on a project involving composing a story around the theme of space. The first stage involved them in making a pictorial plan of their story on a large sheet of paper. They then taped their story with members of the group taking on the role of specific characters or of the narrator. From this point the children's stories developed in many different ways. Having produced a story communally, a process which had supported those who found composing a story diffi-cult and had allowed others in the group to act as educators, the children then produced their own versions of their taped stories singly. Several of the children in the class were now able to write more freely and in greater detail than they had ever done before. Vygotsky (1978) says this shows children working within their 'zone of proximal development', the latter being the distance between their achievements when working alone and their potential as shown when working with the support of an educator or more capable peers.

Peer tutoring

Another way of organising collaborative writing, which can also provide support for young writers who lack confidence, is by pairing younger chil-dren with older children. The example of a Year 2 class paired with a Year 6 class illustrates the variety of ways in which these partnerships could work:

- older child acting as secretary for the younger child;
- older child encouraging the younger child to expand on their initial ideas;
- joint decision making on content of writing;
- sharing the task of writing;
- younger child developing the ideas of the older child;
- younger child doing most of the writing, asking questions of the older child.

The educators involved set up the pairings very carefully so that the chil-dren working together were able to relate to each other socially. Where the older children were leaders in the partnerships they provided invaluable one to one interaction, developing their own skills as encourager and ques-tioner as they sought to extend their younger partner's ideas. This can be seen in an excerpt of conversation between Ruby, a Year 2 bilingual speaker and Seema, Year 6:

Seema   What do you think should happen next?
Ruby   It flies. He (the bird) eats the food.
Seema   (writing)   The bird flies up to the tree and eats the food. What hap-pens to the two girls?
Ruby   They go home.

Conclusion

This chapter has considered young children writing in a variety of settings and for a range of purposes and audiences. Central to all these has been the understanding the educator has of the sorts of responses to expect from the children, which reveal the knowledge, skills and understanding they have about writing. The educator provides writing opportunities which build on these, involving the children in using writing in play situations, writing areas, and when working collaboratively with others. These and other experiences will allow children to develop as confident, motivated writers willing to take risks with their writing. So instead of classrooms where children ask educators:

Can you write that for me?

what can be heard are enthusiastic emergent writers saying:

I can write that myself!

Pointers for writing in the early years

Young writers need:

- an environment to write in which provides real purposes for writing;
- to have ownership of their writing;
- to be able to choose what to write about and for what reasons;
- to have their attempts valued whatever their stage of development;
- to have experiences which link writing with talking and reading;
- to see adults writing;
- opportunities to write in collaboration with others.

References

Browne, A. (1993) *Helping Children Write*, London: Paul Chapman.

Kress, G. (1994) *Learning to Write* (2nd Edn), London: Routledge.

National Writing Project (1989) *Becoming a Writer*, Walton-on-Thames: Nelson.

Smith, F. (1982) *Writing and the Writer*, London: Heinemann Educational.

Vygotsky, L.(1978) *Mind in Society: The Development of Higher Psychological Processes*, Cambridge, Mass: Harvard University Press.

Further reading

Czerniewska, P. (1992) *Learning About Writing*, Oxford: Blackwell.

Goodman, Y. (1986) 'Writing development in young children', *Gnosis*, 8, March, pp. 8–14.

Hall, N. (ed.) (1989) *Writing With Reason*, London: Hodder & Stoughton.

CHAPTER 8

'What's that dog thinking, Mrs Bromley?'

PICTURE BOOKS AND LEARNING TO READ

Helen Bromley

Helping young children become readers has been one of the most exciting parts of my teaching career. Sharing old favourites, introducing and discussing new authors and titles, but, most of all, watching the children's excitement grow as the world of the reader opens up to them (see Figure 8.1).

My own memories of school reading are not exciting. I can vividly recall being sent to the headmistress's study to read some of my 'Happy Venture Reader' book to her. Although I can remember Dick, Dora, Nip and Fluff, it is not with any particular affection. They are remembered more as distant relations who had to be tolerated, rather than as good friends. The books with which I formed the closest ties were those introduced to me by my mother: *Little Bear*, *Fox in Socks* and many others. This was in the late 1950s. Since then there has been an explosion in the publishing of books for children, providing educators with a rich and varied selection to use in the classroom.

Liz Waterland (1992) talks about the difference between 'free range' and 'battery' books. The difference between these being that free range books are written by authors and illustrators who have had freedom to carefully choose and compose their books from the imagination, whilst 'battery' books are products of a factory type approach to literature. 'There is a hint of unnatural practices, of confinement and restriction . . . even a suggestion of the mechanical and the automatic' (pp. 160–1).

THis is a pitcrure of MrsBromeroy. And some peAole cHildron Lisning To Her read a Storey.

Figure 8.1 *The excitement of reading!*

Books as children's friends

In order to explore this difference further, I will return to the analogy of friendship. Children need friends that they can interact with time and time again, they need to share the good times and the bad. Books described as 'free range', that is, high quality, multi-layered texts, provide such opportunities. Amelia, aged four, sat with a copy of *The Teddy Robber*, every morning before school, for six months, just as she might have depended on one child for friendship. She read it over and over again, taking great comfort in its familiarity, and the happy ending. Eventually, she was able to make other 'friendships', but in times of stress, she always returned to *The Teddy Robber*. Brooke, whose aunt had recently died, took *Granpa* (by John Burningham) home, not for herself, but for her mum. As she explained to me, 'It's so mummy will see that everything will be all right in the end.' An example of one friend helping another. I have used many reading schemes during my career and cannot recall examples of any which would have provided such support. 'Battery' books do not provide the sort of friends that stick around for long. They are with you for a short period of time, before you leave them and move on to the next. Lasting ties are not encouraged.

One of the important parts of friendship is the shared conversations that can exist. With your friends you laugh, cry and build a collection of joint memories, whilst all the time finding out more about yourself. Children's literature can provide such experiences. Alyck took *Owl Babies* by Martin Waddell home repeatedly, because he thought that Bill, the baby owl, was so funny. Parents (who like their children to make friends of whom they approve!) frequently mention how much they enjoy Sarah Garland's books, because 'Well, it's just like our house.'

Children need friends that will help them learn, without fear of failure and with the knowledge that risk taking is a worthwhile activity. Friends encourage you to have another go, whether trying to ride your bike without stabilisers or read *Each Peach Pear Plum* for yourself. Books such as those I have mentioned invite re-reading because they offer opportunities to see the familiar and unfamiliar juxtaposed in such a way as to make you want to read them again and again. Just like visiting an old friend, but playing a new game. Texts constructed especially for the teaching of reading may not provide such friendly support, especially if reading does not come easily. It is often difficult for children to recognise themselves in the text (or illustrations) and there may be no chance of trying out a new game until you have mastered the old one.

There is no doubt that the best friends are those that grow and change with you, not just those that were suitable for you when you were five or eight. This is also true of children's reading material. Liz Waterland(1992,

p. 161) quotes Jim Trelease, 'If a book is not worth reading at the age of fifty, then it is not worth reading at the age of ten either.' Look at the books that you use in the classroom as if you were looking for friends. If you do not find them interesting and want to get to know them better, then why should the children? This is not to deny that there will be differences in opinion and in taste, but it's a good place to start.

What I hope for the children that I teach is a rich collection of good friends, to be remembered with affection and pleasure. Friends who teach them that reading is a pleasure for life, not a series of hoops through which they must jump. This chapter intends to introduce activities for using meaningful texts with children, that have been successful in my own early years classroom. It is not intended to be a definitive list of suggestions. Far from it! I hope rather that people would try one (or all) of the ideas out for themselves and be inspired to go on to discover more.

What young children need to learn about reading

It is important to accept that young children already know much about reading when they enter our classrooms. The activities outlined in this chapter, therefore, are designed to allow children to demonstrate what they already know, as well as educating them in new lessons about reading. Henrietta Dombey (1992, pp. 12–15) summarises the lessons that she feels children need to learn about reading; this is an abridged version of her list:

Attitudes

- Pleasure and satisfaction: to see books as a powerful source of enjoyment, information and understanding.
- Confidence: a firm belief that they will learn to read.
- Concentration and persistence.
- Toleration of uncertainty.
- Tentativeness: a readiness to correct error.
- Reflexiveness: a readiness to look with a certain detachment at what they can do and have read, and at what they need to learn.

Knowledge and strategies
Children need to understand:

- that the text is the same on each re-reading and that the marks on the page tell you what to say;
- that language is composed of separable words;
- the conventions of the English language system;

- that words are made up of individual letters;
- the rules of English spelling;
- a reliable sight vocabulary;
- how to use their knowledge of the world and the content of books to aid word identification;
- how to use the information from the pictures (Figure 8.2);
- how to use all these various devices together: orchestration.

HaNNaH andrstas The words Becos of The Pickets.

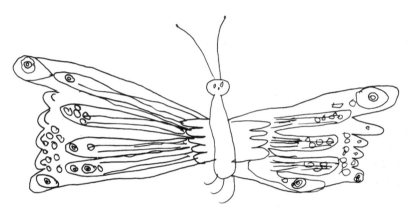

Figure 8.2 *Using information from the pictures*

I feel that the best way for children to learn these vital lessons is through the provision of a variety of rewarding experiences, provided by an educator who is enthusiastic about reading. Some lessons will, by necessity, be more explicit than others, but all will be crucial to the development of the children as readers. There is not room within this chapter to document all the ways in which it is possible to support the emergent reader. I feel that the activities outlined below show a variety of meaningful contexts in which most, if not all, the above lessons could be learned, both implicitly and explicitly.

Big Books

The theory behind using Big Books is well documented. Holdaway (1979), for example, working in New Zealand in the 1970s, looked at children who were already reading when they came to school, to find out what had made them successful. Many of the children had favourite stories that were read to them repeatedly. Gradually, the children were able to take on more of the reading for themselves, firstly by remembering the text and eventually being able to match words and phrases to the known text. Big Books were devised as a way of making stories available to a wider audience. Holdaway noted that all children were able to be successful at their own level, with this approach. Large groups were able to be involved in the shared reading of a familiar text. They provide a shared context for discussion and make it easy for all the children in a class to focus on the chosen text.

The favourite Big Book in my class this year was *This is the Bear*. The children already knew the text extremely well, having heard the small version read out many times. The text rhymes and has marvellous pictures, features which help support the developing reader. Using this story in its outsize version helped to create a situation for the children to learn both explicit and implicit lessons about reading. Each time the Big Book is used, a similar format can be followed:

- Look closely at the cover, find features such as title, author, illustrator, publisher, publisher's symbol. If this is done on a regular basis, then the children will pick up the vocabulary surrounding books and authorship very quickly. They then use these terms for themselves, quite naturally.
- Have a look at each page, ignoring nothing. Some books contain beautifully constructed endpapers, these are all part of what makes a book.
- Look for dedications. Who would the children dedicate a book to?
- What initials would they use?
- Do the cover and the preceding pages tell the reader anything about the story that is to follow?

Developing comprehension skills

The teacher can then follow one of several paths. Skills of prediction and authorship can be encouraged by reading the story part of the way through and asking the children to decide what happens next. To extend this activity, ask the children to justify their reasons for suggesting particular outcomes. This provides an excellent opportunity for formative assessment of their comprehension skills.

Alternatively, the story can be read to the children, not necessarily without interruption, but with as little as possible, so that the children can get the most meaning from the story. This will be the first of many readings, so there will be plenty of opportunities for discussion. The idea is not to encourage passive listeners, an audience powerless to interrupt the reading instructor, but rather to encourage the children to join in and to question what they see and what they hear. This is more effective, however, when the children have heard the whole story through once and have a shared context for discussion.

There are many ways in which Big Books can be used to stimulate discussion. One of the most effective ways I have used is to organise the children into small 'talk groups' and ask them to devise questions to ask about the story. This gives all children some opportunity to be involved in discussion about the text, and provides a safe context for talk for those who prefer not to speak in front of a large group. It also promotes close scrutiny of the text in a collaborative way, providing an ideal opportunity for children to discuss their reading and learn from one another.

As well as promoting comprehension skills, Big Books can be used to look carefully at features of print.

Looking at features of print

- Choose a particular letter. How many of this particular letter can the children find on one page, on a double page spread?
- Can they find any words within words, eg: 'is', 'in', 'the', 'and'?
- Can they find two words with similar endings? (Particularly useful in a rhyming text.)
- How many capital letters can they see? Whereabouts do they appear in the text?
- Introduce the children to the notion of the silent letter. Can any of these be found?
- Use the children's own names as a basis for the print search. Can Jodie find any words beginning with J? Can Matthew find 'at', 'the' or 'he'? My experience has shown that children especially enjoy the activities that involve their names and quickly learn features of not only their own, but also other people's names.
- Children can also be encouraged to devise questions of their own.

Obviously, there is far more to becoming a critical and highly motivated reader than studying metalinguistic features of print! As educators, we want children to know that reading is pleasurable and that there is much to be gained from the re-reading of old favourites. Again using Big Books, it is possible to demonstrate all of this to children and, at the same time, allow them space to air their concerns and perceptions about the books that they are reading. This is achieved by a combination of teacher questioning and, most importantly, providing the opportunity for the children to ask their own questions.

Looking beyond the text

- Children can be put into groups of two or three and asked to devise one question about the story (illustrations included).
- Encourage the children to focus on how the illustrations might be telling a different story to the pictures.
- Look carefully at the body language of the participants.
- Follow the actions of one character throughout the whole story. Use this tracking as a basis for studying character, motive and plot!

Looking beyond the text is especially exciting, as even with numerous readings of the same text, the children always spot something new. This was demonstrated when I discussed *This is the Bear* with a class of five-year-olds. Briefly, this is the tale of a teddy bear who is pushed into the dustbin by a dog and mistakenly taken to the dump. He is found after a long search, by the same dog, and driven home to a hero's welcome! Questions devised about the story included

> Why did the dog push the bear into the bin?
> How does the bear feel about being in the bin?
> How would you feel if you lost your teddy and couldn't get it back?
> Do you think that the dog is jealous of the bear?
> Do you think that the bear likes the dog?
> What's that dog thinking, Mrs Bromley?

I think that it is important to note that there were no questions of the type 'What colour is the van?'. All the questions generated by the children were looking deep into the story, to try and find out more about the characters in it.

Games and play

Whenever I have carried out such activities with my class, I have always told the children that it is part of a game; sometimes them against me, sometimes a collaborative guessing game. For example, individual words can be covered up with a small piece of card, while the children close their eyes. When they open them, they have to guess which word is covered. This promotes close scrutiny of the text and finger/voice match. Then, when the large group session is over, I would always make the suggestion that, if they wanted to play the games themselves later, then they could do so. All that needs to be provided is a Big Book, clipped to an easel, four chairs placed in a semi-circle around it and something to be used as a pointer.

This game was a particular favourite with Eleanor, Hannah and Rebecca, who would often take the opportunity to persuade other members of the class to come and take part as pupils, whilst they operated their own version of team teaching. Rebecca, the most experienced reader in the group, would ask questions like 'Can you find "the" on this page?' Eleanor, who was particularly skilled at memorising texts, would read the book to the rest of the group, pointing with the ruler as she did so. That left Hannah, who had an excellent grasp of initial sounds and was able to devise questions such as 'Can you find a word on here that begins with the same sound as "apple"?' I think that the pupils in the game were getting some excellent teaching from three young experts.

From watching the children play what in my class has become known simply as 'schools', it is apparent that the children reproduce and therefore reinforce the types of behaviour demonstrated by the teacher. Each time the game is played, it is never an exact copy of the previous game, new ideas are added and children negotiate and discuss the questions and the answers.

Developing children's awareness

The children in my class have also had the opportunity to share the Big Books available with their reading partners, children from a Year 2 class. At one session, I asked the children to reflect, in their pairs, on how Big Books might help them with their reading.

Here are some of their comments:

I like Big Books because you can always see the writing.

I think and my friend thinks that a Walker Big Book is good because you can see them better than you can see an ordinary book and you can see the pictures better.

Big Books help you to read properly because they have big words to help you read. (see Figure 8.3)

It will help you write better. Reading will help you think better. It will help you to learn. It will help you think about the pictures.

As you can see, the children are very much aware of how the large format of the books encourages them to become participants in the shared reading process, allowing them to become even more involved than in a normal story telling session. Talk is central to all the activities outlined above. They are operating in the zone of proximal development (Vygotsky 1986) alongside a more experienced reader and their own knowledge and learning potential will only become apparent if they are allowed to explore their knowledge through conversation. Through role-play (such as the game of 'schools') they are able to have the opportunity to act as the more able other, in the company of their peers. Self-esteem and confidence is built up this way, as well as there being room for errors to be made, without the ever watchful eye of an adult.

Figure 8.3 *'Big Books help you to read properly because they have big words to help you read'.*

Group reading

Big Books are not the only way in which children can be encouraged to play with their reading! Group reading around multiple copies of the same text provides similar opportunities, if the right atmosphere for learning and risk taking is created.

Maisie Middleton is the story of an ordinary little girl who gets up one morning and despite attempting to rouse her parents, eventually has to prepare breakfast for herself. It is a story which appealed to all the children in my class, possibly because they too would like to share some of Maisie's independence, however transitory. It was because of the popularity of the book that I chose it as a subject for group reading. All four children in the group had heard the story an equal number of times and could therefore bring some previous knowledge to the group situation.

During the session, the children listen to the story read out loud first, joining in if they wish. They then take it in turn to ask questions about each of the pages of the book, either to each other or to the adult present. I was surprised at how involved the children became with this particular text. I soon realised that I had underestimated its potential. The first page shows the exterior of Maisie's house, framed in an arch with a flower on the top. Eleanor began. 'I wonder who sleeps behind the blind with the stripes on?' she asked, and immediately the others joined in, speculating on the possible occupants of the house. Brooke was trying to imagine herself at the front door, stroking the cat and bringing in the milk. What to me had appeared to be a fairly simplistic picture provided the children with a rich source of discussion for at least fifteen minutes. I thought that we were never going to get any further into the book. Much knowledge was revealed in this discussion and many questions asked and answered. It's wrong to assume that it is always the adult that provides the answers. Thomas wanted to know why the milk was still on the doorstep, he was worried in case the sun turned it sour. It was Brooke that pointed out to him that as the blinds were still down, it must still be early in the morning. Eleanor also pointed out that the stars were still in the sky, so 'That's why the milk hadn't been taken in.' This discussion clearly demonstrated the children's speaking and listening skills, as well as their powers of reasoning and their ability to apply their knowledge of the real world to the imaginary world of the book. It also allowed them to develop ways of taking pleasure from the text that were in addition to those intended by the author.

Whilst we were still considering the first two pages of the book, the children started to do something that I can clearly remember doing as a child. That was to pretend that they were in the book themselves. They began by deciding which room was which in Maisie Middleton's house and dividing them up amongst themselves. Space was also made for siblings and pets, ensuring links between the real world and the imaginary one. I felt that this incident demonstrated an enormous amount, not only about the children's understanding of the book, but also of their awareness of the possibilities that exist for any reader. (Another description of a child talking about Maisie Middleton can be found in Barbara Jordan's (1992) article 'Good for any age'.) I feel strongly that these lessons are as important as the lessons of sight vocabulary and decoding of text. It was very rewarding when, a few days later, Eleanor asked 'Can we play that pretending game again? You know, that one when we were in the book. That was really good.' Following the success of this activity, I built it into further group reading sessions, although the children did not need much direction from me. It was as popular with non-fiction texts as with stories, with children taking on the roles of knights and soldiers in one particular book.

Group reading of texts

- Try to provide a range of texts for this activity – include non-fiction, comics etc.
- Use groups of texts by one author / illustrator, so the children can identify similar features.
- Promote discussion about the characters – who would the children most like / not like to be, etc.?
- Try giving the children a character in the story, while the teacher reads the narration. (The youngest children can manage this if it is a text that they know.)

'Reading out'

This activity was actually devised by my class themselves, and was to provide a source of pleasure to them for many weeks, as well as giving me the opportunity to listen to them read, checking their sight vocabulary, acquisition of known texts and their understanding of what they were reading. Reading standards in the class improved dramatically as did listening skills and concentration spans. It was such a worthwhile activity, that I would definitely introduce it to any new group of children that I taught.

The activity began when Rebecca came in one morning and asked if she could read 'Daley B', her favourite book of the moment, out to the rest of the class. It was agreed that she could, and later in the day, she read the book, with great expression and obvious understanding. The reaction from the rest of the class was extremely positive. Not only did they all, including the most restless children, listen attentively and with keen interest, but many of them offered to read out too. In fact, the whole activity snowballed. Children were allowed to 'read out' either on their own, with a friend, or in a small group. This was to allow some of those children who were not quite brave enough to read by themselves to have the opportunity to participate in what became a very highly regarded activity.

The most popular grouping for the activity was a threesome. Within this group there would be one child who knew the text extremely well, one who knew it quite well, and one who was in the group to gain confidence and add to their knowledge of that particular text. This was a very good example of how children are able to achieve more when in the company of others than they could possibly achieve on their own. It provided great opportunities for the rest of the class to practise texts that were known to them already and add new texts to those that were familiar. Because the children were copying behaviour that they had seen in adults, many of them became adept at reading with the book held next to them, teacher-like, showing the pictures and questioning their very attentive audience.

I tried not to appropriate this activity, although I found this difficult, desperately wanting every one to 'have a turn'. One child in particular, Alyck, could not be encouraged to read out, however hard I tried to persuade him. This situation changed when his friend Sebastian wanted someone to read *Each Peach Pear Plum* out with him. He chose Alyck, who found it impossible to refuse his friend, even though it had been quite easy to refuse my requests. Alyck did read the book out with Sebastian, extremely well, and this provided an enormous boost to his confidence and self-esteem. After this occasion, he frequently read out to the class.

Although I was involved in the activity as a non-participant observer, the children regulated the whole of the sessions themselves. Everyone who wanted to read out would leave their chosen book, with a named Post-it note on the front, on a special chair, waiting for reading out time. They would question each other about the books that were read out and would comment on each other's reading. This was delightful to hear, and was only ever positive. Comments such as 'Your reading's coming along very well, Hayley,' were never patronising, but well meant.

The teacher's role

It is important to realise that the three activities outlined above should not be young children's only experience with good quality picture books. They should exist as part of a well-thought-out set of experiences designed to give children a myriad of opportunities to engage with the literacy heritage that surrounds them. As educators, we have the power to excite and inspire the children in our care and this should not be underestimated. Early years educators should make good use of and familiarise themselves with, the rich variety of books that are published for young children, developing favourites of their own in order to be able to demonstrate to children, that it is OK to have tastes and preferences that are different from one another.

I believe quite passionately, that the picture books of today will provide far more 'good friends' for the children that I teach than 'The Happy Venture Series' ever did for me. However, in order to become known to children, these friends must first be invited into classrooms and introduced to children in ways that make them want to 'play with them', time and time again. As Henrietta Dombey(1992) states:

> All children need the skilled help of informed and sympathetic adults, who appreciate their strengths and weaknesses, have a clear idea of the goal ahead and engage the children's interest and commitment. They also need to encounter texts that are involving, manageable and satisfying, and give them a clear sense that they are making progress.
>
> (p. 20)

If all this occurs in ways that are exciting and inspiring, then young children will certainly acquire many 'friends for life'.

Pointers to supporting the emergent reader

- Take time to get to know a wide range of children's books yourself.
- Act as a role model for the children, demonstrating enthusiasm for and an interest in books and other reading materials.
- Encourage children to talk about what they have read, to you and each other.
- Plan for a wide range of reading experiences.
- Develop effective and informative ways of monitoring the children's progress.

References

Dombey, H. (1992) *Words and Worlds: Reading in the Early Years of School*, NATE.

Holdaway, D. (1979) *The Foundations of Literacy*, Sydney: Ashton Scholastic.

Jordan, B. (1992) 'Good for any age: picture books and the experienced reader', in M. Styles, E. Bearne, and V. Watson (eds) *After Alice*, London: Cassell.

Vygotsky, L. (1986) *Thought and Language*, Cambridge, Mass.: The MIT Press.

Waterland, L. (1992) 'Ranging freely: the why and what of real books', in M. Styles, E. Bearne, and V. Watson (eds) *After Alice*, London: Cassell.

Children's books mentioned in the text

Ahlberg, J. and A. (1980) *Each Peach Pear Plum*, London: Picture Lions.

Beck, I. (1991) *The Teddy Robber*, London, Picture Corgi.

Blake, J. (1992) *Daley B*, London: Walker Books.

Burningham, J. (1984) *Grandpa*, London: Cape.

Garland, S. (1992) *Doing The Washing*, London: Puffin Books.

Hayes, S. (1995) *This is The Bear*, London: Walker Books.

Holmelund Minarik, E. (1957) *Little Bear*, New York: Scholastic Book Services.

Seuss, Dr. (1965) *Fox in Socks*, London: Collins.

Sowter, N. (1994) *Maisie Middleton*, London: Diamond Books.

Waddell, M. (1992) *Owl Babies*, London: Walker Books.

CHAPTER 9

'Penguins never meet polar bears'

READING FOR INFORMATION IN THE EARLY YEARS

Helen Arnold

Reading in some form is part of everyday life for nearly all adults. Many find satisfaction in reading fiction, but far more read for information, so frequently that they are unaware of it. They scan newspapers, absorb advertisements, signs, instructions and warnings. Car drivers do not always realise what skilful readers they must be.

It seems strange, therefore, that children have traditionally learnt to read almost exclusively from narrative texts. This is justified by the belief that response to story is inbuilt, that stories tell about events within children's experience, and that sequential (chronological) text is easier to predict and recall than non-sequential. Non-fiction elements were introduced in the higher levels of traditional reading schemes in the 1960s and 1970s, often called 'supplementary readers'. Even then, these tended to be written chronologically, as history or geography or nature 'stories'.

The assessment of such reading was invariably in the form of comprehension exercises. At upper primary levels 'higher order reading skills' were introduced; until one had mastered 'literal' reading, one could not go on to reading for 'inference' or 'appreciation'. The main purpose of training in higher order reading skills was to prepare pupils for reading in the subject areas when they reached secondary school.

The idea of this hierarchical progression from fiction to non-fiction reading no longer holds. The national curriculum recognises the need to introduce children to reading for information at Key Stage 1. Publishers are now including non-fiction strands from the earliest stages, and there is a growing number of individually published texts in the best traditions of the 'picture book'. Unfortunately many of these texts start with the wrong premiss, assuming that the function of this sort of reading is to include as many facts as possible. They are often not helpful to young readers. It is important to see how non-fiction reading fits into the young child's development, with the most important aim being to help towards concept formation.

Developmental aspects

Young children are intensely curious about the world around them, and from a very early age develop their own ways of classifying and categorising that world. Children probably experience more sharply and directly through their senses than adults. As we develop language to describe what we see and hear, we distance ourselves from the initial impressions. Once we have language it is very difficult to perceive without glossing what is seen with verbal description, response and comment. This is particularly so with regard to the disembedded contexts of reading and writing.

It is important not to push children too early into reading other people's verbalisations just for the sake of it. But it is good for them to realise gradually that there are many different ways of describing the world, some of which can only be done verbally because they involve things that are distant in time and space. Early literacy experiences develop in two main directions (see Figure 9.1), both equally important in the development of thinking and learning. Both may be equally motivating. Some children, indeed, will from the beginning be more interested in 'finding out' than in reading fiction. There is a place for developing both these strands by encouraging children to learn to read from non-fiction as well as story texts.

Life before school: the dinosaur phenomenon

I video-recorded Robert at intervals, not for educational purposes, but because his parents wanted a record of their baby growing up. Robert's mother would spread out a variety of toys and games, and he would choose what he wanted. In one of the early videos he did this by crawling towards them, because he was too young to walk or talk. Amongst the glossy toys was a rather elderly and dog-eared picture alphabet book (this was not a particularly literary family). Robert pushed the train, rolled the ball and crawled to the book. It engaged his interest. He did not eat it or throw it. He held it quite delicately and explored the pages, turned it another way up, pointed at one of the pictures. His mother said 'Duck'. 'Du–' attempted Robert, labelling dutifully. He stayed with the book for some time.

A later video shows Robert, now about two, with the same scenario, but no book on the floor. He exhibits his skill on the tricycle, builds with his

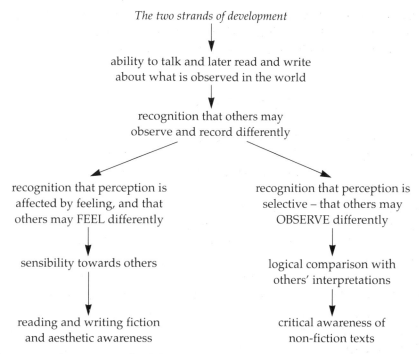

Figure 9.1 *The two strands of development*

bricks and clutches his rubber dinosaur. He walks deliberately to a shelf and removes a book from it, takes it straight to his mother on the settee, and climbs on to her lap. She reads the book to him and he points to the relevant pictures. Daniel, his baby brother, now part of the action, watches every movement from the floor.

At four years old, Robert does not play with any toys. He selects a dinosaur book almost immediately. Again he marches on to his mother's lap. He holds the book, surely turning the pages when he is ready. His mother reads the quite complex text, stumbling over some of the names. Robert seems to be able to pronounce them better than she does. She reads a description of the brontosaurus: 'That's the brontosaurus' points Robert. In fact, Robert knows all the names of the different dinosaurs, knows where their pictures are, and can tell his mother something about each of them. Daniel meanwhile looks on intently, and at one point tries to deseat Robert and climb on to his mother's knee with his own book.

A little girl of four sat by me on a plane journey. As the plane took off, she removed the safety instructions from the pocket and studied every picture carefully, telling herself what she thought each one depicted.

I watched a small boy tracing the letters of a notice in a public-house car-park over and over again. It reminded me of how I did the same as a child with the name of my road – 'Seymour Road' – helpfully embossed in metal on a low-standing notice.

Thalia (four and a half) found a small dead animal on the path. She was interested in animals, and had been to several nature parks. She answered her own questions:

'What is it?
A shrew? . . . No, because its tail is not long enough.
A mole? . . . No, its feet are too small.
A mouse? . . . No, it's not an ordinary mouse – its tail is too long . . .
SO . . . it must be a field mouse.'

On her return home, her mother helped her to look in a reference book, and she was able to check with a picture that she was right.

These are apparently simple incidents. They occurred as part of children's experiences, not as part of teaching programmes. They indicate the vital interaction between adults and children. What is happening is actually complex. Children are turning their world into concepts, slotting them into schemata, understanding secondary symbolisation, assimilating and accommodating in true Piagetian fashion – all long before they start school. Their emerging reading skill is interacting with their conceptual development.

I believe that the way young children learn in the classroom should not only take into account such literacy experiences, but should try to utilise the same sort of motivation. (It is a pity that we do not really know exactly why dinosaurs are so universally motivating, as then we might solve all the problems of helping children to read for learning!)

Into school learning: bridging the gap

Although there are so many information books for young children on the market, I do not think that they are the only, or perhaps the best, way to introduce children to non-fiction. As I have indicated earlier, we are not here asking children to read to collect facts like squirrels collect nuts. Some published information books, even for young readers, are packed with facts which are not expanded or easily connected with each other. How readers conceptualise information is as important as what they remember. It is difficult to store material which cannot first be linked with existing experience. It will be easier, therefore, to engage their active thinking through material that they are already familiar with, and through their own writing, than through reading other people's texts. Labels, notices and advertisements (termed 'environmental print' in the National Curriculum) would serve this purpose admirably.

Using environmental print

A whole curriculum could be built round labels and notices. It is interesting to give children of different ages an assortment of food and drink containers (preferably empty!), asking them to sort them into groups in any way they wish. There is, of course, no *right* way, but there will probably be a progression from random sorting, to personal preferences, to the stage when various properties are more conventionally taken into account. Can individuals or groups explain to one another why they have chosen their groupings?

The wording on labels is often very detailed, but certain aspects can be isolated. There are advantages in studying labels just as 'reading' vehicles. The language is necessarily economical, and is often evocative. Different sizes and fonts of print are used purposefully. What is the biggest print used for? Why? How big is the price label? The text is happily not 'graded' for readability. Labels are real in the sense that they are encountered every day in ordinary life, and usually they are culture free.

Most food packets and tins have both visual and textual information which can be used for classification, comparison and evaluation. It would be valuable to compare two labels for similar products, for instance, chocolate biscuits or baked beans. Children could work in pairs or groups, discussing and recording, first 'What's the same on the labels?' They might find that the weight is the same, that both products contain similar ingredients, or that the names are identical – 'Chocolate Chip Cookies' or 'Baked Beans'.

In doing this, they would inevitable start noticing the differences, and these, too, could be discussed and recorded. For example, one label might emphasise economy, 'Pennywise', another novelty, 'NEW'. One might emphasise healthgiving elements, the other the pleasures of eating. The children will, it is hoped, gradually realise that biscuits or beans which are basically the same products are promoted differently, to satisfy a range of consumers.

So, through looking at labels, often of their own choice, which they bring to school, children will gradually learn to classify and compare, and to read critically.

Environmental print in the street

It is a small step from the examples already given of children noticing the print of street names, to incorporating this curiosity into organised activity in and around the school. Bartlett and Fogg (1992), in their chapter called 'Language in the Environment', give numerous practical examples of ways of looking and recording. Street names, shop names and house names are suggested as fruitful sources. An initial 'print walk' can be taken in an open-ended way, or with pre-planned categories to investigate. If open-ended, a very short walk with nursery age children will reveal what they notice if asked to find 'things to read'. Will they notice the print on water hydrants and grids in the ground? Will they think that logos are words? Older children can collect house and street names and try to guess why they are so named.

Bartlett and Fogg point to the interest of shop names and show how they can be classified – owners' names, puns, alliteration etc. For example:

> Fur, Feather and Fin: I think it is called Fur, Feather and Fin because it has everything that animals with Fur, Feathers and Fins need. The name also sounds good because all the first letters in the name are the same.
>
> (Bartlett and Fogg 1992, p. 47)

Linking reading and writing

Research into emergent writing indicates how developing conceptual frameworks are revealed in the way children choose to write. Thus, by looking at their writing experiments we can see how they are internalising information in the early stages. Marie Clay(1982), Emilia Ferreiro (Ferreiro and Teberosky 1982) and many other researchers, in different parts of the world, have found similar sequences of development.

> The child's written work also provides us with objective evidence of what the child has learned. We have an opportunity to see how the child organises his behaviour as he writes . . . if we see a child write a new word without a copy we can assume the capacity to synthesise information from several sources.
>
> (Clay 1982, p. 210)

Two examples from my earlier snapshots of young children at home show how young children observe and categorise names. Ferreiro and Teberosky (1982) describe in detail the fascination emergent writers show with writing the names of objects and the way in which they distinguish between their written symbols and the picture of the object itself. Robert was already differentiating every dinosaur by its name. The recognition of house names, again, is derived from the desire to label everything. But there are repercussions which go beyond simple labelling. I remember, relating to my own experience with road names, my initial confusion when I found that my house had a number – 4 – and a name – 'Rufford', whereas the house next door was *only* No. 6 – no name! I learnt gradually that the same thing can have several names, and therefore, ultimately, that language defines multitudinously.

As we saw in our earlier examples, the next stage for most children is to want to make lists, combining their interest in naming with a desire to categorise.

> Until I began observing five-year-olds closely I had no idea that they took stock of their own learning. They spontaneously and systematically made lists of what they knew. They consciously ordered and arranged their learning.
>
> (Clay 1982, p. 206)

The most common manifestation of lists in schools is the individual word-book, kept by most children as a spelling check. This is a useful way of helping children to be aware of alphabetical ordering, but they could also occasionally re-order those words in another way. Lists of words might be made which cluster round particular topics. Individuals might keep these books, or groups could be responsible for collecting words for areas within a topic. For example, if the ongoing topic was mini-beasts, one group might collect words associated with spiders, another with snails, another with frogs. Or a different classification could be made, with groups collecting minibeast 'food' words, 'breeding' words, 'moving' words.

I have tried to show here how two of the earliest features of emergent writing – naming and listing – are integral with the beginning stages of reading for information. Other features could be pursued to demonstrate more sophisticated levels of conceptual awareness at later stages.

Ways of reading

Readers of non-fiction should be flexible in the way they process text. Children need to be able to skim and scan and to read certain parts intensively. Reading aloud is not a useful way of approaching text in this case. Can young children use different techniques before they have learnt to read aloud fluently? The following excerpts from a discussion with Clara, who was seven, show that as soon as she became aware of the needs of reading to find out, she was able to apply flexible procedures with very little trouble.

Clara was shown *Writing and Drawing* (Bradshaw 1988). This book poses questions in large print at the top of some of the pages, and answers the questions in the succeeding text. In this case the questions were masked with tape. Here the question was 'What is a ball-point pen?'

Teacher   Can you see where there is a bit that is covered up? There is a question under the tape. See if you can work out what the question might be . . . . It's got all the answers there to the question.
Clara   To do with pens.
Teacher   What sort of pens?
Clara   Biro pens.
Teacher   So what do you think the question might be?
Clara   How does it work?

They went on to a book about spiders.

T   Look at this book. It's about spiders. I want you to think about what you know about spiders before we look at the book.

Clara is presented with a list of statements about spiders, to be filled in as 'TRUE' or 'FALSE' by guessing, without reference to the book. For example:

T   It says here, 'Spiders are vegetarian – they don't eat meat'. Is that true or false? Are spiders vegetarians?
C   No . . . cos they eat flies.

   (and so on through five more statements).

T   Now go through the book and see if you can check from what it tells you whether you guessed right.

At this point Clara turned to the first page of the book and began to read it aloud.

T   You won't have time to read the whole book. Look quickly through it and see if you can spot anything that helps you.

There was a long pause while pages were turned over. Then:

C   The thread *does* come out of its body.
T   Where does it say that?
C   There.
T   Right. Put a tick against that one.

Clara picked up the idea of silent scanning very quickly. Another ploy was tried with a book about signs and symbols:

T   Now you need to look through this very quickly. I'm going to ask you some questions. It's a bit of a race. You won't have time to read all the book . . . you have to jump about a bit . . . . First can you tell me the page number which tells you about road signs?

Clara took three seconds to answer: 'Page 8 and 9'. Some questions related to pictures, some to text; they were not asked in page sequence. The longest time taken to find an answer was fifteen seconds, proof that it is possible to get the idea quite quickly, and to enjoy the fun of 'jumping about' rather than slavishly reading every word.

Preparing to read books

The 'True/False?' exercise is one way of engaging children's interest in what they are going to read about by linking new information with what they know already, known as focusing or 'priming'. With young children a montage of jumbled pictures from books could be made into a large poster. The class or group then discuss with the teacher what the 'topic' might be about. They would then be interested in finding the pictures again in the actual books.

Another method used with seven-year-olds was to divide the class into groups. In this case they were going to read books about different artefacts – bottles, bricks, knives and forks, bubbles. Each group was given a large piece of sugar paper. The scribe, after group discussion, wrote a list of 'What we know about –'. This was prior to seeing any books. In the next session, a similar list was made of 'What we would like to find out about –'.

When they came to reading their books, they focused on two things, whether they had been right in their assumptions, and whether their questions had been answered. Cries of glee came at intervals as they found they could tick items on the first list, or write in the answers to their questions on the second list. The lists were displayed on the wall throughout the project.

The teacher's role

Referring back to the accounts of young children with their parents, it is obvious that the carer's role was important in many ways. The parents in all cases were 'scaffolding' their children by putting them into situations where they could be active, interested learners, and supporting them in response to the children's own initiations. The adults' moves, although maybe unconscious, were subtle, unthreatening and enthusiastic. When children arrive at school, they may bring with them a different image of the new adult , their teacher, who is going to know so much more than they do and expect so much from them – to say nothing of the other children who will be trying to vie for that teacher's attention. The role of the teacher is bound to be more administrative, more aware of the need for total control, and more distant than the parent's. However it is important that teachers and other early years educators should attempt to model ways of teaching on the 'natural' contexts which have been encountered before. Above all, with reading for information, we must not give the impression that we already know everything, and that it is therefore not really necessary for our pupils to find things out independently.

The best way of working, therefore, is to model the different ways in which we find out from texts, showing exactly how we use an index, look up words, find key phrases etc. Just as educators enthuse children to enjoy stories by reading to them with skill and enthusiasm, reading to them from non-fiction books should also be introduced. We shall examine some scenarios in more detail to show how this might work in practice.

Polar bears

A reception class teacher introduced the topic of polar bears to the class, talking to them in the reading corner. She told them some facts, and showed where she had found them in two or three different books, holding the books up to show the pictures, and reading excerpts. As they discussed each point, she recorded it in a simple statement on the flip-chart. Then she gave each child a blank booklet cut out in the shape of a bear. The children were to make their own books, with a sentence on each page, using whatever information they wished. I sat by Jessica , watching her make her book. She received no more help from the teacher. Before writing on each blank page, she looked at the flip-chart, and thought carefully.

She wrote:

Page 1   polar bears live in ice caves
Page 2   polar bears hunt for fish
Page 3   polar bears walk on ice
Page 4   polar bears never meet penguins

(This had interested the children greatly in discussion; they were excited by the fact that polar bears lived at one pole, and penguins at the other!)

There was a long pause at this point. There was one page left to fill, and Jessica had seemingly run out of ideas and information. But she still made

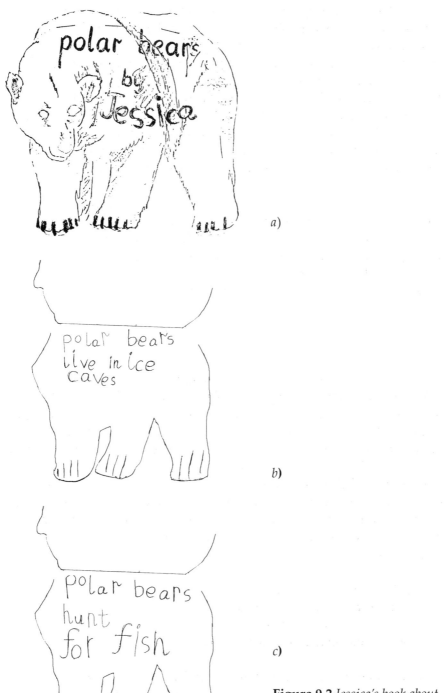

a)

b)

c)

Figure 9.2 *Jessica's book about polar bears: a) the cover, b) page 1, c) page 2*

d)

e)

f)

Figure 9.2 (continued) *d) page 3, e) page 4, f) page 5*

no request to the teacher, and there was no panic. Eventually she turned to the blank page and made her last triumphant entry:

Page 5   and penguins never meet polar bears.

The controlled structure of the task enabled her to produce what was not only a beautiful syntactic reversal, linked correctly by 'and', but a neat piece of logical reasoning.

In this case the teacher introduced the class to specific books. There are very few non-fiction books which could be used independently from the beginning with young children. There are some, however, which lend themselves to be used as models, because they demonstrate different ways of presenting knowledge. It is important to select a few books for this purpose, which fulfil the following criteria:

- They should not be packed with facts.
- The illustrations should relate clearly to the text.
- There should not be extraneous fantasy or story elements.
- Language should be simple but not patronising.
- Close observation should be encouraged.
- The purpose of the book should be clear.
- Texts which ask rhetorical questions or give instructions which cannot practicably be carried out should be avoided.

One book which fulfils my criteria is *Minibeasts* (Butler 1991). Here the photographs are used to encourage the reader to look very carefully, and to compare with similar habitats in real life. The text gives clear definitions, and asks 'real' questions, to draw on existing experience. The text facing photographs of a stick insect on some twigs and a moth camouflaged on a piece of wood, reads:

Where do minibeasts live?
Minibeasts live in many different habitats. They are very small and often hard to see.
Can you find the minibeasts in these pictures? There is a moth and a stick insect.
When animals can hide like this in their surroundings, we say they are camouflaged.

Each page in this book develops conceptually from the previous page. There is an index and a glossary, and words like 'camouflaged' will need to be explained. But it is the total content which should be explored carefully with the children, making sure that the questions are answered, and state-ments verified by checking with the photographs, leading on to taking the children out to look for minibeasts in their own environment.

One reading with the class will not of course, be enough. I suggest that a book like this be tape-recorded, with the questions being asked in one voice, and statements in another, with pauses where indicated for the reader to look carefully at pictures. (This could well be an activity for a pair of Year 6 pupils). The resource is there then for individual prolonged study.

What Makes a Bird a Bird? (Garelick 1989) would be a suitable text to model with older children in Year 2 or 3. This book is built with an interesting con-ceptual structure. The pattern follows exactly Thalia's way of reasoning, quoted earlier. Each page hypothesises about the one question, 'How do we know that a bird is a bird?', and leads the reader through various possibili-ties.

For example, the suggestion that a bird is a bird because it flies is made on one page. However, this is rejected on the next page, because creatures other than birds fly. The mystery tour is an introduction to logical reason-ing based on examples, hypothesis and classification. The very last page offers the solution: 'FEATHERS are the special things that MAKE A BIRD A BIRD.'

Where the Forest Meets the Sea (Baker 1987) is a very different type of non-fiction book, in the tradition of the 'picture story'. It would therefore be read to children first, to evoke intellectual and emotional response. A young boy describes his journey with his father to a tropical rain forest in North Queensland. The text is minimal; the illustrations are superb, built up into collages of the forest from natural materials, forming a wonderful three-dimensional effect. There are hidden elements in the pictures, which merge present and past. The boy says 'I pretend it is a hundred million years ago . . . I sit very still . . . and watch . . . and listen . . . . I wonder how long it takes the trees to grow to the top of the forest!' There are no answers to these questions, but they are just what a young child would ask in sim-ilar circumstances, evoking wonder and dread. The book can obviously be read many times; older children could make similar stories with their own collages made from local materials, around an environment near their homes.

I am therefore suggesting that the introduction of reading for information in the early years will not be directed towards accumulation of knowledge as such, but to widening concepts about the environment, and towards encouraging ways of thinking which will include observation, hypothesis-ing, comparison and classification, complementing the more personal response to fiction. Access will be through the children's own existing knowledge of environmental print rather than through graded reading schemes. The skills needed for reading non-fiction will develop from the beginning, in parallel with fictional reading. The children's writing of non-fiction text will be as important as their reading, and as far as possible will be for real purposes, to list, to record, to share with others, rather than to answer comprehension questions. Some texts will be introduced, of different types. Even very young children will grow into this sort of reading, using active problem-solving and interaction with their educators. Through these experiences and processes they will come to realise that reading for information is just as imaginative and exciting as reading stories.

Pointers for reading for information in the early years

- Children can and should learn to read from non-fiction as well as fiction texts.
- Environmental print is the best introduction to reading for information.
- Children should not just be collecting facts, but building conceptual frameworks to categorise experience in different ways. The processes of comparison, classification and evaluation are part of this development.
- Adults scaffold and model ways of using information texts. It is important that parents and educators should share children's home and school early literacy experiences.
- The processes of learning to read and write are closely interlinked.
- Flexible reading for different purposes, including silent reading, can begin at an early age.
- A few good information texts should be selected and discussed in detail with children.

References

Baker, J. (1987) *Where the Forest Meets the Sea*, London: Walker Books.

Bartlett, R. and Fogg, D. (1992) 'Language in the environment', in R. Bain, B. Fitzgerald and M. Taylor (eds) *Looking Into Language*, London: Hodder & Stoughton.

Bradshaw, A. (1988) *Writing and Drawing*, Story Chest Stepping Stones, Walton-on-Thames: Nelson.

Butler, D. (1991) *Minibeasts*, Take One, London: Simon & Schuster

Clay, M. (1982) *Observing Young Readers*, London: Heinemann Educational.
Ferreiro, E. and Teberosky, A. (1982) *Literacy before Schooling*, London: Heinemann.
Garelick, M. (1989) *What Makes a Bird a Bird?* London: Bookshelf.

Further reading

Mallett, M. (1994) *Reading Non-Fiction in the Primary Years: A Language and Learning Approach*, London: NATE.

The wider curriculum

CHAPTER 10

'How do I do this better?'

FROM MOVEMENT DEVELOPMENT INTO EARLY YEARS PHYSICAL EDUCATION

Patricia Maude

How do you like to go up in a swing
Up in the air so blue?
Oh, I do think it the pleasantest thing
Ever a child can do!'

(from 'The Swing' in *A Child's Garden of Verses*,
Robert Louis Stevenson 1885)

Introduction

The early years are exciting times both for children's physical development as they grow, changing in shape and size, and for children's movement development as they gain in body awareness and as they explore the vast range of available movement experiences within their environment. Not only is movement the main medium of exploration for the young child, but also physical activity is essential for normal growth, providing the necessary stimulus for normal development. Regular, vigorous activity is especially important at times of rapid growth.

We, as educators, have a responsibility for ensuring that the children we teach are exposed to the widest possible world of movement. Within that world of movement children need to experience a varied programme of activity which both balances the demands made on different parts of the body and takes into account the maintenance and enhancement of strength, mobility and endurance, helping to ensure the development of sound physique and posture. Giving children worthwhile movement experience will also develop motor competence and encourage motor confidence and creativity. Confidence in movement is vital for self-expression, and articulate co-ordinated movement ability enhances the development of self-esteem. One of the challenges for the early years educator is to capitalise on the vast movement experience that children have accumulated prior to starting school and then to expose them to a rich and rewarding movement vocabulary from which they can increase physical knowledge and skill and build on that past experience.

In this chapter we shall examine some of the **processes of physical development** from birth through infancy and early childhood and will then explore **motor development**, by looking at ways in which the acquisition of fundamental motor patterns and movement experiences are achieved by the young child. We shall also consider:

- the **role of the child** as a movement learner
- the **role of the educator** as a facilitator and provider of movement knowledge
- some suggestions as to what might constitute **quality movement learning** for children in their first years at school
- some aims and content for the **physical education curriculum** in the early years and in Key Stage 1.

Some processes of physical development

Pertinent to the learner and educator of movement are three key factors in the early physical development of infants, namely the principles of

- cephalo-caudal development
- proximo-distal development
- differentiation.

Cephalo-caudal development

This first principle of physical development is so named because it stems from the Greek word for 'head' which is 'kephale', and the Latin word for 'tail' which is 'cauda'. It denotes the principle that development occurs from the head downwards towards the feet. This seems obvious, since the head houses the brain which is the chief controller and regulator of all bodily functions. The brain also regulates the growth and development of the body. The head is the most developed part of the body at birth, having already achieved half of its adult length. The lower limbs at this stage, on the other hand, are relatively undeveloped and of relatively little importance, lacking in musculature and having achieved barely a fifth of their adult length. This principle will influence our planning and teaching when we are looking to ensure that the children we teach have acquired all the fundamental motor skills to enable them to be articulate movers in both the upper and lower limbs.

Proximo-distal development

The second principle refers to growth from the centre of the body outwards towards the extremities. This, too, is easily understood in the context of the significance of the central nervous system which controls all messages from the brain, running down the spinal column and managing all the life functions of the infant. The vital organs, essential to survival, are housed in the centre of the body, with maximum potential for protection. By comparison, the early activity of peripheral limbs such as the hands is relatively insignificant! For example the hands, the most distal elements at the farthest extremity from the centre of the body, are relatively inactive and non-instrumental in early life. Indeed, at this stage they are not structurally ready for action, since, for example, not all the bones in the wrists are differentiated. Before the wrists are fully prepared and ready to service the complex variety of movement demands that will be placed upon the hands when older, some of the wrist bones will separate and will develop appropriate musculature.

As with the principle of cephalo-caudal development, the principle of proximo-distal development is also important for the educator in creating a movement programme which takes account of the length of time necessary to achieve movement competence in those parts of the limbs that are relatively more distant from the centre of the body. Classroom learning can also be significantly dependent upon this principle, where, for example, the learner may not have achieved the moment of readiness to hold a pencil with the pincer grip and feels more comfortable using the palmar grasp. The product of work produced using the palmar grasp is usually less accurate than that of the pincer grip with which it is possible to achieve greater control.

Differentiation

The third principle is that whereas the new-born child offers an apparently global response, the more mature child is more discriminatory in response. For example, the infant cries, pulls the limb away and generally thrashes about in response to a pin prick on the hand, and whereas the older child will withdraw the limb and may cry, the adult is unlikely to do more than consider withdrawing the affected limb. As neurological development takes place and the child matures, so the ability to differentiate responses grows. This developing ability to discriminate responses with increasing maturity is an important element of learning for the early years child in school.

These three principles not only provide us with many insights into the process and rhythm of development of the infant, but also underpin for us many aspects of child development. They are particularly relevant as we move on to consider the movement (motor) development of young children. Movement is the lead area of functioning for the infant in acquiring information about the environment and in learning about self. The principles and processes of movement development therefore, hold many of the keys for the educator, in developing an appropriate movement curriculum for children.

Some processes of motor development

Motor development, along with other areas of development, follows the principles of cephalo-caudal, proximo-distal development and differentiation.

In relation to **cephalo-caudal development**, success is achieved in movement involving the upper part of the body before that involving the lower limbs. Control of the head, as in turning to look towards a stimulus and later lifting and holding the head, precedes management of the shoulders, to push up from front lying to raise the head. Thereafter further control of the trunk and hips enable the infant to learn to sit. This in turn precedes control of the hips, knees and ankles and later the feet and the increase in strength required for weight-bearing on the feet and for achieving the standing position, prior to learning to take the first step and later to walk.

The sequence of learning to walk, then, is significantly influenced by the principle of cephalo-caudal development. Whilst it is very rare that the mainstream educator of young children needs to be involved in teaching locomotion, this is a very significant sequence of development for some physically and mentally disabled children and for children with delayed movement development who are integrated into mainstream schooling. All early years educators will, however, be involved in developing and enhancing the efficiency and quality of this fundamental movement pattern and of the motor patterns that emanate from it, such as running, jumping and all other locomotion skills. The significance of cephalo-caudal development and its influence upon children's success in movement is of great importance both in the planning of the movement curriculum and in the general education of young children.

The equally logical principle of **proximo-distal movement skill development** can be observed as the infant explores the immediate environment and subsequently gains control over the arms, starting at the shoulders as the central or proximo part of the limb, before gaining controlled movement in the hands, the more peripheral or distal elements of the arms. Early exploration of the environment takes place through movement. Even from the relatively still supine lying position, the infant is seen to use the entire arm, flailing in the air, as if to swipe out and later to reach for objects in sight. In a similar way, apparently indiscriminate movement of the arms results in the infant discovering the mouth with the hands and subsequent success is achieved in grasping at objects with both hands, followed by trying to put them into the mouth.

Much movement experience is gained using the entire arm as a single lever, with relatively little **differentiation** between the arm joints. It is not until distance from an object becomes significant that flexion of the elbow is used to shorten the arm, for example. Much later, when one hand rather than two is required to achieve a movement task, the infant is dependent upon the development of the wrist joint and the joints of the fingers and thumb having acquired appropriate structure and musculature. Significantly, the principle of 'readiness' by which the child is unable to attempt a more advanced procedure until the structure and musculature are sufficiently mature, dominates motor development. We thereby do not see the infant progress from two-handed grasping to the use of one hand until that readiness is in place.

The sequence of growth and development

This leads us on to consider the sequence of growth and development including motor development, which is invariable, from one infant to the next. Helpfully for us as educators, the order in which all infants acquire movement skills is usually the same, every child follows the same sequence. Normally, for example, infants learn to roll over, then to sit and later to stand before learning to walk (see Figure 10.1).

Similarly, in terms of sequential development, prior to acquiring the skill of hopping, children must gain the strength to fix the pelvis, so that it remains horizontal when holding the body balanced over one foot. They then need the balance and co-ordination to transfer the body weight to that single foot before learning to take off, usually to hop along before hopping on the spot.

The fact of all children following the same sequence of movement development is very helpful. However, the challenge for the educator comes from the knowledge that the rate of development is unique to each child; no two

Figure 10.1 *The regular sequence of motor development in infants. From Rathus (1988, p. 202)*

children, even in the same family, follow the same pace of development. In preparing movement programmes, therefore, we must take account, particularly in the nursery and reception years, of the need for some children to complete their learning of some fundamental motor skills.

Gross and fine motor skills

Linked with the three preceding principles of motor development is another invariable and not-surprising feature of child development, that of 'gross' and 'fine' motor skills. The child achieves greater control in large (gross) body movement before managing control in smaller (fine) movements. For example, walking, jumping and running are more advanced in their performance and control at a relatively younger age than is drawing, cutting, or colouring-in, where detailed management of the developing muscles of the wrist and hand can be extremely challenging for the young child. Since much learning activity in the classroom involves drawing, painting, writing, measuring, cutting, sticking etc., the more mature the child's wrist and finger development and the stronger the musculature, the more successful will be the practical elements of the product and the least inhibition will have been experienced due to muscle fatigue. Some children's classroom behaviour may have been observed to be off-task or demonstrating lack of concentration when the true inhibitor was lack of maturity in the structure and functioning of the wrist and hand.

We rely on children arriving at school already articulate in movement, with mature movement patterns already established in the fundamental motor skills, and sometimes we have not incorporated this movement learning into the curriculum. On arrival at school, with a wealth of pre-school movement experiences, children should expect to rely on and draw from their existing movement vocabulary, using established and efficient movement patterns to enable them to participate fully in the activities on offer, to enjoy their learning and to be successful. My own experience would be that even where articulate movers arrive in school, reinforcement of mature movement patterns should continue to be a part of the curriculum, as the child grows, as body levers lengthen, strength increases and body awareness is enhanced. The child is in a state of readiness to become even more skilful and to acquire an even greater movement vocabulary.

Developing an appropriate movement curriculum for young children

As a starting point for devising a movement curriculum we may ask ourselves what constitute the most useful movement skills that children bring with them to school. Certainly efficiency in all daily living tasks, including feeding, toileting, dressing and moving safely around the environment will enable the child to operate independently in school. Additionally, children bringing a range of the gross and fine motor skills that are needed for full participation in class activities, such as those previously discussed, have an advantage over children who are less experienced or whose gross and fine motor skills are less developed.

Many children also bring with them a rich movement vocabulary developed through play. The importance of play as a basis for all aspects of education, cannot be overestimated, as has been ably discussed in previous chapters within the present volume. The importance of play involving gross and fine motor skills is of paramount importance in children's movement development and must underpin the devising of the physical education curriculum. Indeed, the physical education curriculum should be founded upon the natural movement vocabulary of the playing child.

Aims of the physical education curriculum

However, before deciding on the content of the physical education curriculum we should explore what we might consider to be the aims of that programme. In order to enhance the child as a learner and to ensure that you, as the educator, offer the best possible provision for that learner, the following broad aims for the physical education curriculum for early years children need to be developed. These relate to physical and movement development, movement skill acquisition, confidence in movement, and general education.

Physical development:

- to stimulate growth
- to enhance physical development
- to provide healthy exercise

Movement development:

- to build on existing movement vocabulary
- to develop co-ordination and body tension
- to extend movement vocabulary

Movement skill acquisition:

- to develop fundamental motor skills to the mature stage
- to introduce new motor skills
- to increase knowledge of dynamics of movement
- to develop co-ordination
- to teach accuracy in movement

Movement confidence development:

- to teach movement observation skills
- to develop movement experimentation and expression
- to enhance self-expression
- to enhance self-confidence, self-image and self-esteem

General education:

- to teach movement observation
- to teach appropriate vocabulary for discussing and explaining movement
- to stimulate thought processes
- to expect quality work from children

- to encourage independence in and ownership of learning
- to learn respect in co-operation and competition
- to enhance positive attitudes towards health-related exercise
- to provide experiences that teach children to plan, perform and evaluate their movement learning
- to sustain feelings of enjoyment and well-being in physical activity

Are there other aims that should underpin a curriculum plan for early years children in movement and physical education, such as providing stimulating, challenging and imaginative learning experiences for children? These can then be built into the curriculum.

The importance of play

In developing a movement curriculum for young children, the notion of building upon play is a compelling aim. Play is important for:

- encouraging discovery of movement abilities
- allowing for exploration of the movement environment
- offering practice time to enhance fundamental motor skills

The provision of a stimulating environment, both for children's pre-school play and for developmental play during the school day is a matter for detailed planning for parents and educators of young children. This might include:

- an adventure playground
- a secret garden
- a playground with suitable markings to encourage challenge in movement
- a tarmac area with wheeled toys including trucks, tricycles, bicycles and other ride-on and push-along toys
- an indoor space with soft-play or gymnastics apparatus
- grass and hard areas with balls of various sizes and textures, beanbags, hoops, bats and velcro catchers

These and other home and school provisions can significantly enhance the movement-learning experience for young children.

The development of skilled movement

The route to the acquisition of skilled movement has been plotted by Gallahue and Ozman (1995). They name three progressive stages in skill learning:

1. The initial or rudimentary stage

This is the emergent movement pattern, or early experimentation stage.

2. The elementary stage

At this stage, in which co-ordination is improved, the movement is still incorrectly performed and incomplete, perhaps lacking in strength, mobility, balance or speed.

3. The mature stage

Finally the child achieves the mature stage in which all the elements of the movement pattern are integrated and in which the movement includes appropriate preparation, followed by the accurate action and ends with follow through and recovery.

Watch a professional cricketer throw the ball in from the boundary and compare that action with the overarm throw of the average five-year-old and your mind's eye will no doubt provide ample evidence of potential for further development in the young child's achievement! (see Figure 10.2). Note the trunk flexion, rather than rotation.

Figure 10.2 *A beginning thrower. From Haywood (1993, p. 145)*

Figure 10.3 illustrates the movement development between a beginning and an advanced runner. With the advanced runner there is a much fuller range of leg motion and the thighs and arms drive forward and back rather than swinging out slightly to the side.

Bearing in mind that the elementary and mature movement patterns are normally achieved during the primary school years, the educator has considerable responsibility for recognising the three stages in the various fundamental motor skills of locomotion (walking and running), jumping (including taking off and landing) and projection (throwing, kicking) and in analysing the child's achievements, in order to improve performance.

Recognising the moment of readiness in the child, is a skill in itself to be acquired by the educator. Spatial and body awareness as well as appropriate maturing of the body structures and brain functioning are influential in attaining that moment of readiness. Have you ever tried to teach a child to ride a bicycle before readiness has been achieved? Holding the saddle, you walk or run along behind the bike growing ever more exhausted, as the child tries to stay upright and pedal, without success as far as independent balance is concerned. Put the bike away for a matter of weeks (or months if you or the child had been over-ambitious) and then notice that when the child gets the bike out again she climbs on and rides away unaided. The frustration of anticipating readiness too soon is outweighed by the satisfaction of helping a child to be successful in enhancing a partially learnt skill or in acquiring a new skill!

Figure 10.3 *A beginning and advanced runner. From Haywood (1993, pp. 128–9)*

The early years physical education curriculum

So, what should we include in our physical education curriculum that will meet our selected aims and provide satisfaction and rich movement experience for our young learners? The National Curriculum for Key Stage 1 promotes experience in dance, games and gymnastics, with swimming as an option in either Key Stage 1 or Key Stage 2. These activities seem entirely appropriate for children whose pre-school movement experience has been made up of broad-based and varied play. They are also appropriate activities as between them they offer extensive movement vocabularies, opportunities to develop creative as well as functional movement and opportunities for exercise and the stimulus for physical development and growth. Through dance, games, gymnastics and swimming the child can achieve the mature stage in fundamental movement patterns and can derive challenge, enjoyment, confidence and movement competence.

The range of movement vocabulary on offer can also be advantageous to the child with delayed movement development, who could be enabled to work within personal constraints and push out the boundaries of those limitations.

The child illustrated in Figure 10.4 has acquired by the age of six a sophistication of skill in kicking that is rarely seen in Key Stage 1.

The child seen in Figure 10.5 has achieved a quality of body and spatial awareness in leaping that should be our aim for all children in Key Stage 1.

Figure 10.4 *An advanced 6-year-old kicker*

Figure 10.5 *The leap*

For the normal child there need be no constraints beyond those imposed by the limitation of the developing body and brain, the confidence of the learner, and the bounds of reasonable safety imposed by the environment, the equipment to be used and the other children sharing the same space.

For me, the early years programme must be one of discovery and achievement, of valuing the learner, with evidence of excitement and satisfaction in learning. Can you recall an experience similar to that quoted above by Robert Louis Stevenson? Do you remember the effort of getting the swing started and then of discovering the knack of leaning back and then forward to increase the height of the swing and then the fear of going over the top, having seemingly swung too high?

Perhaps it is here, in the young child's physical play that we should start observing in an attempt to discover the 'lifeworld' of physical education for young children. If we are to provide worthwhile learning experiences that challenge the children, give them ownership of their learning and enable them to build on pre-school play experiences, we must seek out appropriate starting points. From these we can build upon:

- the fantasy and exploratory expressive play that becomes **dance** in twirling, galloping, leaping, reaching up and away and pausing;
- the **games**-like play that involves chasing, dodging, sending, receiving and kicking;
- the rolling, jumping, climbing, swinging and balancing play that becomes **gymnastics**.

We may need to take a closer look at what children actually do when they engage in physical activity and from our observation, put ourselves in touch with the nature of children's physical development before proceeding to influence that development by the pedagogical framework that we provide.

The role of the educator

One area of educator competence that is essential, in addition to that of understanding children's physical and movement development, is knowledge of the progressions for, and techniques of, the basic skills to be developed in physical education. The remainder of this chapter attempts to illustrate what is involved here using an example from each of the areas of dance, games and gymnastics. Enabling children to leap, to catch, or to do a forward roll, which are our three examples, requires a minimum level of technical knowledge, which can be acquired from observation, from demonstration or from videos, pictures or books.

Dance: learning to leap

Learning to leap involves transferring the body weight off the ground, from one foot to the other. Lead up skills for children who cannot leap include the basic jumping skills of take-off and landing on two feet and on one foot (hopping). Striding (taking very long steps), trying to make the knees straight to extend the stride length, can also be a lead up skill. Many children who find leaping difficult take a run and then take off and land on the same foot, i.e. they do a sort of long, fast hop. Encourage these children to take long strides and to try to push off the floor and do the step through the air.

Once the child can leap through the air from one foot to the other, the quality of the technique can be developed. Look for an upright body position, arms swinging to help elevate the leap, and then extending, probably sideways and symmetrically, to help control the shape in the air. Finally, look for height, distance, a clear shape in the air and a controlled landing.

Games: learning to catch

Learning to catch is best achieved by using a range of progressions, rather than by repeating experiences of failure, if it is clear that the child cannot catch the object being thrown. Progressions can be considered in at least two aspects:

1 **missile used** – size, weight, texture, shape, surface; encourage the child to choose a missile that is easy to catch e.g. a velcro catcher, a soft bean bag or a foam ball

2 **receiving activity** – the progression here is as follows:
   - receive from a slow roll sent along the ground towards the two waiting hands of the receiver
   - receive from an underarm feed with bounce so that the ball comes up to the waiting hands of the receiver
   - receive from an underarm throw

The technique of the catch involves three phases:

1 **the preparation** – including the stance, arms extended towards the missile, the open palmed ready position of the hands and the eyes watching the missile rather than the sender
2 **the action** – the hands closing around the ball, the arms bending or recoiling to control the impact of the missile
3 **the recovery** – in which the catcher regains a controlled position

Gymnastics: learning to forward roll

As with the catch, there are many progressions that can precede practising the forward roll for children who cannot readily perform this complex roll. (The forward roll is made up of at least 17 flexions and extensions of joints as it is performed!) Give children a vocabulary of other rolls that they can practise on the floor, on mats and on and from apparatus. Start with the log roll in which the child lies in a straight line and rolls over sideways. This roll can also be practised tucked. Teaching the ending of the forward roll is also a helpful progression, namely how to stand up from rocking on the back in a tucked shape, by keeping the knees bent and by placing the feet on the floor near the seat and reaching forward with the hands and arms to help transfer the weight from the seat to the feet. Learning to transfer the weight from the feet to the hands and then onto the shoulders in a forward roll is best learnt going down a soft, gentle incline, such as a foam ramp onto a mat, before practising the whole roll on a mat.

These are some of the main teaching points for three basic skills. Other texts provide greater detail of these and other skills (see list at the end of this chapter). What else should be included within the pedagogical framework is a question to be answered by the competent curriculum planner, in devising an appropriate developmental physical education programme for young children.

Satisfying the 'skill hungry years' of children in primary school and answering the myriad of questions, of these same children, such as 'How do I do this better ?' is a constant and often insatiable challenge for the educator.

My own view is that this is not an insurmountable challenge. The educator first observes and studies the lifeworld of physical activity as experienced by the young learner in natural movement development. The child is then put at the centre of the learning experience and the educator enables the joy of indulging in physical activity to be sustained and enhanced as the child matures and engages ever more skilfully in the wide range of physical activities available.

Pointers for physical education in the early years

An effective physical education curriculum for the early years will help to cultivate in children movement that is skilful, articulate, creative and satisfying. In order to help young children develop these motor skills the early years educator needs to:

- acquire knowledge of the physical development of young children in relation to motor development and the achievement of mature motor patterns;
- acquire knowledge of the techniques of movement skills;
- develop observation skills to enable appropriate developmental feedback on the child's performance;
- build the Physical Education curriculum from natural movement and play.

References

Gallahue, D. and Ozman, J. (1995) *Understanding Motor Development* (3rd Edn), London: William C. Brown.

Haywood, K.M. (1993) *Life Span Motor Development* (2nd Edn), Champaign, Illinois: Human Kinetics.

Rathus, S.A. (1988) *Understanding Child Development*, Fort Worth, Texas: Holt, Rinehart and Winston.

Further reading

The Physical Education Association of the United Kingdom (1995) *Teaching Physical Education at Key Stages 1 and 2*, London: PEA UK.

Teaching and learning movement skills

Gymnastics

Maude, P.M. (1994) *The Gym Kit* (video and handbook), Albion Television, the Health Promotion Research Trust and Homerton College, Cambridge.

Benn, T. and B. (1992) *Primary Gymnastics*, Cambridge: Cambridge University Press.

Games

Cooper, A. (1993) *The Development of Games and Athletic Skills*, Hemel Hempstead: Simon & Schuster.

Read, B. and Edwards, P. (1992) *Teaching Children to Play Games*, Liverpool: British Council of Physical Education/Leeds: National Coaching Foundation/London: Sports Council.

Dance

Harrison, K. (1993) *Look, Look What I Can Do*, Sevenoaks: Hodder & Stoughton.

—— (1989) *Bright Ideas for Dance and Movement*, London: Scholastic.

CHAPTER 11

'Can I play the drum, Miss?'

MUSIC IN THE EARLY YEARS

Jane Edden

The task ahead

It would be altogether too easy to be deterred from teaching music to children. After all, in an investigation carried out in a college of education, it was discovered that 'By a wide margin . . . music is the subject in which most students have the least confidence as teachers' and that 'Some students thought that they needed to have musical skills customarily associated with music specialists, e.g. piano playing, fluent music reading and an inside-out knowledge of the Classics' (Mills 1989). This somewhat gloomy picture is offset, however, by those who have faced the challenge head on, and in one case, emerged with recommendations from the county music adviser as providing good practice in the classroom. A teaching head in Warwickshire (Dancer 1991) who had 'never been on a music course of any kind', began her written guidelines with the words 'You don't need a piano, a guitar, a wonderful singing voice or a special room to enjoy music making with children'. Her commitment to 'bringing children into contact with the musician's fundamental activities of performing, composing and listening' (DES 1985, p. 2) in order that they 'can best discover something of its nature, its vitality, its evocative power and the range of its expressive qualities', (ibid.), serves as an illustration for this chapter, which aims to outline the ways in which the world of sound can be presented to young children in an exciting, meaningful and yet non-threatening way. It is also hoped and expected that, during this endeavour, students and other early years educators may very well rediscover the key to their own previously lost world of sound. As such, the chapter will address the following:

1 The recognition, exploration and manipulation of sound and the beginnings of composition;

2 Integrating musical activities into a broader framework;
3 The question of singing;
4 Introducing rhythm and movement;
5 Listening as part of a wider curriculum.

Exploring sound: starting points

The simplest way of beginning an exploration of sound in the classroom , is by helping children to develop the art of listening.

> Learning to listen – both to sounds around them and sounds that they can make themselves – is fundamental to children's music making. By encouraging children to think about these sounds, to be aware of them, to talk about them and to experiment with and manipulate them when they are in groups or by themselves, we provide a framework within which musical activities can take place and a real musical awareness can develop.
>
> (Davies 1985, p. 8)

Through a series of questions, children can be introduced to some listening games in order to help them focus on the sound world around them.

What sound?

Listening game: What can you hear?

1 Ask the children to close their eyes and to listen to any sound they can hear within the room. Discuss with the children.
2 Next, ask the class what they can hear outside the room, but inside the building. Discuss.
3 Finally, ask them to listen to any sounds they can hear outside the building. Discuss.

As will be discovered, children will initially talk about any sound they hear regardless of its origin, but on repeated exposure to the game (it can be used as an infill at the end of a session, or as a contrast to a lively activity – no two playings will ever be the same!), it can be seen that the children are developing not only their powers of concentration, but also the ability to discriminate – two vital ingredients of the listening act.

The whole notion of games to explore musical learning is of significance. Storms (1983), suggests games are nothing new, but increasingly recognised as a valuable preparation for music education. He believes moreover, that games are a way of overcoming barriers for children and their educators alike – they can aid the personal, social and creative development of the children, whilst perhaps allowing the person lacking in confidence to explore ways of delivering music in the classroom.

It is important to give young children the opportunity on a regular basis to play some of these earliest listening games in order to develop their listening skills. It is worth remembering that an ability to listen is a crucial part of a child's whole development and essential for day to day life in the classroom! Something as simple as asking the children (with eyes closed) to wiggle their fingers when they hear keys being shaken will sharpen their concentration whilst aiding their motor skills.

Listening tape

Collect together on tape some household sounds e.g. tap running, clock ticking, kettle boiling (it may be appropriate to group them together in order to enhance a topic – Water/Machines/Myself – early morning routine).

This could be used as a 'Guess the sound' game by itself as a classroom activity, or 'Match the picture to the sound' by providing visual representations of the sounds on the tape (such as those in Figure 11.1).

This could then become an individual listening task which could be set in an area with a small tape recorder and the picture cards – an activity which would contribute to the development of children's autonomy, whilst at the same time acquainting them with the operation of simple technology.

Once children have been given practice in listening skills, it is time to move on to ask the next question.

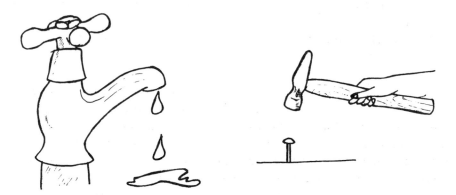

Figure 11.1 *'Match the picture to the sound'*

What kind of sound?

Listening game: listen to my sound!

1 Gather together a collection of percussion instruments (if possible, an assortment of tuned and untuned, wood and metal).
2 Seat the children in a circle with an instrument in front of each child.
3 Ask the children to take turns in making one sound on their instrument, but only playing when they can no longer hear the sound made by the previous instrument.
4 Go round the circle, avoiding as far as possible any comments from the children. In this way full attention will be given to the sounds made and a sound picture will emerge.

A slightly different version of this game – How long does my sound last? – can be found in *Soundwaves* (Davies 1985).

The discussion which follows the game can include a variety of questioning. A good way of beginning is to ask the children if they noticed if everybody waited until the sound had finished, thus focusing on their previously acquired skills (it is worth remembering however, that an early entry may very well have more to do with an over-enthusiasm than an inaccurate hearing!). Other questions might be:

1 Who thinks they had a longer sound? (e.g. metal instruments.) Invite those children to play their sounds again.
2 Who had a shorter sound? (e.g. wooden instruments.) Ask the class to listen to the differences between the two.
3 How do the materials affect the sound?
4 Can anybody change the sound they made? It may be necessary to demonstrate at this juncture. A particularly good point to make is how a drum can be played very quietly indeed (even with finger tips), thus putting paid to any preconceived ideas that it is always to be beaten as loudly as possible! It is also worth showing more imaginative transitions e.g. how a long ringing note on a glockenspiel can be changed into something much duller and shorter by dampening it with one's hand.
5 What kind of sound is that? Can you describe it?

This last question is central. In setting up opportunities and games in which they can experiment and play with sound possibilities, children can be encouraged to respond in a variety of ways. For example, from the simple shaking of a maracca comes initially a recognition of the sound of a shaker. Through questioning, they can come to understand that they are making a series of 'fast' sounds. Furthermore, in encouraging them to talk about any related feelings or images that come to mind – 'It sounds like rain', 'It makes me scared 'cos I think of mice running' – they can use their imaginations to invent their own sound images.

Thus it can be seen that the exploration of sound with young children can elicit both a cognitive and an affective response, in addition to working hand in hand with the acquisition of language. Through this playful, experiential process with the raw materials of sound emerges a new vocabulary, neatly set out as the list of musical elements in the national curriculum document:

pitch – high/low
duration – long/short; pulse or beat; rhythm
dynamics – loud/quiet/silence
tempo – fast/slow;
timbre – quality of sound, e.g. tinkling, rattling, smooth ringing
texture – several sounds played or sung at the same time/one sound on its own;

and the use of the above within

structure – different sections, e.g. beginning, middle, end; repetition (e.g. repeated patterns), melody, rhythm.

Some of this technical vocabulary may seem daunting, but it is much less so, for educators and children, when the concepts have already been explored and described. The word 'timbre', for example, might be threatening in isolation, but when known to be dull or bright and, most importantly, recognised as the difference between the clashing cymbal or the one which falls with a thud to the floor, it is much more acceptable as part of a new vocabulary. Sound must be experienced before symbol to sow the seeds of joyous musical discovery. Gone are the days when the stave was taught in a vacuum without any meaningful purpose.

What makes the sound?

The third question addresses soundmakers, and it is important to remember that the child's first resource is his or her own body.

Listening ideas: my body

Get the children to listen to the sounds that they can produce themselves – this may well come out of a topic on 'My body'. e.g.

playing with hair

fingers on cheek – mouth open / mouth closed
fingers in cheek – pops
tapping / scraping teeth
tongue clops / clicks

(See *Pompaleerie Jig* (Baxter and Thompson 1978) for further ideas).

This only goes as far as the head! What can they think of for the rest of their body? What kind of sound are they making? What words can they use to describe the sounds they make? Encourage the children to listen firstly to their own sound, but then to the effect of the same sound made by the whole class – what do they think of when they have their eyes shut but are listening to the sound of thirty arms being lightly rubbed? Talk about the sound images that emerge.

Can they invent their own words for their very own soundmakers? If children are given permission at a young age to think creatively this will serve them well in every other area of life.

Listening game: tropical storm

1 Stand the children in a circle.
2 Ask the children to very lightly rub the palms of their hands together. Gradually get louder.
3 Change to tapping two fingers against their palms.
4 Increase the volume and use the whole hand to clap.
5 Use the hands to slap the thighs.
6 Move the feet in quick succession.

The object of this game is to achieve a continuous increase and decrease in volume (no sudden lurches!) to represent the appearance and disappearance of a storm. It is an ideal opportunity to discuss *dynamics* with the children, and in particular the meaning of a *crescendo* and *diminuendo*. (It is only meaningful to do this because the children are experiencing it.)

Once the class have a grasp on the sequence of the actions, divide the circle up into four groups. The conductor (it could eventually be a child) then points to a group at a time to indicate when they start and move onto the next sequence. In this way the storm gradually increases in ferocity and will ultimately die away. Voices can be used (only use a few children at a time!) depending on how tropical the class want the storm to be. Keep this in reserve, however, for when the game has been played before, or possibly as an introduction to a discussion on the possibilities of the voice.

The voice

The voice of course, is a very important soundmaker in its own right. Children should be given ample opportunities to use their voices inventively in order for them to appreciate that each one has their own very special instrument with its own wealth of possibilities (Chacksfield and Binns 1983, have some interesting ideas). The author appreciates that there are some amongst us who may feel very uncertain about exploring this area, but it is to be remembered that young children are a very uncritical audience and only welcome the opportunity to be allowed to make their own discoveries. As will be seen later, the larynx is a muscle that needs developing like any other.

Other soundmakers

Once children have been encouraged to use their voices, bodies and instruments in inventive ways, they can broaden their horizons by recognising that anything is a potential soundmaker. They might be asked to bring in any discarded packaging from home which can then be explored in exactly the same way as any other resource. An instant listening and response game can be conducted around different kinds of paper for example. This may well fit into any kind of work on conservation or be linked with a blitz on litter!

'The freedom to explore chosen materials' (Paynter 1978, p. 7) gives children the vocabulary with which to express themselves. If the word 'composition' (potentially threatening to some!) is to be seen as 'a way of saying things which are personal to the individual' (Paynter's definition of 'creative music' – an earlier description of the composition process), then by this stage children are ready to compose.

Combining sounds

Having had the experience of playing with sound, manipulating it to their own ends and realising that there is no right or wrong way, it is now time to give the children a framework in which to explore further. John Paynter has clear ideas about the role of the educator which might well be encouraging to many: the educator's role 'is to set off trains of thought and help the pupil develop his own critical powers and perception . . . as far as possible this work should not be controlled by a teacher' (Paynter 1978, p. 7).

The simplest 'trains of thought', useful as starting points for composition are action packed pictures or picture books with a few words on the page (e.g. *Rosie's Walk*, Hutchins 1968; *Dinnertime*, Pienkowski 1980) . After two or three readings of the story, the children can be asked to suggest some ideas for sound effects as illustration. This can emerge from discussion on characterisation and events, and use any sound sources the children consider appropriate (they may need to be reminded about their voice and body possibilities due to over-eagerness to play instruments!).

'The processes of composition in any art are selection and rejection, evaluating and confirming the material at each stage. It is essentially an experimental situation!' (Paynter 1978, p. 7). So it is that the educator becomes an enabler and facilitator to help children explore, discuss and select the sounds they want. It is a case of constantly checking that they are happy with their choices. If, for example, they felt that the woodblock didn't sound 'bad' enough for the fox, the educator could open up a line of questioning on what kind of sound might sound more menacing – longer, shorter, metal, wood, vocal even? It is important to take time and for the class to listen with care to each other's suggestions (an ongoing reinforcement of the skill of listening) Maybe someone were to favour some longer sounds on the cymbal. This might be a forerunner of the processes of discrimination and refinement – 'Could we get louder then quieter?' Time will then need to be spent in fine tuning, until the children are satisfied with their results.

In the initial stages of this work, one would need to make this a whole class activity, but ultimately small group work is desirable, as independent learning and social skills can come into play. The finished product can be committed to tape and played back to the children for appraisal. A series of questions can elicit to what extent the class are satisfied with their piece. Did it sound as they wanted it to sound? Is there anything they would like to change/improve upon? An opportunity for them to make further refinements is empowering and helps them to adopt the ownership of the work. Part of the role of the educator is to assist the children in taking a pride and a sense of responsibility for their creative acts. Encouraging positive comments to begin with before accepting constructive criticism can give the children a model with which to work.

We as educators can, during this critical listening time, be open to opportunities to reinforce any musical elements that might have been used. For example, Rosie walking over the haycock might have served well as an illustration of *pitch*, or a blend of voices/instruments and other soundmakers could have created a particularly interesting *texture*. If we can heighten children's awareness of what they have produced, we are making a substantial contribution to their musical development.

What then has the learning been in this compositional process? Over and above John Paynter's key summary, we can list the following:

1 *Social skills and co-operation*: taking turns, working together and sharing would have been in evidence (even more so when group work is begun).

2 *Motor skills and co-ordination of hand, ear and eye* would have been practised: e.g. holding a beater and playing at the right time.
3 *Imagination* would have been heavily engaged.
4 The children have been involved, not only as *performers* and *composers*, but as three different kinds of *listeners*: as composers – 'which sound is better for the splash?'; as performers – to each other; and finally as audience listeners – when they stand back and listen to the tape (and ultimately to their peer groups).
5 They have been introduced to the first stages of *appraising* their work.

Recording the sound

The final stage of the compositional process – finding a way to store the information on paper, can be an important breakthrough for adults and children alike in discovering its accessibility. In helping children explore pictorial representations of sound, the word *'notation'*, threatening for so many in the past, can have new meaning when expressed graphically. Figure 11.2 shows some early examples of starting points.

Figure 11.3 shows a full score in graphical notation, entitled 'Red Dragon's cave', from *Dewi the Dragon* by Gill Wilson (Edden *et al.* 1989).

Before performing this, the children could look at, discuss and play each line separately, noting the obvious changes in *pitch* and *dynamics*, for example. For further reading in this area, see Gilbert (1981).

Figure 11.2 *Young children's graphical notation for music*

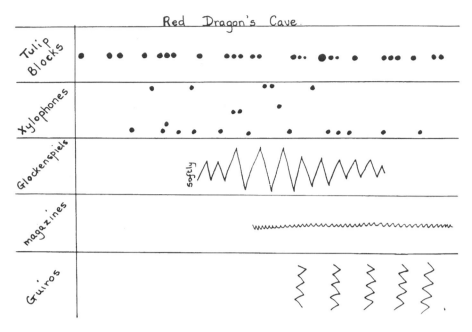

Figure 11.3 *Red Dragon's cave: a full score in graphical notation*

A holistic framework

It has been seen that composing, performing, listening and appraising skills can sit together very comfortably under the developmental umbrella of exploring sound. Such integration can be viewed as a model for working in a holistic fashion. Not only does this make sense from the child's perspective, but it can be most reassuring from our point of view to realise that music can be approached from any angle and in particular from our own strengths.

> Good primary school practice is based on teachers recognising the opportunities to fertilise work in one part of the curriculum with work in another. The unifying and integrating aspects of the arts give them a particular value in this respect.
>
> (Arts in Schools 1982, p. 53)

Let us take an example. *Rosie's Walk* (Hutchins 1968) can be read to the children as part of a topic on journeys. To give it musical depth two elements are pre-selected to focus on, although this does not mean that others are not acknowledged! *Pitch*, *pace* and *duration* all give particular scope (but it is hoped that during the course of the year all elements will be explored in some depth through various activities). Already, attention has been paid to pitch through Rosie walking up and down the haycock. Further endorsement of this might come at another time by showing children the xylophone and working with some high and low notes. Science can be introduced by carrying out pitch experiments with levels of water in bottles which could then be played like a xylophone. Geography can be covered by recreating Rosie's journey as simple mapping work for a classroom display, and maybe helping children map out their own journeys to school, which could then be used as scores for graphic notation. Language of course, has been explored alongside the selected sounds.

Games can be played to reinforce the concepts and there are many useful books to explore. Mary York's (1984) choice is particularly appropriate in her book *Gently into Music,* and *Hi Lo Dolly Pepper* (Clark 1991) includes a comprehensive exploration of all the concepts together with some attractive graphic scores. Nursery rhymes like 'Hickory Dickory Dock' lend themselves ideally as a good illustration of both *pitch* and *pace.* Stories like 'The Three Bears' and poems like 'The Four Friends' (in York 1984) provide wonderful opportunities to consolidate the idea of *pitch,* but also feed into other areas of the curriculum. The flow chart in Figure 11.4 might be used not only as a model for any kind of comprehensive musical input to any topic, but as a basis for the kind of holistic framework that has been discussed.

Also not to be missed as valuable sources of topic ideas:

Topic Anthology for Young Children (Gilbert 1991) – includes
    Water, Machines, Toys, Fairs and Circuses, Cowboys and Indians
Music Through Topics (Clark 1990)

The question of singing

One of the best links that can be made between topic areas and the musical elements is singing.

> For both children and teacher the importance of regular classroom singing is greater than realised. It can stimulate and calm the children, bring class and teacher together and provide an enjoyable controlled activity to balance the programme of a busy day. It develops the child's musical abilities and social skills whilst also acting as a valuable aid in reading and language development, in building basic concepts and in linking and extending other areas of the curriculum.
>
> (Gilbert 1981, p. 15).

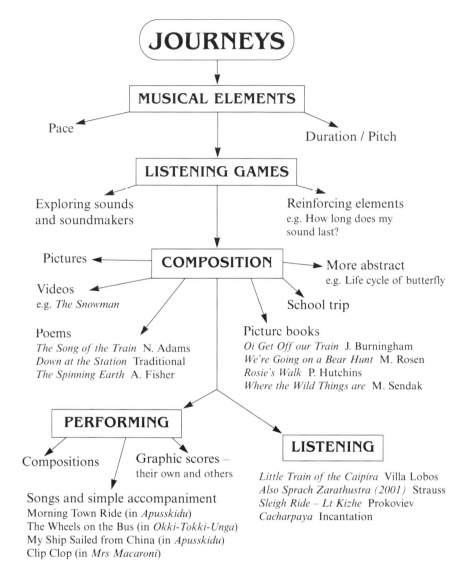

Figure 11.4 *Flow chart of musical activities related to the topic of 'journeys'*

Ideally singing should be a daily activity and should fulfil a variety of criteria. Songs of different kinds will perform different functions

Songs with repetition and action songs

These are particularly important to young children. The action song 'Jack in the Box ' (Scott Wood) with its descending scale and its final leap 'Yes I will!'

in answer to the question 'Will you come out?' is a perfect example of how to illustrate *pitch* to children. Some children might join in with a xylophone, stepping from high to low, whilst others could take it in turns to be Jack, and leap from low to high. Many songs can be used in this way to consolidate musical learning through a focus. Increasingly, there are books available which use songs in this kind of broader context. Try exploring other songs used to feature *pitch* and other elements in:

Game Songs For Infants (Richards 1990)
Mrs Macaroni (Tillman 1985)
Managing Music with Infants (Edden *et al*. 1989)
Gently into Music (York 1984)
Hi Lo Dolly Pepper (Clark 1991)

Two and three note songs

Children also need to be given opportunities to work with two and three note songs (e.g. 'Rain, Rain Go Away', 'Bell Horses') to help them find their voices. Singing the register using the Soh–Me interval, or responding to a sung question can be of great value. Nicki Bennison and her intensive work with children at Chichester Central school, proves how valuable this kind of work can be, and the success story of her choir (Sainsbury's Choir of the Year 1990) is living proof that constant exposure to singing and making it a highlight of the school day can pay rich dividends. 'I believe that all children can be taught to sing if and only if somebody bothers to find their voice' (Bennison 1991).

Singing with confidence

But what of those who have very low self-esteem when it comes to their own singing, and are fearful of leading children in song? There are no magic cures for this dilemma, but there are reassurances that can be given. The first of these is that young children are just grateful to have an opportunity to sing. They are not a critical audience. Be encouraged with older infants, moreover, to allow the stronger singers to assist in leading the class. There is a distinction to be made between those who are unwilling to sing in front of their peers but will 'have a go' behind closed doors, and those who have absolutely no confidence whatsoever. For the latter kind, pre-recorded tapes are a useful prop. The author has witnessed a very successful use of such a strategy in a situation where confidence was low, but a commitment to children's singing was high. Ten minutes before each break time, the teacher would gather the children from their various activities to sit together on the carpet and sing with the tape. It was a joyous sight, particularly in the light of the teacher's own perceived difficulties. It is important to realise that a willingness on the part of the unconfident educator to expose children to the joys of singing can be infinitely more beneficial than the 'expert' who quite erroneously blames a child for singing out of tune. After all, at seven years old, only about 50 per cent of children can represent a given pitch.

Rhythm and movement

Another area which gives particular concern to early years educators is that of introducing rhythm to children. Yet simple activities can serve children well in this area. All children have had the experience of a steady beat (mother's heart beat, rocking, knee bouncing) and, by the time they come to school, many have a developed sense of pulse. Helping children reinforce this skill by using body percussion to accompany simple rhymes, songs, jingles or any piece of recorded music with a steady beat is a good starting point .

Rhythm game: Follow my leader

1 Select a piece of recorded music with a strong beat.
2 Establish the pulse.
3 Ask the class to copy what you do – 'follow my leader'.
4 Use a variety of different body percussion to keep a steady pulse e.g. tapping hands on head, shoulders, thighs; clapping, clicking etc.
5 Alternate the actions.
6 If appropriate, invite a child to lead.

This game is not only helpful in terms of developing a sense of *pulse*, but improves concentration and is fun! It can also be used as a five-minute 'filler' for those occasions when there is time to spare at the end of a session. Maybe the music that is selected (and this is certainly an opportunity to introduce the class to different genres) is chosen as part of the holistic framework, and can thus feed into an integrated curriculum.

Simple echo clapping, where the educator claps four beats (*pulse*) and the children follow, can move into an understanding of 'walking' beats – walk, walk, walk, walk – and can ultimately be drawn on cards as a demonstration of simplified crotchets (this is the very beginning of staff *notation*). The natural progression moves to clapping patterns (e.g. names, topic words, the words of a rhyme, e.g. 'Rain, Rain, Go Away'). The following example demonstrates how children can begin to understand simple rhythm patterns in terms of walks, slow walks and runs.

Big	Chief	Sitt	ing	Bull
(walk	walk	run	run	walk)

Hi	a	wa	tha	brave
(run	run	run	run	slow walk)

Pain	ted	tee	pee	Arr	ow	head
(run	run	run	run	run	run	walk)

War	drums	grave.
(walk	walk	slow walk)

Each one of these lines forms a *pattern*, as opposed to a *pulse*, and a line said repeatedly becomes an *ostinato* (repeated pattern). This can be an exciting way of introducing simple song/rhyme accompaniment and the following can be used as a model for any simple song or rhyme.

Using an ostinato:

1 Familiarise the children with the song or rhyme.
2 Select a short phrase from the words of the text, which lends itself to being repeated e.g. Big Chief Sitting Bull/Rain, Rain Go Away.
3 Ask the children to repeat it several times in rhythm.
4 Ask a small group to continue to do this whilst the rest of the class say the rhyme. This is vocal *ostinato* in action!

As a progression, try substituting the phrase with either body percussion or untuned percussion, asking the children to say the phrase silently in their heads. This internalisation helps develop musical memory. Linking patterns to words is a security and a learning tool for educators and children alike! It is important to state here that it is best to only work with the staff *notation* with which one is comfortable. It would be foolish to topple confidence which has gradually emerged in other areas by putting too much emphasis on delivering what might well be at the heart of our fears. This is in no way intended to undervalue the traditional form of recording music, but is much more an observation on unrealistic expectations .

Rhythm through movement

Many rhythmic ideas can be experienced through movement activities. 'Music is not heard by ear alone but the whole of the body' (Mothersole 1921, p. 23). Movement is an ideal vehicle for consolidating learning whilst at the same time enabling children to make creative use of their energies.

Games are a perfect medium to explore movement activities. Try the following:

Movement Game: 'Journey of the animals'

1 Divide the class into four groups of different syllabic animals (cat, ti – ger, po – lar bear, al – li – ga – tor).
2 Send each group into a corner of the room.
3 Tap out each of the rhythms in turn, and encourage them to move to the secret cave in the centre by stepping out their pattern, when they hear their particular rhythm.(You may need to demonstrate first!) They must stop when they hear the pattern change.
4 When the children are secure with their rhythms, be more unpredictable in your sequencing!
5 Change the groups in order for them to experience all the patterns.

Some movement games need instrumental players: e.g. 'Charlie Chaplin went to France' and 'Punchinello' (Edden *et al.* 1989) both need a two note drone (i.e. the same two notes played repeatedly throughout.). Games to reinforce any of the musical elements can be led by someone without pianistic skills. With *pitch*, for example, children can be asked to 'walk tall' if they hear some high notes on the piano or move as low as they can when they hear low notes. This, of course, is further practice in listening skills.

Listening as part of a wider curriculum

In a world bombarded with sound, young children do not necessarily find listening as easy as in years gone by. There has already been discussion earlier in the chapter about the crucial role it plays in a child's musical development, and as such educators are encouraged to expose the child to a variety of listening activities. Affective responses can be made through the medium of paint or words (a 'journey' to South America to hear 'Cacharpaya', played by Incantation, is an ideal starting point here: 'How does it make you feel?', 'What can you imagine?'), whilst the cognitive response can even at an early stage be developed (Prokoviev's 'Sleigh Ride', for example, from *Lieutenant Kizhe*, features the sleigh bells the children may very well have on their music trolley. Can they hear them?) Attention to *pace* can be given through Villa Lobos' 'Little Train of the Caipira', where they can hear the train increasing in speed, but they can also be asked if they think it sounds like a train, and why? We need to try and present a focus for listening and to take the 'musical' questioning as far as we are able. Recorded music, it has been seen , can be played in a variety of different contexts all within a cohesive programme. Try finding a piece of music as a follow up to children's compositions, or something relevant to the topic which could be used for movement purposes. If children can be in touch with live music (either attending concerts or inviting musicians into school) then it becomes an exciting, living reality.

Conclusion

It is hoped that after reading this chapter early years educators will come to see that whatever their own musical history might be, they have an important role to play as an enabler and inspirer of young children's music. If you can make music an integral part of the school day, you will be using the your own and the children's creativity to build a new way of being for yourself and the children you teach. 'Every creative act involves a new innocence or perception, liberated from the cataract of accepted belief' (Arts in Schools 1982, p. 22).

Pointers for early years music

- Don't assume you need to have had a traditional music training in order to facilitate young children's music making.
- Use simple games as a means of reinforcing a musical idea.
- Exploring sound and sound sources can stimulate the imagination whilst developing language skills.
- Look for any opportunities to reinforce the elements of music.
- When planning a topic look for ways in which music can be naturally linked with other areas of the curriculum, thus making it a daily and relevant activity.
- A song a day keeps the grumps away!
- Make music fun!

References

Arts in Schools (1982) *Principles, Practice and Provision*, London: Calouste Gulbenkian Foundation.

Bennison, N. (1991) *Singing is Central*, BBC 2.

Dancer, A. (1991) 'Every child has a song to sing', *Times Educational Supplement*, 8th February.

Davies, L. (1985) *Soundwaves*, London: Unwin Hyman.

DES (1985) *Music from 5–16*, London: HMSO.

Gilbert, J. (1981) *Musical Starting Points with Young Children*, London: Ward Lock.

Mills, J. (1989) 'The generalist primary music teacher', *British Journal of Music Education*, 6, 125–38.

Mothersole, A. (1920) 'La Rythmique est-elle une lubie?' *Le Rythme*, 5, 23.

Paynter, J. (1978) *Sound and Silence*, Cambridge: Cambridge University Press.

Storms, G.(1983) *Handbook of Musical Games*, London: Hutchinson.

Source material referred to in text

Baxter, A. and Thomson, D. (1978) *Pompaleerie Jig*, Exeter: E. J Arnold.

Chacksfield, M. and Binns, P. (1983) *Sound Ideas Books 1–6*, Oxford: Oxford University Press.

Clark, V. (1990) *Music Through Topics*, Cambridge: Cambridge University Press.

—— (1991) *Hi Lo Dolly Pepper*, London: A. & C. Black.

Edden, J., Edwards, R., Malcolm, A. and Wilson, G. (1989) *Managing Music with Infants*, Cambridge: Cambs County Council.

Gilbert, J. (1991) *Topic Anthology for Young Children*, Oxford: Oxford University Press.

Hutchins, P. (1968) *Rosie's Walk*, London: Bodley Head.

Pienkowski, J. (1980) *Dinnertime*, London: Orchard.

Richards, C. (1990) *Game Songs For Infants*, (available from Acorn Percussion Ltd., Unit 34, Abbey Business Centre, Ingate Place, London SW8 3NS.)

Tillman, J. (1985) *Mrs Macaroni*, London: Macmillan.

York, M. (1984) *Gently into Music*, Harlow, Essex: Longmans.

Other source material

Birkenshaw, L. (1974) *Music for Fun, Music for Learning*, Toronto: Birk–Holt Rinehart & Winston.

Farmer, B. (1982) *Springboards*, Melbourne, Australia: Nelson

Gamper, E. (1986) *Music with Mr Plinkerton*, Woodford Green, Essex: International Music Publications.

Mills, J. (1991) *Music in the Primary School*, Cambridge: Cambridge University Press.

Maddocks, A. and Stocks, M. (1991) *Growing Up with Music KS1*, Harlow, Essex: Longmans.

Wheway, D. and Thomson, S. (1993) *Explore Music through . . .* (9 subject areas), Oxford: Oxford University Press.

CHAPTER 12

'I can't do horses'

DEVELOPING CHILDREN'S DRAWING

John Lewis

If you read about children's drawing you will become aware that the authors tend to be either child psychologists or art educators. Their different perspectives are not altogether compatible. This chapter begins with a review of these different perspectives before looking at how they might guide the early years educator in helping children to develop their drawing.

Research by psychologists

The psychologist is examining a child's drawing as evidence of what is going on inside their head. When they witness changes in the drawing it is seen as a change of the child's perception. Measurements of intelligence, and states of mental stress, have both been made on the basis of drawing, but ironically they tend to be related to the degree of realism portrayed.

Numerous studies of the development of children's drawings have been made throughout this century (see Thomas and Silk 1990, for a useful review). They are usually different in the detail of their findings but they generally conform to a pattern that starts with:

Stage 1 Scribbles.
Stage 2 Symbolic shapes that are given names.
Stage 3 Descriptive drawing based on a degree of analysis.

Progress is generally seen to be made by acquiring techniques and skills towards a 'photographic' realism. This is not surprising as the research focuses on the drawing of objects. Correlations are made on this basis between ages, stages and intellect.

Some art educators as well as psychologists use these stages as markers for assessment. One is Robert Clement – the influential member of the committee who devised the National Curriculum for art. His recommended assessment procedure is to measure progress of the child's work on the basis of how far they have moved towards a goal of descriptive realism (Clement and Page 1992a, p. 104).

Researchers have focused on particular aspects of children's drawing in an effort to understand it. Listed below are interpretations of a selection of some of the ideas developed and terms used.

Stages in drawing

Traditional theory is based on research of children's drawing of objects. It traces a path from early scribble marks towards visually realistic images. There are always exceptions to the rule but a change from about the age of seven to nine years is identified between a predominately 'symbolic stage' and a predominately 'analytical stage'. There is a body of opinion, beginning to grow, that discredits this theory on the basis that it is too narrow a definition of drawing.

Scribbles

A scribble is a set of marks that is the very antithesis of order and control. It is often seen as a gesture to obliterate or an outpouring of uncontrolled energy. Underneath the solid black charcoal drawing in Figure 12.1, for example, is a line drawing of a figure. Adele, a three-year-old nursery class child, appears to have deliberately erased the figure by working heavy rhythmic marks over the top. This caused much distress to her teacher!

It is often difficult for adults to see more to drawing than simply representation, but for children it serves a range of different purposes and provides different pleasures. These might include enjoying the texture of the marks made by different instruments. Hayley (aged four), in her charcoal drawing (Figure 12.2), appears to be involved in simply exploring vertical marks. She has repeated her vertical strokes over and over again. She was not trying to describe anything.

Children will sometimes ascribe meaning to their scribbles, however, which is evidence of an early understanding of symbolism, and may have important links to emergent writing. George (aged three), for example, described his scribble (see Figure 12.3) as a 'monster'. To produce this he used a soft felt pen that wouldn't last long if he continued to draw as he did here. School finances would soon force alternative media. He dive bombed his pen to make the small dots and pressed down extremely hard to make

Figure 12.1 *Scribble by Adele, aged 3*

Figure 12.2 *Vertical lines by Hayley, aged 4*

Figure 12.3 *Monster by George, aged 3*

his 'scribble' marks. The drawing has little to do with the observed description of a monster. Perhaps it parallels the aggression perceived in the animal
or perhaps it is merely a sequence of rhythmic movements. One way of
assessing George's drawing might be to monitor a range of his work and
look for the extent of variation.

It may seem a contradiction in terms but John Matthews argues that even
in their earliest scribbles children are making marks that are intentional and
involve making decisions. (Matthews 1992, p. 26)

Symbolic drawing

A symbol is an image that identifies the object. Children begin to develop
their own symbols for objects at quite an early age. As they continue to
draw them over the years they change and modify their images but they
continue to remain symbols. For example, children's first drawings of
houses are likely to be just a few scratchy lines. Drawing the same object
many times after this often involves modifying previous images but it

usually remains essentially a generalised drawing of a house and has involved only the minimum analysis of what houses actually look like.

Analytical stage

This is said to start occurring at the end of the symbolic stage. At this point the child begins to analyse the visual appearance of the world. They begin to measure the differences between their own drawing skills and other images in the world around them. Direct teaching seems to be largely irrelevant to the timing of this change of perception but there is some consensus that drawing instruction is useful once the analytical stage has been passed.

Occlusion

The old and often repeated phrase about young children is that 'They draw what they know and not what they see' (Kierchensteiner 1905, quoted in Cox 1992, p. 88). In their early drawings children usually want to give each item that they draw its own individual identity. Maureen Cox's four-year-old daughter insisted on drawing a handle on a cup even when she knew that she couldn't see it (Cox 1992, p. 93). In her words the cup with a handle 'looked better'. One suspects that she didn't want it confused with a jar or a vase. Young children are reluctant to obscure all or part of an object behind something else, a tendency which can sometimes lead to 'transparency' in their drawings. In the remarkably descriptive drawing of a horse and rider by Abi (aged four), for example (see Figure 12.4), note the reluctance to obscure one of the rider's legs.

Even when drawing

Figure 12.4 *Horse and rider by Abi, aged 4*

from observation a child will often draw a group of objects on a table as separate items with their own space around them, and nothing overlapping.

Tadpole figures

Western researchers have given a great deal of attention to children's drawings of the human figure. They have tried to identify the first signs and then examined some reasons for the 'tadpole' forms that children draw in their early years. Characteristically these appear to have the head and body as one closed shape and lines – usually interpreted as arms and legs – extending from this shape. Four-year-old Sophie's portrait of a man (Figure 12.5) is a typical example.

The development of figure drawings is a fascinating subject which illustrates well the development of young children's graphic vocabularies. Three-year-old Alex, in his drawing of 'My mum, my bike and me' (Figure 12.6) illustrates a stage on from the 'tadpole', including a clearly identifiable 'body' separate from the head. He has shown himself large and his mother very small but there could be a number of reasons for this (he ran out of

Figure 12.5 *Portrait of a man by Sophie, aged 4*

Figure 12.6 *My mum, my bike and me by Alex, aged 3*

space or she is less important?). Notice, however, the detail on the bike, and particularly the marks for the front lamp – one wonders where he acquired this graphic device at such an early age.

Space

One way in which children begin to indicate a sense of space in their drawings is by showing two viewpoints at the same time, the front and side view of a house, for example. This is the beginning of the complex skill of describing convincing depth on a two-dimensional picture plane. The failure to master this is the main reason why many adults have feelings of inadequacy about their drawing ability. The drawing by Abi (aged six) entitled 'In the bedroom' (Figure 12.7) is an example of a drawing with two independent viewpoints. We look horizontally at the three standing children but we see the figure in bed from above. It looks also as if the paper was turned 180 degrees before drawing one of the views. The drawing of two of the figures from a side perspective is another quite sophisticated aspect of this drawing.

Figure 12.7 *In the bedroom by Abi, aged 6*

Baselines

The feeling of 'rightness' about the right angle begins to appear quite early in the young child. Drawings are often developed by adding a line or shape in relation to what has already been drawn. Thus if a child starts their drawing of a person by drawing the two eyes at an angle, rather than parallel, to the edge of the paper, then the rest of the figure is likely to lean over at right angles to an imaginary line linking the two eyes.

Reference to the right angle can often explain a great many of the characteristics of a child's drawing. The figures often are at right angles to the edge of the drawing paper. Sometimes new baselines are set up and subsequent objects respond to them rather than using a consistent vertical throughout. An example of this is the familiar image of the chimney stack that shoots off at right angles to the pitched roof of a house. Another example is the splayed out figures sitting around a table, their bodies perpendicular to the table's edge which acts as the baseline.

Six-year-old Nathan's drawing of animals on the farm (Figure 12.8) illustrates a number of these characteristics. It is related strongly to the edges of the paper, the bottom of which acts as a baseline. The chimney pots are drawn at right angles to the roof. Note also the orientation of the windows in the corners of the house-front. A number of other familiar characteristics of young children's drawing can be also seen here, for example, avoidance of overlapping, transparency and the varying sizes of the human and animal figures.

Figure 12.8 *Animals on the farm by Nathan, aged 6*

There is a natural tendency to draw in this way right on into adulthood. Adolescents observing and drawing streets from a rooftop are still likely to draw house walls slightly off the vertical and splayed out alongside the road. Because most figures are perpendicular to a baseline there is a tendency for them to appear rigid. See Goodnow's research on how young children are least likely to articulate the human figure (Goodnow 1977, p. 141).

Imagination and artists

There is a lot of research interest into the development of representation but imaginative skills tend to get overlooked.

This is ironic as it was the interest in the child's imaginative abilities that was the original reason for art becoming a curriculum subject in school. This resulted from the combined efforts of psychologists and artists who, for their different reasons, became enamoured with the art of the child. Modern artists at the beginning of this century valued the freshness and spontaneity in children's work. They recognised a truth and honesty that academic art had lost and towards which they strove. Paul Klee wrote, 'The pictures that my little boy Felix paints are often better than mine because mine have been filtered through the brain' (Weidmann 1979, p. 224).

Franz Cizek was an artist and influential art educator who worked in Vienna at the beginning of this century. It is still possible to get a sense of what it was like to be taught by him by reading Wilhelm Viola's transcripts of some of the lessons – and quite amazing and endearing pieces of reading they make! (Viola 1942, p. 112). He taught all ages from the very young to adolescents but it was the work of the young child that he most valued. He believed that as they grew older they forfeited real art for empty adult skills. Children aged seven can often express themselves confidently and be still unaffected by adult concepts. But this is, nonetheless, a state of transience, which Cizek expressed in the memorable phrase, 'There is so much of the summer and autumn but the spring never comes again' (Viola 1942, p. 31).

Drawing and writing

In early years education there is some overlap in the development of drawing and writing (see also chapter 7 in this volume). Given that the early forms of writing were often pictographs perhaps this is not so surprising. The push–pull marks, the arcs, the zig-zag and the rotation marks that can be seen in children's early drawing is a basis for their early forms of writing.

Later on from this children can often be seen reversing letters because they get into a habit of starting somewhere other than the prescribed place or go in the opposite direction. This then causes the order of the strokes to get out of synchronisation. In drawing too it is crucial where the child starts on the paper and the nature of the first few marks. The rest of the drawing can only be thought out and made in relation to these. The character of a child's drawing is often determined by the order in which the various lines are drawn.

The value of drawing

More recently a growing number of writers have sought to show the value of drawing to a child's education. The central basis of this argument is that drawing is essentially a way of learning about something. This is a truism if one considers the amount of organising, thinking, and making decisions in any kind of drawing. The argument tends to be used however when referring to drawing from observation. Drawing from an object prolongs the looking and learning. In the words of Maurice Rubens and Mary Newland, 'Children who learn to look, learn to question, to discover and to understand' (Rubens and Newland 1989, p. 15). Drawing, it is argued, is an essential tool for learning activities across the whole curriculum.

A way to proceed

I have outlined below a programme for teaching drawing to early years children. Some of it is based on research, some on personal experience and beliefs and some on recommendations of other professionals. All of it is consistent with the recommendations of the National Curriculum for art, but at the same time I hope that it is not without one or two controversial remarks to encourage debate.

The early years educator's role in developing drawing has to be very different from those teaching older pupils. Children who are drawing in a predominately symbolic way are very resistant to analytical approaches. Formal directional teaching is usually counterproductive and even those advocating the teaching of drawing skills acknowledge that this is not the time to start. Formal teaching is best begun when children begin to be analytical and question their own work. This is not to say that the teacher should put their feet up and wait until the child reaches the age of eight. The early years educator has to work hard to encourage a wide range of drawing.

A range of media

It is easy and convenient to continually give children A4 plain paper and some coloured felt tips. But this limits the range of expression and colours can easily confuse one's aims. Different media demand different handling. If children are to develop their mark-making skills then they must use and develop as wide a range of media as possible.

There is an endless array of tools and surfaces on which to make marks and similar tools are capable of great differences. Even the humble pencil comes in degrees of hardness depending on how much clay is mixed with the graphite. The soft 5B or 6B has only a little clay and can make a very black line. It smudges easily, causing distress to those who need precision but sensuous enjoyment to those who don't.

Children are rarely given the opportunity to explore drawing in more than one or two media from the long list of possibilities. From fingers to pens and brushes, from paper to computer monitor screens the various different media will produce different solutions. They will encourage new skills, create new problems to solve, and encourage more imaginative responses.

Drawing materials are only limited by the imagination of the child and the educator. One of my old teachers draws on driftwood by beaming the sun's rays through his magnifying glass. As a 'starter kit' the early years educator could introduce the children to the following mark-makers:

soft graphite pencils
charcoal
electronic computer marks
water-based ink with felt-markers and fibre tips
ball point pens
ready-mixed black paint and brushes
chalk

and the following surfaces:

paper of all kinds (including white cartridge paper sometimes as, although costly, it does show the marks to their best advantage)
fabrics
boards (blackboards, whiteboards, cardboard)
walls
the playground

Obviously, with some surfaces it is only appropriate to mark them with materials which will wash off, but this is well worth doing occasionally. If the focus is on drawing, then colour can confuse. Experiencing and experimenting with colour is best saved for other times.

A range of tasks

Young children will often make a different kind of drawing when spontaneously working compared to when they are given a specific task. It is important to have time for both in the classroom if one is to fully assess an individual child's work. As for tasks you ask of the child, let them be wide ranging and, over the course of time, include the many different purposes for drawing. Include drawings which express feelings, convey ideas, provide information and tell stories. Symbolic drawing is particularly appropriate for many of these tasks. It enables children to tackle very complex themes that are usually too difficult for older children.

The introduction of different drawing 'genres' can be a valuable means of extending young children's range and showing them new possibilities. Children are natural and enthusiastic imitators. Look, for example, at the richness of the drawing in six-year-old Abi's front cover for her own children's story comic (Figure 12.9).There is a sense of movement and fluency in this drawing that is not common in the work of many children. She has added many new figures engaged in completely independent activities. This would seem to indicate a good deal of thinking and decision making.

Some drawing from observation is important as well. They will not spend much time looking and analysing an object but it will produce a different kind of work; a fusion or struggle between the appearance of the objects and the symbolic drawing method. Clement and Page see it as providing an

Figure 12.9 *Story comic front cover by Abi, aged 6*

important bridge between the two developmental stages (Clement and Page 1992b, p. 16). They see it as a way of giving the older child a basis from which their work can develop after they begin to lose their confidence.

The drawing of myself (Figure 12.10) by Denise (aged six) is a good example of young children's observational drawing, and the important observational and perceptual skills they can learn from it. Denise has focused on the details of my clothes – my check shirt, dark trousers and a tie with a squiggle pattern. She is learning to look.

Figure 12.10 *Observational drawing of Mr Lewis by Denise, aged 6*

Resources and discussion

Whatever the nature of the task, stimulating material is likely to produce a more motivated response. A bicycle drawn from observation by a young child is always going to be a more profitable than a drawing of a wine bottle. Morandi made profound art using bottles as motifs but the agenda for the early years child is very different.

When setting children tasks that involve memory and imagination, encourage incidents that involve some kind of movement as well as the more static scenes. For example, the school gymnastics session can make different demands from a drawing of a family wedding.

Literature, drama and music are all particularly rich resources from which to develop drawings which express feelings outside the child's immediate experience. A story such as *Peter and the Wolf* is capable of stimulating a large number of differently drawn responses, particularly if these are enriched by discussion beforehand. When working from observation it is also important to have discussion about the appearance of the objects and the media being used. A two-way discussion can be helpful for both adult and child.

A developmental approach

The educator has a responsibility to encourage children to develop their drawing, but they also have to be realistic about the nature of this development. It has to be appropriate to the age of the child. Some aspects of research into young children's drawing were outlined at the beginning of this chapter and these have to affect the approach to teaching.

For example, to an adult's eye a figure in a child's drawing may seem to be lying down at the edge of a pond but to a child it is a way of recording a standing figure on the edge of a pond. To the child it is probably important to show the roundness of the pond whilst at the same time showing the shape of the figure from the front viewpoint. This, after all, does identify the figure better. The child is showing the scene from two viewpoints at the same time whilst many (but not all) adults would attempt the scene from only one. They might well feel inclined to ask the child why the standing figure is lying down, but is this not likely to inhibit, rather than expand, the range of the work?

Assessment

There is a view that it is not possible to assess art, but this is to misunderstand the role of art within education. We must not judge children's work as if we were at a Sotheby's auction. Assessment procedures have to be based on the approaches to the work as well as to the final product. They have to be related to the aims in the lesson plans – which means that different things will be assessed at different times. If a great deal of learning takes place when a child draws, assessment ought to be able to record/measure that learning, though this is not to deny the difficulty. It is easier to assess descriptive drawing. A note can be made of the 'stage' the child has reached on the path towards analysis and realism. In order to measure more fugitive concepts such as imaginative ability it is necessary to look closely and compare the different ways in which children organise their drawing and mark-making.

To do this well one has to be fairly systematic about it. Work has to be collected, dated and a note of the task and assessment criteria has to be made somewhere. Many teachers find it helpful to meet and talk about the children's work together. They find it helps them to develop some patterns for assessment.

Discussion with young children about their drawings is also vital to determine their intentions. It would be difficult to interpret four-year-old Sophie's drawing shown in Figure 12.11, for example, if you did not know that it shows her in bed watching the video and includes the stairs, the TV screen and the bedcovers up to her neck.

Figure 12.11 *In bed watching the video by Sophie, aged 4*

The educator's role

To conclude this section, it ought to be said that the teacher doesn't have to be an artist or skilled in drawing. The most important requirements are probably a personal interest in art, an enthusiasm for the children's work and an ability to appreciate what they do. Armed with these, the teacher's enthusiasm will be 'caught' by the child. They will able to create situations which will develop skills, learning and imagination – all through drawing!

Conclusion: a simple task!

Having read this chapter it would be helpful to try out a little task. The aim of this is to help you understand a little more about children's drawing in a more personal and less academic way. You can do it in the privacy of your own room and no one else need see the results.

Just think back to yesterday and focus on a simple incident that happened to you. It can be something that you have done many times before; e.g. crossing the road in the same place or making the bed. Or it could be something special like meeting someone who you've never seen before. The choice is yours! Having chosen your incident spend ten or fifteen minutes drawing it and whilst drawing try to speak into a tape recorder saying as much as you can about what is going on inside your head. When you have finished the drawing play back the tape recorder and listen. Perhaps you could even scribble down a transcript.

(10–15 minutes later!)

Many readers will have been tempted to skip this part and get on to reading for some insights that will help them with their teaching. This is understandable, time is precious, the task sounds gimmicky and what real use could it be for an understanding of the subject?

My rationale is that the human brain has a tendency to run ahead of itself at times. In our heads we can imagine that we understand about something but find that it is often only after some practical experience we gain real understanding. This task is a case in point. If you do spend some time on it you are likely to approach the subject of children's drawings with a different perspective. By struggling (yes struggling – you weren't the only one!) to record this event that happened to you yesterday you are able to ask all sorts of questions that would not have been possible had you only thought about it. It is, after all, something that we as teachers, might ask our five- or six-year-olds to do; and it is interesting to compare our approaches to the same subject. You might also be interested to know that it is a very old academic technique that was regularly practised to develop a visual memory.

Because I would not presume to know how you went about your drawing I can only ask you to ask yourself the questions. I can however record just a few of the feelings that I had as a result of trying out the task. My drawing is shown in Figure 12.12.

There was an initial feeling of uncertainty of what to do. I couldn't seem to think of anything that I did yesterday that would make a picture. I knew that I had to make a quick decision. Chose to 'picture' me washing up at the sink. Where to view from? Decided from window on far side of sink. This allows the washing of the pans to be seen even though it is not a view normally seen. One would have to be a window cleaner up a ladder as the

Figure 12.12 *Washing up by John Lewis*

kitchen is on the first floor. Chose pen and ink, something different from pencils which are always too readily available. Start with an unthinking tentative diagonal stroke, the side of my head. Have to stop, concentrate. Work a little more on the head, but before it gets too resolved and definite, move the pen down to briefly indicate some aspects of the rest of the figure. Draw edges of sink basin. This gets me into perspective eye levels. Redraw over sink basin making it much bigger. Tap. Can't think how one turns it on. Then redraw this. Briefly indicate plates in rack, light single lines, contrast with the heavy overdrawing of tap. Now back to drawing myself. Now I have to be much bigger. Overdraw earlier marks. Begin to draw in an ear. Change it to an eye. This changes the direction of the head. Scribble in other eye, slightly lower. Nothing about the figure resembles me. Not too cartoony, but still nothing to identify that it's me. Work over the tee shirt a little more heavily though no one would know that it was a tee shirt. Try to make the body have more solidity. Emphasise the light on one side of the head. Work on the cupboards that can be seen behind me. Put in the radio (always listen to it when washing up). Rework hand to show fingers around pan.

Now overdone, cannot get it back, need some white crayon or correction fluid. Now realise that the window cleaner would only see me obscured by plants on the window ledge. Shall I put it in? No! Perhaps another time. Stop now. Ten minutes drawing time is up!

These are only some of the thoughts that raced through my head. If I hadn't talked through it my concentration would have been greater and I would probably have been more directly visual. Nevertheless enough has come out of this exercise to ask a few questions.

What, for example, are the differences between my adult approach to this task and a child in their 'early years'? The level of confidence in the child's approach to the task is almost certain to be greater than mine was. Despite the fact that I enjoy drawing, I feel particularly inadequate in this aspect that involves memory recall and a more open inventiveness. Quite honestly I have not been methodical enough to train up this aspect of 'visual realisation'. Some artists are very strong in this – one thinks of Tiepolo and Titian. But there are many who depended heavily on having something in front of them to get the imaginative juices working, Manet and Cezanne, for example.

In addition to the confidence issue, my choice to use perspective, to concern myself with viewpoints and qualities of light, make for obvious differences in my approach to the task.

But now look at some similarities in the activity. I drew myself as I had drawn myself before when working from memory or imagination – I used a 'scheme' that had a minimum amount of information of what I really looked like. I changed my first lines, developed them and made them a bit more descriptive. I remembered more information as I went along and added this to the drawing where I could, but there were lots of things that I couldn't remember very clearly and I only vaguely suggested them.

What all this shows is that many of the factors which lead us to design and organise a drawing are perhaps not so very different from that of a six-year-old. The concept of children's perception being so different from an adult's and the concept of 'stages' in children's drawing can mask this. No I didn't use a baseline or splay my figures out in different viewpoints, but I was still using a system (one-point perspective) based on what I knew rather than what I could really see. In many ways my one-point perspective was a particularly unimaginative approach. Not only has non-western European art got by very well without this particular drawing system, but Uccello, Velasquez and numerous other western artists used and continue to use multi-viewpoints in their paintings.

Drawing by anyone of any age is always going to be a complex affair and something that we are unlikely to fully understand. It is capable of displaying magic and invention. But although it is often promoted as a vehicle for creativity it is clearly not always creative and neither should it have to be. On many occasions it may be bound by rules and routines, but in any case it can develop a kind of thinking that may not always be possible in other areas of the early years curriculum. Drawing is essentially making marks that can get ever more complex and increasingly sophisticated. It can it involve logical organising, planning, and thinking in a purely visual way on one day whilst on the next it can also be capable of developing imaginative qualities by taking risks and adopting new sets of 'rules'.

Pointers for developing young children's drawing

- Be sensitive to the developmental stage of a child's drawing.
- Try to relate researchers' terminology to actual drawings produced by your pupils.
- Use a wide range of materials. Remember that the nature of the medium can influence the nature of the drawing.
- Have a broad perspective in your plans for your pupils drawing e.g. use drawing as a medium for creative thinking as well as developing analytical skills.
- Be empirical! Develop your teaching skills by observing children drawing and questioning the nature of the activity and its product.

Acknowledgements

I wish to thank the staff and pupils of the following schools for their help in making this chapter possible:

Henwick Primary School – Greenwich
Soho Primary School – Westminster

References

Clement, R. and Page, S. (1992a) *Principles and Practice in Art*, Harlow: Oliver & Boyd.
—— (1992b) *Investigating and Making in Art*, Harlow: Oliver & Boyd.
Cox, M. (1992) *Children's Drawing*, London: Penguin.
Goodnow, J. (1977) *Children's Drawing*, London: Fontana Open Books.

Matthews, J. (1992) 'The genesis of aesthetic sensibility', in D. Thistlewood(ed.) *Drawing Research and Development*, Harlow: Longman.

Rubens, M. and Newland, M. (1989) *A Tool For Learning*, Ipswich: Direct Experience.

Thomas, G.V. and Silk, A.M.J. (1990) *An Introduction to the Psychology of Children's Drawings*, Hemel Hempstead, Herts: Harvester Wheatsheaf.

Viola, W. (1942) *Child Art*, London: University of London Press.

Weidmann, A. (1979) *Romantic Roots in Modern Art*, Surrey: Gresham.

CHAPTER 13

In Search of the Elephant's Child

EARLY YEARS SCIENCE

Penny Coltman

But there was one Elephant – a new Elephant's Child – who was full of 'satiable curtiosity', and that means he asked ever so many questions. (from 'The Elephant's Child' in the *Just-So Stories*, Rudyard Kipling 1902)

A common response when matters of science are raised during adult conversation is a total shut down. Many of us have an antipathy to the subject founded on hours spent in school laboratories which smelled of coal gas, had walls lined with shelves of unspeakable parts preserved in jars of formalin and a teacher who presented incomprehensible hypotheses attributed to a cavalcade of assorted historical personae.

Happily over the past few years science teaching has emerged from this chrysalis in an almost unrecognisable form. The inclusion of science as a core subject throughout the national curriculum was an initiative which resulted in a national review by early years practitioners. How could we use the prescribed material to enhance the learning of young children, to help them to fit together the jigsaw puzzle of their world, and to promote positive attitudes towards science, its knowledge and methods? As a result of this reappraisal it is becoming rapidly more widely appreciated that science in the early years, including Key Stage 1, can be a springboard for activities which are novel and creative, which stimulate children's interest and enhance the learning environment.

However to begin to see such opportunities for innovation it is helpful to step outside the national curriculum to consider those skills and qualities which are possessed by successful scientists. These are the attributes for which we can be laying secure foundations in our early years classrooms.

The prospect is at first daunting, but the aim of this chapter is to demonstrate that a great deal of sound scientific understanding can be engendered by developing a fresh approach to the provision of opportunities for discovery, and a positive appreciation of the contributions to learning which can be made by purposeful play.

Good science and good fun!

Science should be enjoyable

Primarily, although it is neither realistic nor desirable to hope that all infants, however positive their perceptions of the subject, will grow up to be scientific professionals, it is an assumption worth considering that those who do so undoubtedly *enjoyed* science as children. With this thought in mind, we should not hesitate to present activities in forms which are designed to provide fun and enjoyment as well as learning.

Science should clarify understandings

This does not imply dilution of the rigour of the curriculum. It is vital that we consider very carefully exactly what scientific concepts it is that we are presenting and that adequate preparation and thought are given to the ways in which these concepts are going to be highlighted to the best advantage. Whilst in no way apologising for the emphasis on creativity, imagination and delight incorporated into the planning of successful science, these aspects must not be seen as ends in themselves. The central focus of the activity must remain scientifically sound. The enjoyment must not be allowed to evolve from packaging to smokescreen. To this end we need to ensure that as educators we have a secure knowledge of the principles and justifications underlying the activities we introduce to children. Their scientific implications and the way in which we will respond to questions or unexpected findings need careful anticipation.

An example: cars and ramps

Even apparently foolproof ideas may contain hidden pitfalls. A standard scientific investigation widely recommended to early years educators during the introduction of the national curriculum was, in fact, a prime example of a scientific minefield: the cars and ramps classic. It was a good choice in that it used equipment found in most classrooms; a few toy cars and a table top or piece of wood which could be sloped to form a ramp. Cars were placed at various points along the ramp and released, their stopping place being noted and the distance travelled measured. It was relatively easy to see that the cars should be the same size and shape, and that the slope of the ramp and the surfaces involved should be constant. This was how to do a fair test. If we ignore the fact that even apparently identical toy cars behave quite differently according to the amount of rough play they have endured, and that it is very difficult to release two cars with exactly the same degree of 'push' then as a phenomenon to observe, with opportunities for measurement and comparison, it is a reasonable suggestion. The car which was started at the highest point will go the furthest. However unwary teachers who employed this idea in their classrooms found that all went well until they were asked the obvious question. Why does this happen? Is it because the longer the distance the car travels along the ramp, the more time it has to speed up, so the further it goes? No. The answer concerns the vertical height of the object, at its starting point, above the ground. The greater this value, the more potential energy (stored gravitational energy) the object has. Unless we are confident ourselves in our understanding of this type of concept and the way in which it could be rendered accessible to young children, it is better by far to answer with a simple 'I don't know, but isn't it interesting?' than to attempt an explanation based on half truths and inaccuracies.

Investigative skills

The popular image of a scientist is that of an experimenter and there is a temptation to view science in the classroom predominantly within this context. The section of the national curriculum which relates to experimental and investigative skills at Key Stage 1 to a large extent reinforces this perception, as 'planning experimental work' is the first aspect for consideration. The impression is given that in order to fulfil the demands of the curriculum even the youngest of children should be carrying out simple investigations. However, the processes involved in turning ideas into forms which can be investigated and then carrying out a fair test with accurately measured and recorded observations, are extremely sophisticated. To achieve this is to knit together a complex pattern of skills which must be first mastered individually. We need to look much more closely at the nature of these skills, identifying much smaller units of learning which can gradually be combined as we work towards structured investigations at the end of the Key Stage. These will include elements of exploration, articulation of ideas, perception of detail, measurement and description. Later, children will begin to relate concepts encountered in different contexts to build the ideas which they can extrapolate as informed and reasoned predictions and attempts at considered explanations.

First-hand experience

Children cannot acquire these scientific concepts by hearing about them. It is not good enough to sit with a class 'on the carpet' describing the wonders of the universe. Direct exploration using all the senses and hands-on experience is the route to infant learning. Consequently we must capitalise on every opportunity to facilitate this, thinking carefully about the presentation of every activity and how its value might be increased by considering sensory implications.

Learning science through purposeful play

To illustrate this it may be helpful to look at some everyday activities and to reflect upon how they can be used to assist in the development of scientific skills and understanding. In the early years classroom many of these activities will be predominantly play-based. The provision of purposeful play is no easy option. It is not a way of 'occupying' children, but is a demanding component of the early years curriculum. It is crucial that we acknowledge the value of planned play and develop a pro-active approach towards recognising and taking full advantage of its scientific potential. To achieve this requires a commitment to the ethos of learning through play and a willingness to be a contributive, though not over-interventionist, participant in it. Playing with children, engaging them in relevant conversation, following their lead but at the same time interjecting suggestions or questions, will enrich the activity and stimulate creative and imaginative thinking. At the same time, by joining in with the play, we are providing a positive role model. Play is OK.

Playing with dough: making the most of sensory experiences

An example of play which is consistently undervalued is that with dough (see Figure 13.1).

The value of dough and clay in building the hand muscles needed to control a pencil or brush is accepted, but only linger near a table where children are using dough to discover its potential as a forum for linguistic development. Opportunities to touch, smell, manipulate and talk about dough will assist enormously in the acquisition of the skills involved in investigating materials and their properties. These skills will develop to include abilities to explore and describe the way in which materials behave, to discover how they respond to the impact of forces and to make sensible suggestions regarding their suitability for different purposes. By focusing on the tex-

Figure 13.1 *Making and playing with dough: May, aged 3, making the most of sensory experiences!*

tures, colours and smells which can be added to dough and resisting the temptation to load the table with cutters and rollers which diminish the hands-on exploration of its properties, vocabulary is elicited and promoted which can then be related to other contexts:

- How does the dough feel when you touch it?
- When you squash it in your hands is it hard or soft?
- What does its colour remind you of?
- Have you smelled anything else like this?
- Can you roll it or stretch it?

The standard recipe for cooked dough (see Figure 13.2) is extremely good tempered and can be adapted in all sorts of ways to provide a range of stimuli:

- *Bath oil* replaces cooking oil to make a dough smelling of anything from strawberry to coconut, mango to tangerine.
- *Cooking essences* add touches of lemon, almond or peppermint.
- *Herbs,* fresh lavender flowers, lentils or rice add texture.
- *The rind of fruit* can be added for the same reason — try marmalade dough made using orange food colouring and flavouring and grated peel.

<u>Cooked dough</u>

2 cups plain flour
1 cup salt
2 tbsp cooking oil
2 tsp cream of tartar
colouring
2 cups water

Cook all ingredients in saucepan over low heat stirring continuously. Mix the food colouring with the water before adding for solid colour or add separately for a marbled effect. Remove from heat when mixture leaves sides of pan. Knead, adding any dry products designed to add texture and store in an airtight container.

Figure 13.2 *Recipe for cooked dough*

A few seconds in an oven or microwave before the dough is brought into the classroom gives a wonderful surprise. Handling warm dough is one of life's pleasurable sensations!

Adventurous experimentation with food colourings adds yet another dimension, using paste rather than liquid food colourings gives a denser result. Glitter and sequins add sparkle but are fairly quickly tarnished by the salt in the dough, so these mixtures will need to be used soon after making.

Other dough recipes do not require cooking and can be made with the children. Using wholemeal flour and water a dough with a strong smell of wheat is produced which has a granular texture. A mixture of self-raising flour and water which is not cooked gives a dough which is pliable and elastic (see Figure 13.3).

Linguistic exploration takes on a different perspective as productive questioning accompanies the making of the dough:

• The flour, salt and water can be poured, but what about the resulting mixture?
• Where has the water gone?
• What happens when we stretch the dough, squash it, pull, push or press it?

Stretchy dough

1½ kilos S.R. flour

500mls water

Mix together. The longer you knead, the stretchier it will become!

Figure 13.3 *Recipe for stretchy dough*

A wealth of scientific concepts is encountered including physical properties of materials, absorption, forces, and states of matter. A 'runny powder' mixes with a 'liquid' to provide a sticky mixture forming a 'squashy solid'. Using a salt dough recipe (see Figure 13.4) provides experience of yet another change as the pliable dough becomes a hard material which can be painted and varnished.

Language development is one of the primary aims in early years teaching, and there is no doubt that an ability to communicate is vital to success in science. Scientists need to be able to describe clearly and accurately what they have observed. They need to relate their methods carefully and logically to others so that experiments can be replicated and will need to argue their reasoning coherently to convince others of the validity of their claims.

Salt dough

2 cups plain flour

1 cup salt

¼ cup of lukewarm water

1 tbsp cooking oil

Mix the flour and salt before adding the oil and water. Knead thoroughly – the more the better. After modelling dry in a very low oven for at least 12 hours.

Figure 13.4 *Recipe for salt dough*

By maintaining and developing an atmosphere in the classroom in which children's excitement in enquiry is manifestly shared we engender an ethos of enthusiastic curiosity. Through the respect and appreciation of opinions, ideas and contributions, we also generate a climate in which thoughts are freely communicated and questions asked. Articulating ideas helps the speaker to clarify thinking and the sensitive listener will use this insight into children's thoughts to identify present understandings and future learning needs. As vocabulary grows, so the difficulties of putting thoughts into words will lessen. We can assist the development of the vocabulary of science in even the youngest of children through activities which may not yet necessarily be perceived as relevant to this area at all.

Looking, feeling, exploring, sticking – talking!

In every nursery, children are familiar with collage activities. If we take collage in this instance to mean a collection of materials glued onto a background rather than a composite picture, there are a myriad of opportunities to reinforce those areas of vocabulary dealing with the properties of materials, which will later be used to describe observations with accuracy and detail. Collage facilitates an exposure to a wide variety of types of material, with differing textures, colours and properties. Through encouraging children to select items carefully, using as many senses as possible, and to talk about their choices, we can promote linguistic progress from the general to the specific and from the prosaic to the particular, ('curly' to 'spiral', 'shiny' to 'reflective', 'see-through' to 'transparent').

One approach is thematic. A range of materials can be carefully selected, all of which demonstrate the same particular property. Suitable materials might include dyed pasta, pieces of textiles, papers of varying types and qualities, wool, feathers, wood shavings dyed with food colouring etc. Early concepts will concentrate on colour and texture, (hard, soft, bendy, spongy, furry, spiky, rough, smooth), but it is also quite possible, with a little time and imagination, to find materials which, for example, 'smell like flowers' or which can be made to 'make a rustling noise'. More sophisticated ideas might include a 'natural materials' or a 'metallic' collage, or even an 'elastic' collage.

The selection of items available for use should be attractive – sorted and presented in containers which invite exploration. If a background medium appropriate to the task, such as a shaped piece of coloured paper or card is prepared, then an attractive result is ensured and building blocks of observational vocabulary will have been founded. Initially only relevant materials should be provided. Before children can identify and discard materials which are not shiny, a secure idea of exactly what shininess is needs to be established. Too much choice given before concepts are fully digested serves only to confuse. Later, as a progression, a choice of materials can be offered from which the child selects those which demonstrate the chosen attribute.

Eureka! in the classroom: putting children in control

Children are naturally curious and gain enormous pleasure from exploration and discovery. Planned activities will provide these experiences to a great extent but inventive use of the classroom environment can provide opportunities for children to make serendipitous discoveries which will excite and delight. There are many classrooms in which displays are produced solely as a response to children's work. Whilst applauding the philosophy of valuing achievement, such a narrow view of the purposes of display denies children a source of stimulation which enlivens their learning. Of course interactive displays can be complex, full of ideas for children to investigate and extremely time consuming to prepare – not to be undertaken every other week. But opportunities for scientific discovery do not need to be elaborate, and indeed it is neither needful nor necessarily advantageous to always draw particular attention to them.

A scientist needs to notice things; small changes or aberrations from the ordinary. Similarly it is important that children take note of their surroundings, and that their classroom is managed in a way which allows a touch of unpredictability, affording surprises waiting to be found whilst still retaining the security of superficial sameness. We can aim to produce an inquisitive climate in the classroom, in which incidentals are seen as sometimes unexpected but nonetheless valuable opportunities for learning.

In its simplest form a way of enlivening the room and encouraging observation skills is to introduce new artefacts for children to spot. A basket which always hangs by the window can one day be seen to contain a teddy, which a few days later has been replaced by a toy rabbit. Older children enjoy looking out for small but inappropriate objects, such as the plastic toy soldier hiding in the bunch of flowers, or the very realistic toy snake winding its way through the library books.

Access to more explicitly scientific learning can be similarly provided. To both embellish the classroom and to demonstrate aspects of transparency and colour, pieces of coloured acetate can be mounted in card surrounds and suspended on long ribbons in front of a window. If blue, red and yellow filters are provided children can look through two or more acetates held together, mixing magenta, green and orange. Hanging the frames in a slightly overlapping formation will also produce areas of secondary colour which will be seen both against the window and in the pattern which appears on the carpet, wall or table top whenever the sun shines through them. Indeed this pattern will obligingly move around the room to help promote discussion in older infants about the apparent movement of the sun. The same effect can be achieved by hanging suitably transparent balloons in the window or the strategic placement of models made from a kit such as Galt Super Octons, which consists of interlocking pieces of coloured transparent plastic.

The joy of allowing for these moments in the classroom is that children make use of them at will. In a small way they are in control of their own learning and the time that they wish to spend in exploratory play. The discoveries made are, at that moment, every bit as exciting as Archimedes' bath. The interest and encouragement shown in response to these impromptu investigations will result in an enthusiasm towards scientific discoveries in other, perhaps unplanned, contexts which must then be equally well received.

Mirror, mirror on the wall! Play and progression

There is a perceived pressure to be actively 'teaching' *all* the time, but the relentless delivery of information regardless of the readiness of the child to receive it, is not productive. Similarly we need to be wary of presenting formal tasks too soon. Imagine, as an adult, being given a new and rather complex construction kit, with cogs, wheels, axles, connectors and very strange looking linking devices and mechanisms. Now imagine being asked to use that kit 'immediately' to make a model vehicle. Such a request would be, to say the least, unreasonable. Before making specific items there is a need to explore the kit, look at the pieces, discover how they connect, look at the angles it is possible to make and the way in which the wheels fit on. In short there is a need to play with it. In exactly the same way an infant needs to explore and play with phenomena before we insist on specified tasks (cf. Bruner's experiment, p. 10).

Looking at the concepts of reflection and the use of mirrors illustrates this well. If we present a child with a mirror for the first time and request the completion of a given task, for example 'Look at and draw your own reflection', we are doomed to a disappointing result. For a while the task will be attempted, but before very long the ways in which the mirror behaves, the way it mists up when you breathe on it, the way in which a funny face can be made by holding it against your nose, the way a square of light can be made to dance across the ceiling, will all prove irresistible distractions. And so they should. These are all properties of mirrors which invite exploration and investigation, and by active enquiry into these aspects children become familiar with them and with the ways in which a mirror can be reasonably expected to behave.

The next time a mirror is encountered there will be a need to revisit these experiences, and the next. But on each occasion the revisiting time will be less and gradually a rounded picture of mirrors and reflection is pieced together. It takes a confident and committed educator to allow this play to happen as a natural course of events.

During play the children will be setting a great deal of the agenda and it is easy to feel almost superfluous. This is far from the case. Now is the time to be observing, listening, assisting, questioning, responding and encouraging. This is the opportunity to spend some time with the child who may not be joining in the activity but who may be watching carefully all that goes on and who consequently may be involved in a very active process of thinking.

It is not difficult to facilitate play with mirrors. Ideally there will be one in the dressing up area before which budding models admire themselves, but if not, small unbreakable plane mirrors should always be available in the room and easily accessible to the children. Reflection provides one of the simplest concepts on which to base an interactive display. Undulating mirrors, which can be made from synthetic foil wrapping paper mounted onto card, provide all the fun of the Victorian side show. On a smaller scale, a pair of plane mirrors mounted at head height, at right angles in a corner of the room, will result in children investigating for themselves the spectacle of multiple images.

As the desire for uninhibited exploration nears exhaustion, now is the time to set tasks. Having established the potential of mirrors through play the child will have a much better idea of how to approach the task and will also be able to concentrate on just those aspects of reflection to which the task relates. This approach of a progression from free exploration to structured activity is equally applicable to an enormous range of scientific equipment and concepts and its implications extend throughout primary education and beyond.

Children do not outgrow the need for unrestrained experimentation, or play. How many of us, as adults, will still pick up a magnifying lens and examine the pores of our skin? Given a pair of magnets, we continue to enjoy the feel of the force of repulsion as we use one to push the other along the table. A more widespread recognition and acceptance of the necessity for this type of activity and its contribution in developing both the concepts and investigative skills of science, can only be to the subject's advantage. Science is essentially playful. Discoveries are made when scientists are playing with ideas, albeit in a thorough and methodical manner. If, as educators, we relax a little and learn to play with science again, we will not only greatly enhance the learning of our pupils, but we may produce future generations for whom science is less hostile territory. The opportunity is exciting!

Pointers for early years science

To summarise:

- Science should be enjoyable.
- Investigative skills should be separately identified and developed.
- First hand experiences are fundamental to early science.
- Play can make a major contribution to this process.
- A positive contribution to scientific learning is made by providing opportunities for small discoveries in the classroom.
- Structured activities should not be introduced until exploration through play has been encouraged.

Suggestions for further reading

Allen, P., Harris, M. and Tozer H. (1991) *Children First, Vols 1–4*, Crediton: Southgate Publishers Ltd.

Cornell, J.B. (1990) *Sharing Nature with Children*, Watford: Exley Publications Ltd.

Harlen, W. and Jelly, S. (1989) *Developing Science in the Primary Classroom*, Harlow: Oliver & Boyd.

Richards, R., Collins, M. and Kincaid, D. (1987) *An Early Start to Science*, London: Macdonald Educational.

Richards, R. (1990) *An Early Start to Technology from Science*, Hemel Hempstead: Simon & Schuster.

Sherrington, R.(ed.)(1993) *The ASE Primary Science Teachers' Handbook*, Hemel Hempstead: Simon & Schuster.

CHAPTER 14

'Maths – is that a kind of game for grown ups?'

UNDERSTANDING NUMBERS IN THE EARLY YEARS

Annie Owen and Laurie Rousham

The quotation in the title of this chapter is something asked of Laurie Rousham by a three-year-old called Mark. He had heard Laurie say that he did 'maths', but wasn't sure what it was. Of course, Laurie answered 'Yes! That's exactly what it is!' Unfortunately, we have to report that this rosy pre-school view did not survive Mark's encounter with school mathematics.

Mathematics is an area of great concern to teachers, parents and the general public. For many, their own learning of the subject ended with feelings of confusion or failure. Adults pass these feelings on to young children through such statements as 'I could never do maths' or 'I hated maths!', but teachers of the early years can also have a more directly negative effect.

When we feel insecure, whatever the situation, we play safe. A drowning person will not use a swimming stroke he has only just learnt to get himself to dry land. Less dramatically, a cook will not experiment with a new recipe if important guests are expected. Similarly, there is a temptation in the classroom for the teacher who feels insecure mathematically to fall back on traditional procedures and teaching methods.

Unfortunately, most traditional methods are very didactic in style and regard the young child as a blank sheet onto which the teacher writes mathematical knowledge. Hilary Shuard put this very well in the 1985 *Horizon* television programme 'Twice Five Plus the Wings of a Bird' for the BBC:

> We've had very much in mathematics education the idea that the child is an empty vessel and you pour in mathematics. Often I think we have thought of the child as a rather leaky vessel and mathematics has flowed out as well as in!

Such an approach will not only ignore the understanding a child already has about mathematics but also assumes that all children will learn the subject in the same way, in the same order and at the same rate. A short time spent in a nursery or infant mathematics class soon shows the deficits in this model of learning! Shuard continues:

> But I think that, if we are to be more successful in helping children to learn mathematics, we need to see them as people who think about their experiences and build on them . . . . We are coming to see children as mathematical thinkers in their own right, trying to develop their thinking, and we need to provide the experiences from which they can build mathematics for themselves.

This so-called 'emergent' approach, which begins with the child and not with the mathematics to be learned, is the focus of our chapter. It is a methodology which has developed gradually from the days of the Nuffield Maths project (1968), through the recommendations of the Cockcroft Report (1982) and the guidance of the PrIME (Primary Initiatives in Mathematical Education) project (1986–9), on to the present day. Whitebread (1995) has recently produced a very useful review of the essential elements of this 'emergent mathematics' approach together with the psychological research evidence about children's learning which crucially underpins it. Our national curriculum emphasises mathematical *process*, that is the need for children to ask their own questions, to explore them and to form their own conclusions.

We have concentrated on the area of number, this being the area causing most concern to the new teacher, but the issues which we raise are pertinent to all areas of mathematics. The chapter is organised under two headings:

- *Understanding, knowledge and application*: How do children come to understand number concepts, know important number facts and learn to use their understanding and knowledge to solve number problems?
- *Learning factors and the educator's role*: How can we facilitate this understanding, knowledge and learning?

Understanding, knowledge and application

Trying to untangle the three areas of understanding, knowledge and application may be seen by some as fruitless. Each is vitally important and all are interdependent and supportive. Understanding addition without ever being able to remember such number bonds as 5 + 3 = 8 would be extremely limiting. Knowing multiplication tables without understanding what multiplication is would be pretty meaningless. Solving a multiplication problem is impossible without a recognition of the operation required and is tedious if the answer cannot easily be remembered or computed.

However, the failure to recognise the distinction between these three elements will lead to poor teaching and hence poor learning. Although the children may see their mathematical experiences holistically, the teacher needs to keep the distinctions in the forefront of her planning in order to ensure balance. Over-emphasis on rote learning of facts and procedures produces children who cannot adapt or use their knowledge. Traditional 'drill and practice' methods are notorious for such failure. A child who understands what she is doing but has poor memory skills is less handicapped, as there are always other ways to reach an answer, but the tedium of relying on elementary procedures is very demotivating. Such an approach gave the 'discovery' learning of the 1960s such a bad reputation.

Therefore, let us take a short look at each area separately.

Understanding

The world of the pre-school child is full of numbers. Whether setting the table, feeding the ducks, sharing their sweets or building with blocks, they are involved not just in counting and pre-counting skills but are also making assumptions about how numbers work. They begin to see partitions in numbers (e.g. their six building bricks can be split into three red and three blue or perhaps four green and two yellow – the beginnings of addition and subtraction), to recognise that sometimes sharing doesn't work exactly (you can't share five sweets between yourself and your sister, but you can share four and give one to the dog), and other simple beginnings of pattern and structure.

Take the 'Five Little Ducks' rhyme:

> Five little ducks went out one day
> over the hill and far away.
> Mother duck said, 'Quack, quack, quack, quack'
> but only four little ducks came back.

On the surface, this is a 'counting back' rhyme, but subtraction can be introduced through such questioning as 'So, how many little ducks have gone altogether now?' (2, say) , 'How many has mother duck got left?' (3) and 'So, what is 5 little ducks take away 2 little ducks?' Martin Hughes (1986) found that children as young as three can add and subtract small numbers, as long as the problem is one which has meaning for them. His book, *Children and Number* is an essential read for anyone involved in early years education.

Children do not always need adults to spark thinking in this way. They can automatically make connections and form their own conclusions. They cannot always verbalise them in a form adults recognise, as they lack formal mathematical language, and their assumptions are often incorrect. However, they slowly build up their own personal view of the world of numbers, their properties and their interconnections. Take Tim (aged 5 years 6 months), who was playing with a calculator and wrote down spontaneously the addition sums reproduced in Figure 14.1.

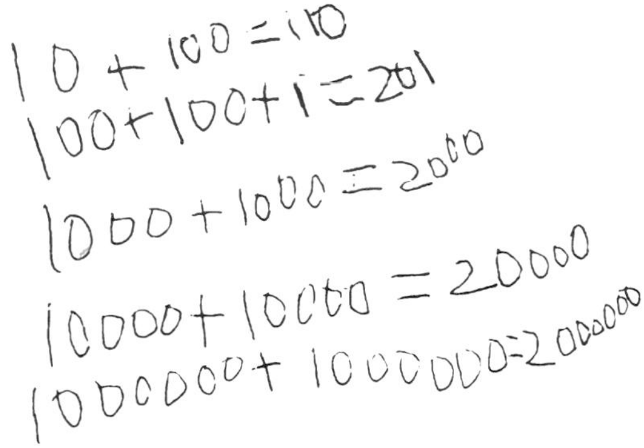

At this point he brought his paper to an adult and asked 'What's the next number?' Tim was exploring within a free play situation. He clearly knew how to recognise and write 100 and this was most likely his starting point. (It is worth reflecting on the fact that many mathematics schemes for children of this age are just beginning to introduce the numbers 11 to 20!)

Figure 14.1 *Addition sums produced by Tim (aged 5 years 6 months) while playing with a calculator*

Barbara Jaworski (1988) views this type of activity from a constructivist stance, quoting two principles of knowledge and learning:

1 *Knowledge* is actively constructed by the cognising subject, not passively received from the environment.
2 *Coming to know* is an adaptive process that organises one's experiential world; it does not discover an independent, pre-existing world outside the mind of the knower.

Teachers of mathematics at all levels know only too well that, no matter how careful their explanations, children can misunderstand a concept, make incorrect connections or just plainly 'fail to learn'. Unless they can incorporate the new idea into their existing view of mathematics (what constructivists would call their 'schema'), and hence make sense of it, children are very unlikely to take it on board. The old adage 'you can take a horse to water but you can't make it drink' fits perfectly! Look at the example in Figure 14.2, in which Dean, a six-year-old, is counting the sides (edges) and corners (vertices) of some plastic shapes, a fairly common activity.

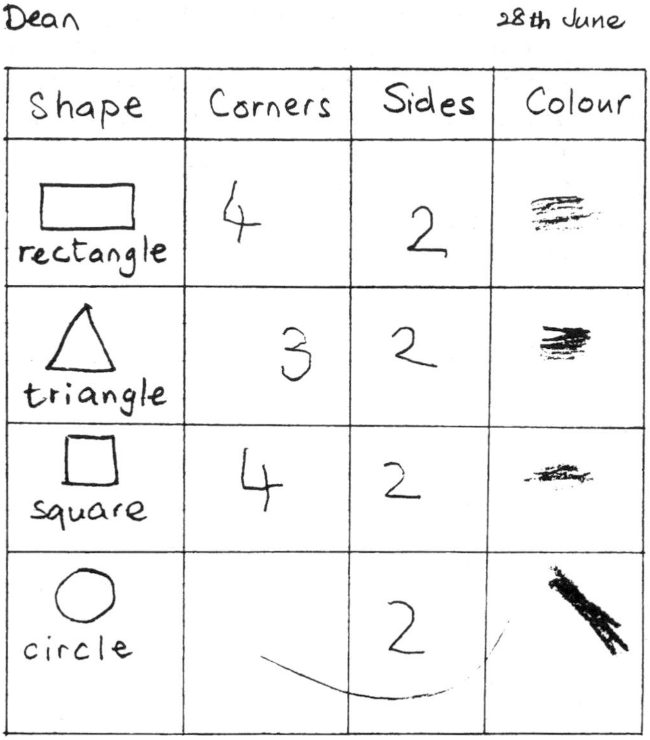

Dean   28th June

Shape	Corners	Sides	Colour
▭ rectangle	4	2	
△ triangle	3	2	
▢ square	4	2	
○ circle		2	

Figure 14.2 *The corners and sides of common shapes as recorded by Dean, aged 6*

Dean has filled in a teacher-prepared grid. As you can see, he appears to be able to count corners correctly, but not sides. What might be going on here? Well, one point of view might be that we already knew Dean isn't very able and this proves it. Alternatively, he could be making mistakes out of sheer wilful naughtiness. Fortunately his teacher chose not to operate on the basis of either of these views, and instead opened negotiations with him to try and see what he was thinking:

Teacher Dean, I'm not sure this is right, is it? Do all these different shapes have two sides?
Dean [Belligerently] Yes.
Teacher Well, can you get your shapes and show me the two sides?
Dean [Returning with his set of plastic shapes.] Look, [holding triangle in one hand and using his other hand to point, he places his index finger in the centre] one . . . (turns shape over) . . . two.

If Dean had been told to 'Go away and do it properly', or to 'Go back and think again', he would perhaps have begun to believe that maths is some strange activity with its own rules which do not accord with common sense. And from his point of view he would have been exactly right! It may be experiences like this that demoralise and undermine the initial confidence with which young children approach mathematics and we have included this exchange to illustrate how sensitive we need to be in responding to 'mistakes'. Often children's errors are the best indicators of their thinking and of how conceptual development is coming along. The biggest problem with this 'negotiability' approach is that of teacher time: all teachers are busy, and at a time when class sizes are rising again, it is difficult to investigate individual pupils' mistakes as thoroughly as we would like. We have all certainly been guilty of saying 'No, go back and do it again' on occasion, particularly if we were trying to attend to another group or hear readers at the time! Nevertheless we recommend negotiation to you whenever you can manage it.

Knowledge

As previously stated, there are mathematical facts and procedures which it is useful for children to know if they are to be confident and competent mathematicians. The controversy comes in deciding which are essential and which can be seen as optional. Being able to multiply a three digit number by a two digit number may be seen as useful in a junior child (and in fact can be used to promote understanding – particularly of place value), but not exactly essential in these days of cheap calculators. Also, the teacher who does decide that her children need this skill must decide whether to encourage the children's own methods or teach the standard algorithm (method). At a simpler level, take subtraction facts and the following short conversation (pupil is in reception):

Teacher   What's twelve take away seven?
Pupil   [Five-second pause] Five.
Teacher   How did you do that?
Pupil   Well, I knew that two sixes make twelve, so if I took one six away it would be six. But it's twelve take away *seven*, so that would be one *more* than six, But like I said before, um, twelve take away six would be six, so it would be one *less* than six, so it must be five.

The teacher's eventual aim for the pupil is that she be able to recall automatically the number fact $12 - 7 = 5$, and will most likely be engaging the pupil in practical activities involving counting out 12 objects, removing 7 (counting again) and finally counting the remainder. The pupil may also be encouraged to use her fingers and count backwards. Much consolidation and practice will be done to ensure that she eventually attains the required 'instant recall'. Yet this child is thinking on a much more sophisticated level, and needs encouraging to build on her present ability. The failure to do so leads to lack of self-confidence (as teacher always does it in only one way, then my way must be wrong) and boredom. Ian Thompson (1992) describes children as old as ten and eleven relying on simple counting strategies to solve arithmetic problems, most likely because they lack the confidence to do it any other way. Our own experience of researching top juniors' knowledge and application of multiplication facts shows that less able children constantly revert to counting strategies when in a stressful situation (eg. being interviewed by a stranger!).

To show what we mean about the crippling effects of lack of confidence in maths, look at the following subtraction, done by seven-year-old Katy, who has made a very common error.

$$\begin{array}{r} 23 \\ -18 \\ \hline 15 \\ \hline \end{array}$$

Laurie R Hello, can I talk to you about what you are doing?
Katy Yes.
LR What are these? What do you have to do?
K You have to . . . you have to take this away from that.
LR Tell me about this one. What numbers are these?
K Twenty-three . . . take away eighteen.
LR Twenty-three take away eighteen. Right. So how did you do it?
K Well you say eight take away three is . . . five, and two take away one is one. That's how I did it.
LR Good. I see. Um . . . why do you take the top number away from the bottom here, and then you take away the bottom one here . . . that's what I was wondering.
K That's . . . that's just what you have to do.
LR How do you know when to do what, that's . . .
K [interrupting] You have to always take away the smaller number . . . away from the bigger number, that's why.
LR Why do you have to always take away the smaller number, do you think?
K I don't know, that's the way my teacher told me to do it.
LR But why do you think?
K [laughs] Teacher told me to do it!

LR   And . . . this answer, fifteen, twenty-three take away eighteen leaves fif-
      teen . . .
K   Oh, it isn't right, I know it isn't right.

Laurie showed Katy mercy at this point, but she was a bright child who
knew perfectly well that the answer she had written down was wrong.
Parents sometimes ask 'Why do you spend all this time trying to get them to
understand, why don't you just *tell* them?' Katy's example illustrates why
'because that's the way my teacher told me to do it' is an inadequate reason
for doing a sum a certain way. This sort of difficulty does not arise so often
when children are encouraged to devise their own methods, perhaps
because then they *expect* to make mistakes and correct them as they go
along, adapting their processes as they meet harder numbers and so on. It is
a great pity that in many mathematics classrooms, children are so afraid of
making mistakes that they will cheerfully write down answers they know to
be nonsense. This does not seem to happen so much in other subjects. It is
the notion which attaches to maths, that it must be done at great speed but
without making any mistakes, that bedevils the teaching of it.

Application

Ever since universal education began, there have been complaints that children cannot apply their mathematical knowledge to varying contexts. When
the curriculum is delivered in separate bundles, called subjects, as in almost
all secondary schools and in an increasing number of primaries, children fail
to make connections between them and cannot identify the required mathematical processes even when they have only very recently studied them
(Brown and Kuchemann, 1976). Employers complain that mathematics
graduates lack application skills, secondary science teachers complain that
pupils cannot draw graphs (though they magically produce similar ones in
their maths lessons) and primary educators are familiar with the blank stare
when children are given word problems (what *is* it asking me to do?).

The thematic method

Since the time of the Nuffield Project, British primary educators have
attempted to improve the situation through thematic teaching, but many
have found mathematics difficult to build in to their topics. Some have aban-
doned the task completely, teaching mathematics as discrete from the rest of
the curriculum. At the other extreme, some have sometimes produced links
which are so weak that both the mathematics and the topic have suffered.
For example, a popular theme within history teaching is that of 'shopping',
which on the surface offers many opportunities for cross-curricular work.

When the mathematics is analysed, however, the units are usually too diffi-cult (e.g. using number bases different from our own – not a good idea if the children are still struggling with base 10) or are inappropriate (imperial units no longer forming part of early years mathematics). One solution is to sim-plify the numbers by giving incorrect prices or measures, but what does this do to the historical accuracy? And can we really say that the mathemat-ics is being applied to a real situation? Similarly, at the junior level, a recent pack of cross-curricular material on the Egyptians included a maze inside a pyramid which a cat must solve in order to reach a mouse. Certainly, this is a mathematical skill worth developing but it gives children erroneous mes-sages about the structure of the inside of the pyramid!

Cross-curricular themes *do* exist which contain rich mathematical oppor-tunities – for example, 'shopping' in the present day:

- Items can be sorted – edible / not edible; animal / vegetable; liquid / solid; etc.
- Articles can be compared by weight, or weighed if the children are ready.
- Packages can be explored for the packing properties, or cut open to look at the nets.
- Layouts of supermarkets can be explored – plan the best way round with a particular list of items.
- Prices can be entered into a calculator, or into a computer and then printed to make their own till receipts.
- Tallies can be made of when parents shop, who goes with them etc.

All these have relevance to children, and all the mathematics is worth doing. If the mathematics does not grow naturally out of a topic, and hence has no *real* purpose, then it is better left out.

Mathematics as a theme

An alternative to both the thematic method and the context-free method is to follow a theme which is particularly rich mathematically and which runs concurrently with other classroom topics. This method is used by the pub-lished scheme *HBJ Mathematics* (Burton *et al.* 1990). For example, the title 'Bigger and smaller' provides impetus to look at how numbers grow (as Tim was doing in our example earlier), to explore number patterns (early alge-bra) and shape patterns, to get a better feel for the concepts within measurement and to represent growth pictorially (data-handling). Hence, the mathematics curriculum is united.

Atkinson *et al.* (1994) adopt this approach even more explicitly within their *New Cambridge Primary Mathematics* scheme, building in both 'mathe-matical' and 'contextual' themes throughout. Both these texts support an emergent approach and can be used to encourage children to devise their own methods of calculation and problem solving. Without the existence of such support it is often a difficult task for the teacher of young children to avoid, even unwittingly, an over-directive approach, since the author(s) of the scheme may have decided on the 'best' way to do almost everything for them. Whatever texts are used, however, it is always advantageous to get into the habit of taking every opportunity to challenge children to utilise what mathematics they already know in fresh contexts and situations.

Whichever thematic approach is employed, opportunities arise for problem solving within a context which will interest and hence motivate the children. Mathematics without a context is not only dry for young children, but is also harder to visualise and hence harder to engage with. Visualisation and practical engagement also help children to decode the mathematical language, finding equivalent everyday alternatives.

Real contexts

Even better is to use a real context from the children's environment. For example, if a new playground is to be laid out, children can investigate different arrangements. If a picnic or party is planned, the children can plan the sharing out and the cost – using a calculator, please, *not* doctoring the numbers! If a party is not planned, organise one for the (mathematical) purpose. You are the teacher, who can make things happen! Suggest to them that they invite the local over-60s club in for a tea-party, or their parents, or just another class.

Of course, even the most energetic teacher cannot make things happen every day, and hence real problem solving, as such an approach is often called, cannot be the only method used. With practice, however, you can get into the habit of using the available environment whenever possible to practise the mathematics you have already taught. This is not a time to 'teach' new knowledge, rather a chance for children to enjoy being creative with what they know, and to learn through playing around with numbers.

So, for example, you might say

> I wonder how many bricks there are in this school. How could we find out?

No starter is infallibly successful, but this one has often produced fierce enthusiasm and much incidental learning. Children have all sorts of suggestions as to how to do it. Calculators and clipboards and anything else they want should be provided. We have seen this done with children who were too young to have met multiplication yet, and who began simply by counting every brick in one outside wall. They began to realise that the task was going to be a daunting one, but wanted to persevere. After some time, one pair came running up in tremendous excitement so the whole group (half a class in this instance) was quickly assembled to hear what they had to say – it was obviously very important!

> Look, look, you don't have to count all the bricks! You count how many in a row and if it's twenty-seven, you see how many rows there are and it's that number of twenty-sevens!

They had not been taught multiplication so, faced with a great need, had simply invented it for themselves. Not all of the rest of the group really understood what these two were saying, but some did. It also provided a very useful experience later, when multiplication *was* being introduced formally. We all built little walls out of bricks and the original pair proudly explained their discovery again.

Another time, this class enjoyed some mathematical 'play' on the parquet floor of the hall. We began the activity by drawing squares of different sizes with chalk on the floor, then counting to see how many of the little wooden rectangular blocks had been enclosed. The original idea was to see whether anyone spotted a relationship between the sizes of squares and the number of blocks, but this didn't happen. Maybe it was too ambitious, but in any case the children quickly subverted this purpose by drawing all sorts of different shapes. It didn't really matter that they did this: they had a very enjoyable time and recorded their findings in all kinds of different ways.

The impact of the activity was shown by the paintings they produced on the following and subsequent days, based on the patterns of the rectangular blocks but with lots of different arrangements and colours. The only drawback to what had been a relaxed morning of maths came when the caretaker saw what we had done to his highly varnished floor. When doing this again, we experimented using frames made from paper and with string, but nothing had quite the same appeal. They just enjoyed drawing all over the floor, so we went back to doing that, but being much more careful to clean it off before the caretaker got in! Your children will nearly always enjoy activities invented or inspired by you more than the ones invented by the writers of books, however eminent, so be bold and experiment, whilst remembering the caretaker.

Games and puzzles

Equally motivating are games and puzzles with a mathematical content. Children are hopefully already enjoying card games and board games at home and during wet play time at school. Most of these require counting and number recognition – both symbolic (numeral) and iconic (pictorial) —

and only slight adaptation is needed to introduce addition, subtraction and higher order concepts. Usually, such games are used to reinforce and practise skills already acquired, though concept formation can happen spontaneously as children make their own connections. Little investigations and puzzles can be introduced too:

- What do the opposite sides of a dice add up to? (partitioning of 7).
- What is the difference between the opposite numbers on a dice? What sort of numbers are these? Why do we only get this sort of number? (odds and evens).
- Can you put two dice together so that all the touching numbers add up to make the same?
- Are you a lucky person? Do you get a 6 more often than other numbers?

Competition need not be a negative element – for many it can add to the enjoyment – but if a game is to be played competitively then the teacher needs to choose partners carefully. A bad ability match can lead to a poor experience for the loser. One way around this is to introduce a large element of luck independently from the mathematics, though this can reduce the amount of time available actually to *do* mathematics. Alternatively, aim for co-operative games or large group efforts. Student teachers are often surprised by the willingness of children to help one another even within a competitive situation.

Puzzles are an excellent way of introducing mathematical problem solving. Children who are already interested in numbers will enjoy mathematics for its own sake, but others need motivating and hopefully the intrinsic interest will grow. As with all problem solving, discussing the results and strategies is very important. Young children find it difficult to explain their methods formally, but informal chat with their peers about what to do next, what would be a good 'next move' is an important step along the way.

It is difficult to do justice to this very wide subject in a single chapter, and we therefore recommend that those wishing a more in-depth coverage read *Mathematics with Reason* by Sue Atkinson (1992). This excellent book provides many useful ideas alongside examples of children's work.

Learning factors and the educator's role

If we therefore regard the child as an active learner – choosing what to learn and what to reject, making their own mathematics rather than ingesting ours – then what role is there for the early years educator? Obviously, children cannot create for themselves the body of knowledge we call mathematics, nor can we afford to let them develop only in certain areas of the subject. We have a responsibility to the children not only to expose them to the fascination mathematics can engender but also to equip them for the adult world. Educators by necessity exert control over the curriculum by the questions they ask the child, by the experiences they provide for concept formation and the challenges they set for application of those concepts. We become their guides and their mentors.

In order to fulfil this role to the best of our ability, it is vital to keep in mind some important factors: language, visualisation, differentiation and, finally, self-respect and personal responsibility.

Language

Mathematics has to some extent its own language – a combination of what are often referred to as ordinary English (OE) and mathematical English (ME). Our explanations and discussions with the very young begin with OE, as otherwise the language would be meaningless, but ME needs to be introduced gradually and continuously. There are a few myths in this regard, for example the idea that young children cannot cope with large proper names for mathematical concepts or objects. We are told by some that young children cannot cope with such words as 'subtract' and that therefore 'take away' is better. Yet these very same children have no difficulty remembering and using names like Diplodocus or Brontosaurus! It is important to use both the correct language and also a variety of language as there is therefore less room for misunderstanding. 'Take away' represents only one aspect of subtraction. 'Difference between', 'more than' and 'less than' are others in which nothing is being removed. What one must be careful to avoid is confusion, and hence these different aspects – with their correct language – are not tackled all at once.

There is also the danger of misunderstanding through the ME word existing with a different meaning within OE. A good example of this occurred when one of our students asked a group of young children if they knew what volume was. Up went one hand very firmly, but on asking the student was told 'It's the button on the remote control that makes things louder'!

To aid children's learning of ME, much discussion is required, both teacher–pupil and pupil–pupil. The latter will often use everyday alternatives, but this in itself helps as children draw connections between the new concept and the familiar. A more formal situation such as 'show and tell', where discoveries and achievements of the day are shared by individual children with the rest of the class, encourages them to use ME correctly. For a fuller discussion of language issues in mathematics please read *Maths Talk* by the Mathematics Association (1987).

It is vital to keep in mind language confusions when trying to assess children's mathematical knowledge. When a local education authority set up a working group to try to devise assessment items which would avoid language difficulties, they opted for a minimalist, orally presented script which was to be very closely adhered to, for example:

> I will read out some questions and I want you to write down just the answer to the question, You will have plenty of time. Write down the answer to:
> 1   One more than seven [pause]
> 2   Two less than ten [pause]
> 3   Three more than eight . . . .

On taking in the work, they discovered that several children had written:

1   No
2   Yes
3   No

Well, 1 *isn't* more than 7 and 2 *is* less than 10! We feel this illustrates the dangers of trying to avoid language difficulties by avoiding language. Far better to take a language-enriched approach than an impoverished one. Always simplifying 'difficult' words or even, as here, cutting them out completely, is not helpful to children in the long run. Discussion should be a vital part of maths, and expanding a child's mathematical vocabulary is as important as it is in other areas of the curriculum, so accept responsibility for promoting your children's powers of expression in mathematical situations as you would in any other.

We have noticed that educators of young children will go to enormous lengths, and use hundreds of words, to avoid using a precise term like 'parallel'. It would be better, and less patronising, to introduce the term, defining and explaining it when the opportunity arises, even if you think that the children are too young. Better still would be to do this, then make a point of using it correctly yourself a few times over the course of the next few days. Children are brilliant little learners and we underestimate their potential far too frequently in the early years.

Visualisation

Young children cannot easily work in the abstract, and learn to do so only gradually. If they cannot visualise the situation, they will most likely fail to understand it. Martin Hughes (1986) describes an experiment with pre-school children to investigate their conservation of number, a concept of which Piaget had thought them incapable. When the questions were couched in contexts which were familiar to the children (using teddy stories), and hence which they could visualise, then far fewer children failed to conserve number.

The following is an account by a teacher in a CAN school (see Note) of a discussion with a seven-year-old boy.

> Daniel was finding as many ways as he could to make 8. He had filled a page of his book with fairly short examples (like 10 − 2, 6 + 4 − 2, and so on). Now he was using a calculator to produce long, interesting strings of numbers, using the calculator to keep a check on the running total.
>
> Looking over his shoulder, I could see that he was able to range up into thousands and below zero into negative numbers and still end up with a number sentence that equalled 8.
>
> I said to him
> 'Don't you ever think that you'll never be able to get back to 8?'
> He looked at me scornfully and said
> 'I can always get back to 8.'
> 'How can you be sure that you'll always be able to get back to 8?'
> 'I can get back to 8 any time I want to. See this (the calculator) is like a video recorder.'
> I was genuinely puzzled by this.
> 'What do you mean?'
> 'You see *this* (the addition key) is like "play". Now this one (multiplication) is like "fast forward". The take-away key is "rewind", and this one (division key) is "fast rewind".'

Children like Daniel have years of experience of putting videotapes into video recorders and running them backwards and forwards to find the recording they want. While they are doing this, the four-digit display of the tape counter reels past their eyes, from 0000 to 9999. Some machines even show negative numbers. Daniel was relating this familiar vision to the school work he was doing with his calculator.

It is important always to keep in mind the 'child's eye' on the world. Talking to children informally – as they arrive at school, in the playground, etc. – helps the educator to get to know how they think, what interests them and what are their common experiences. An early years educator cannot afford to keep a distance between herself and her pupils.

Another aid to visualisation is practical activity. All nursery and infant schools use practical, or 'structured' apparatus for mathematics to a greater or lesser extent. It makes explanations easier, it helps the children keep a check of where they are up to, and it provides a pictorial image of the answer which can be used for assessment (very helpful with children who are not yet recording formally). Nowadays, it would be unthinkable to teach mathematics without this hands-on experience, and we would never wish to discourage such activity, but a word of warning is necessary. It is possible for children to learn a practical procedure by rote – similar to a standard written algorithm – and work through the stages with little understanding of what they are doing or why. Such children find it very difficult to transfer from the practical method to the mental or written forms as they can make no connections. The visualisation is not happening – they are only going through the motions. Unless the practical manipulation builds on their previous understanding – and if at all possible is a method devised by themselves – then it will be no more meaningful than playing 'Simple Simon says'. This is equally true of computer work, calculator methods, etc. Without a solid understanding of how children think and learn, these aids become gimmicks and finally are unfairly discredited.

Differentiation

Every child has the right to an education delivered at a level which is within their grasp and which challenges them, pushing them ever forward. Easy to say, but far less easy to deliver to a large class of small children. Groupings by ability are a part solution, though even with a group size of only two, we can find significant differences between children.

Open-ended working is a different way to tackle the problem, which provides more opportunity to learn from one another and more room for discussion. At a very simple level, this can mean the difference between asking children to solve such sums as 2 + 7 or 9 – 3, etc. and asking them instead to find all the partitions of 9 they can (as in how many different ways can they put 9 cows in two fields). The latter can easily be extended – choose your own number of cows, choose the number of fields – saving teachers from producing endless, repetitive worksheets. In this way, consolidation and practice (a vital element of learning if such number bonds are to come to be 'known') is kept interesting. It can also tell you much more about the children's abilities as they will explore and push forward their own frontiers, sometimes into areas different from those thought of by the educator.

Figure 14.3 shows a six-year-old's attempt at partitioning money. Notice how he begins each section by finding solutions using only one type of coin. He is obviously comfortable with this, and needs further activities leading to exploring multiplication and division. This piece of work also

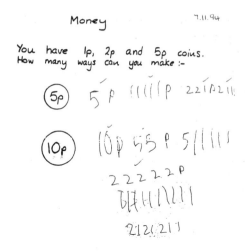

Figure 14.3 *A 6-year-old's attempt at partitioning money*

tells the educator that this child has a well-developed feeling for pattern (10p being made with 2, 1, 2, 1, 2, 1 . . . 1) and works fairly systematically (starts with the larger coins, looks for equal additions, and then moves on to mixed coins). Quite a lot from a small piece of writing, and perhaps too presumptive, but the educator will base her assessments on many such items from one child.

Self-respect and personal responsibility

Finally, while planning mathematics for young children, we cannot help but consider our wider role in the young child's personal development. We need to help them become effective, autonomous learners; they must also learn to work co-operatively, to listen to others and to respect others. None of this is possible without an element of self-respect, and this will not come about unless their work and their responses in mathematics are respected by the teacher. They need to know that you are genuinely interested in the work they do, the things they say, and the way they are thinking as they try to solve their problems. 'Tell me about this: how are you getting on? Is it difficult and what are the difficult bits?' are better interactions than simply marking things right or wrong. Children also need praise; they need appropriate work which they tackle with some success and they need to see their own lives, interests and experiences valued and reflected in the business of the day.

These are, of course, issues which pervade the whole curriculum, but there is a specific role for mathematics. In the outside world, the popular image of a mathematician is of a white male – probably wearing glasses and equally likely to have a calculator in his pocket or be sitting at a computer. These images give subtle messages to children about what is appropriate behaviour for them, causing disaffection which becomes manifest from older primary children onwards. Because the effects are not evident at the nursery and infant stage does not mean that the damage has not begun. In nursery and reception classes, boys can be seen dominating the construction tables. Teachers often have to engineer time specifically for girls, rather than having free choice time, as construction work is vital for their growing understanding of shape and space. As boys are more likely to be bought calculators and computers by their parents than are girls, early years educators need to monitor carefully girl's attitudes to these aids, and to ensure girls use them as much as necessary.

It is 'well known' that girls are neater than boys, and hence do better at standard arithmetic work – they can at least get the tens and units in the right columns! – but this is more a reflection of teacher attitude than any innate difference between the sexes. Close monitoring of teacher–pupil interaction shows girls being praised for neatness, while boys are praised for creativity. The children respond with whatever will gain your approval.

Conclusion

Teachers entering the profession in the late 1990s, and others beginning work as early years educators, do so at an exciting time. Dogma on all sides has been tempered by experience and to some extent the appearance of the national curriculum provides a breathing space for us to sit back and re-evaluate mathematics teaching and learning. People are again questioning what education is really about and mathematics is no exception. It can be an exciting time if we allow it, and much depends on our new recruits. Get in there and experiment – you have nothing to lose and a great deal of professional satisfaction to gain!

Note

CAN is an acronym for the Calculator-Aware Number curriculum project which was a part of Hilary Shuard's much larger PrIME project, referred to in our opening section. Schools which joined the project agreed to make a calculator permanently available to each child, allowing them to use it at any time *they* chose, and undertook not to teach any standard 'right' way of doing the number operations for addition, subtraction, multiplication and division. There were many exciting results which are reported in Shuard *et al.* (1991), but noteworthy in the example cited is Daniel's confidence and sense of ownership of what he was doing. An enhanced ability to do calculations mentally was another result, probably because of increased understanding of place value and the way the number system works, which of course are built into the calculator, thus making it a very powerful teaching tool. For a fuller discussion of meaningful calculator use, see Rousham (1995).

Pointers for early years number work

- Children are mathematical thinkers in their own right, and have already made many connections and conclusions before they start school.
- Educators need to be aware of children's perceptions about mathematics (through observation and discussion), so that they can build on the children's correct understandings and help them amend their misunderstandings.
- In order to understand mathematics, and be able to apply it to solve differing problems, it needs to be couched in understandable language and within a context which is relevant or interesting to the child.
- Educators can provide appropriate experiences (through, for example, play, investigations or practical tasks) and encourage children's thinking through discussion and exposition, but children maintain control over what and how much is learnt.
- Mathematics has its part to play in children's personal development. Their attempts must be respected, no matter how trivial to the adult observer and no matter how they perform compared to their peers.

References

Atkinson, S. (1992) *Mathematics with Reason: The Emergent Approach to Primary Maths*, London: Hodder & Stoughton.

Brown, M. and Kuchemann, D. (1976) 'Is it an add, Miss?', *Mathematics in School*, 5, 5.

Cockcroft, W. H. (1982) *Mathematics Counts*, London: HMSO.

Hughes, M. (1986) *Children and Number: Difficulties in Learning Mathematics,* Oxford: Basil Blackwell.

Jaworski, B. (1988) ' "Is" versus "seeing as": constructivism and the mathematics classroom', in D. Pimm (ed.) *Mathematics, Teachers and Children,* London: Hodder & Stoughton.

Mathematics Association (1987) *Maths Talk,* Cheltenham, Glos.: Stanley Thornes.

Rousham, L. (1995) 'Can calculators make a difference?', in J. Anghileri (ed.) *Children's Mathematical Thinking in the Primary Years: Perspectives on Children's Learning,* London: Cassell.

Shuard, H., Walsh, A., Goodwin, J. and Worcester, V. (1991) *Calculators, Children and Mathematics: The Calculator-Aware Number Curriculum (CAN),* London: Simon & Schuster.

Thompson, I. (1992) 'From counting to calculating', *Topic: Practical Applications of Research in Education,* 7, 10, 1–6.

Whitebread, D. (1995) 'Emergent mathematics or how to help young children become confident mathematicians', in J. Anghileri(ed.) *Children's Mathematical Thinking in the Primary Years: Perspectives on Children's Learning,* London: Cassell.

Maths schemes

Atkinson, S., McClure, L., Harrison, S. and Williams D. (1994) *New Cambridge Primary Mathematics,* Cambridge: Cambridge University Press

Burton, L., Harvey, R., Kerslake, D., Street, L. and Walsh, A. (1990) *HBJ Mathematics,* London: Collins Educational (HarperCollins).

Nuffield Mathematics Project (1968) *Mathematics Begins (1); Computation and Structure (2); Computation and Structure (3),* London: W & R Chambers and John Murray.

Further recommended reading

Ainsley, J. (1988) 'Playing games and real mathematics' in D. Pimm (ed.) *Mathematics, Teachers and Children,* London: Hodder & Stoughton.

Anghileri, J. (ed.) (1995) *Children's Mathematical Thinking in the Primary Years: Perspectives on Children's Learning,* London: Cassell.

Burton, L. (1994) *Children Learning Mathematics: Patterns and Relationships,* Hemel Hempstead: Simon & Schuster.

—— (ed.) (1986) *Girls Into Maths Can Go,* London: Holt, Rinehart & Winston.

Buxton, L.G. (1981) *Do You Panic about Maths?: Coping with Maths Anxiety,* London: Heinemann.

CHAPTER 15

'I think DT should stand for Deep Thinking'

DESIGN AND TECHNOLOGY – THE EARLY YEARS

Babs Sweet

Design and technology, as a curriculum subject, has a major role to play in developing in children the lively enquiring minds needed to cope with the technological demands of the twenty-first century. A carefully structured contextual involvement with materials, tools and associated equipment offers to all children enjoyment, excitement and expectation as 'designers and makers'.

Working through the design process, children are encouraged to make judgements having aesthetic, functional, moral and economic implications for their own work and that of others. Communication skills will be broadened and the ability to work individually, or as a member of a team, will be developed.

Design and technology in the early years is the meeting ground for many of the thinking, practical and process skills which are developed elsewhere in the curriculum and which reinforce and are reinforced by the skills of designing and making. It develops the capability to see the job through from first ideas to finished product.

Children begin to develop this capability long before they arrive in school. Playing with toys and the many objects around them at home or at playgroups are their first taste of designing and making activities. Good design and technology teaching in the early years builds on these early experiences by broadening the range of materials and associated tools alongside the introduction of appropriate construction kits.

Children love to please and to be accepted, and here lies the potential danger in a subject such as design and technology. For, unless the right messages are given clearly, children are more likely to produce what they think the educator wants in order to gain praise and approval, than to risk rebuff with innovative and unconventional ideas. 'Oh, what a lovely house' implies 'That's just what I was expecting' and 'What sort of a house is that?' says 'Don't you know what a house looks like?' The bottom line should be that every child's effort is totally acceptable and equally important because it is their statement about themselves.

This is a little anonymous story about John. Although fictitious it is a timely warning to us all:

> John always wanted to explain things, but he couldn't always say them.
> So he drew.
> Sometimes he would just draw and it wasn't anything.
> He wanted to carve it in stone or write it in the sky.
> He would lie out on the grass and look up in the sky and there would only be the sky and things inside him that needed saying.
> And it was after that that he drew the picture.
> It was a beautiful picture. He kept it under his pillow and would let no one see it. Because it was him.
> And he would look at it every night and think about it.
> And when it was dark and his eyes were closed he could see it still.
> And it was all of him and he loved it.
> When he started school he brought it with him, not to show anyone, but just to have it with him like a friend.
> It was funny about school.
> He sat at a square brown table like all the other square brown tables.
> And his room was a square brown room, like all the other rooms.
> And it was tight. And close. And stiff.
> He hated to hold the pencil and chalk, with his arm stiff and his feet flat on the floor, stiff, with the teacher watching and watching.
> Then they drew. And he drew all yellow and it was the way he felt about the morning. And it was beautiful.
> The teacher came and smiled at him. 'What's this?' she said.
> 'Why don't you draw a proper picture like Ken's ? Isn't it beautiful?'
> After that he always drew airplanes and rocket-ships like everyone else.
> And he threw the old picture away.
> And when he lay out alone looking at the sky, it was big and blue, and all of everything, but he wasn't anymore.
> He was square and brown inside and his hands were stiff.
> And he was like everyone else. All the things inside him that needed saying didn't need it anymore.

It had stopped pushing. It was crushed. Stiff.
Like everything else.

If this is the sort of child we are aiming to produce, devoid of imagination and with no independent thinking, then read no further. In fact, close the book and find a good novel instead. If you are determined that the tragedy that beset John at four years old is unacceptable, then read on.

If we are to avoid creating a world full of 'Johns' we need to look carefully at the means and measures we employ to help produce children who have the confidence to:

- try out their own ideas;
- produce alternative solutions;
- develop their full potential;

in a climate that is wholly supportive and free from censorship.

Ins and outs: input reflects outcome

The main problem area in encouraging children to be innovative, inquisitive, inventive and investigative has very little to do with their age, their environment, gender, birthplace or even their ability. In a society such as ours the only inhibiting factors are the restrictions imposed by the attending adults.

We all mostly live in houses that are cuboid in shape with square or rectangular windows, rectangular doors and apex roofs. Therefore, if we want our children to construct a house, we are likely to supply them with the materials and colours that match our preconceived expectations of what the result should be. With such a narrow start these intuitive children – and most of them are intuitive to a very high degree – will build our idea of a house, because that is what has been implied by the materials given. Nothing inventive or innovative here because the input has been imposed upon the outcome.

We probably need to consider the question, 'What is a house?' The answer of course is a dwelling place, somewhere safe to live. But who said that dwellings had to be of regular shape? Not the caveman of long ago, not the shanty town refugees of today and maybe not even the space explorer of future years. So, along with the regular-shaped materials, the shoe boxes and cereal packets, we should also provide a range of seemingly unlikely materials, such as tubes, lids and egg cartons, in order to promote imaginative ideas. One four-year-old recently constructed a three-dimensional lorry using only small rectangles of flat corrugated card.

There is inevitably a percentage of children whose developing minds can not yet extend further than the conventional image, but at least the options are there along with freedom of choice and unspoken permission to make their own decisions. To the adventurous majority, we are saying 'over to you', and then we must give them licence to be inquisitive, inventive and innovative.

This permissive scenario allows plenty of scope for important, unobtrusive input for the teaching of aspects of safety, appropriate language and a range of skills. But, as in any interaction with children, timing is crucial.

Teaching approaches

The most difficult thing for any teacher of design technology must be – **Hands Off!** So often one sees the teacher doing and the child watching because the child has asked the question, 'How?' There are times, of course, when physically helping may have to be the way forward but, mainly, children can achieve by themselves if the appropriate strategy is employed.

Verbal instruction

Give the children verbal instructions by talking through the processes step by step, allowing them time to complete one instruction or process before moving onto the next stage. Resist the temptation of doing the work for them even though it would mean a quicker and more expertly accomplished job. How will a child learn without the practical experience, and who will claim the finished product? You or them?

Demonstration

Demonstration allows the teacher to show how to solve a problem by using similar materials, but not by working on the actual model. The children can then either copy the example or adapt the presented idea but ultimately the work will be their own.

Disassembling

Disassembling is a useful technique allowing the teacher to show the solution on the child's own model and then to disassemble, or take apart, the teacher input leaving the model in its original state. This then enables the child to do the actual work.

Manipulative skills, using basic tools and equipment

With very young children, their skills in using basic tools, such as pencils and scissors, is dependent upon the physical development of hand / eye co-ordination, muscle strength, and to a certain degree, hand size. In the early stages they should have the freedom to draw and cut to their own abilities, unless a child is perceptive enough to realise that performance and requirements don't match up – for example 'I want a window but I can't do it straight.' Strange shaped windows and taped down box edges are completely acceptable if it means freedom to proceed, unaided, and fosters the element of independent working, which must be the ultimate goal. However if teacher input is requested, then simple but correct procedures should be adopted.

In fact, even quite young children can be taught to use a range of tools effectively and safely. Figure 15.1 shows a scene from a first sawing lesson.

Figure 15.1 *5-year-old Tristan practising the correct way to use a junior hacksaw and a bench hook to saw wood*

Giving assistance

If a child requests help to 'make a window straight', then by using a ruler, and allowing the child to assist in holding it firmly as the line is drawn, the idea is established that rulers are used to make lines straight. Then, if rulers are readily available, children will attempt to use one without assistance. At five years a child should be able to use a ruler, if somewhat inexpertly.

If asked for help to cut out and the line was 'wiggly' it would be necessary to establish if the line was to be followed exactly, so offering the opportunity for the child to see that the line was not straight. Then, if desired, the teacher and child together can use a ruler to make the corrections. If the line is not perceived to be crooked, then one must have the courtesy to cut on the presented mark, and not impose one's own criteria. An alternative to the teacher doing the cutting would be for them to hold the materials and the child to operate the scissors whilst suggestions for improving technique are offered. For example 'open the jaws wide' etc. This is as good a way as any to improve on the child's skills.

As children mature then expectations of them grow and care and accuracy at their own level become just as important as independent thought and work.

Safety

Safety is paramount and should be taught by

1 Instruction – 'This is how we hold the scissors'.
2 Reinforcement – 'Well done, Sarah, you're holding that just as it should be held'.
3 Example – 'Sam, will you just show everyone how carefully you carried those scissors'.
4 Demonstration – of the adults always using the safe practices we instil in children.

Designing and making activities are, in the majority of cases, safe and enjoyable. During these early years it is essential that children are taught safe practices. A balance should be achieved between autonomous learning and the necessity for close supervision. The range of materials offered to the children will determine the tools the children need to use, allowing the teacher ample opportunities to demonstrate correct and safe tool usage.

It is so easy for the safety aspect to be forgotten in the excitement of 'making', so the teacher must be vigilant and actually remove from the child anything that is being handled in a dangerous manner. One good practice is the 4 Rs policy.

1 Re-instruction – 'Remember, this is how we . . .'.
2 Reminder – Show me how you . . .'.
3 Remonstrate – 'Show me how to . . . . Good, now if you can't remember to do that, I will take it away from you'.
4 Removal – simply take away the offending article with a rueful smile and a 'sorry'.

This gives children three chances to remember, and if that isn't enough, we must ask whether they are sufficiently mature to handle the material, tool or piece of equipment in question. A final chance could be given but only under direct supervision for the rest of the lesson. The individual teacher must decide if second chances are allowed but the safety of all the children in the class must be their number one priority. Safety in D&T lessons is achieved through a combination of good teaching and common sense. Irrespective of age, children should have a healthy respect for all materials, tools and equipment.

Language

Terminology

Correct terminology can and should be introduced right from the start. In the same way that we hand a child a writing tool and say 'here's your pencil' rather than 'here's that bit of wood that makes a mark', so we can use the correct name for tools, shapes, materials, equipment and procedures. The children will absorb the information as and when they are ready, and we can help by using the reinforcing tactics of 'double-talk'. That is a term for offering a simplified description to back up the technical language. For example, 'Now you need a bench hook, the wood block that we saw on,' or 'Shall we get that tape you can paint on because it's not shiny, the masking tape?' In the same way, we would be looking for a toilet roll cylinder, a shoe box cuboid and so on. This way we are teaching, not preaching, and this continual reinforcement reaps its rewards.

Encouragement

The way language is used can greatly influence the listener, so care must be taken. Phrasing is important. The next logical step in Sarah's house construction would be to put the roof on, but is that what Sarah is thinking? If the teacher asks Sarah, 'What are you going to use for the roof?' it does give her the opportunity for choice of materials but it also presupposes that she is going to have a roof and that's the next step to take. All alternative ideas Sarah might have had will probably now give way to the educator's expectation of a roof. Instead the question, 'What next, Sarah?' allows her to tell you her plans or the gentle prompting of 'Does your house need anything else?' may stimulate more ideas. With a little thought a negative or 'closed' phrase can be transformed into a positive or 'open' one.

Here is a list of some open and closed phrases:

Closed	*Open*
That's not a straight line	Is that how it should be?
Get a ruler and draw it	What could you use to help it go straight?
Now you've got to . . .	What next?
Put the glue here	Where will the glue go?
Right, now glue it	What's the best way to fix it?

It is noticeable that the most useful, helpful phrases are non-directive and usually contain those magic words 'how', 'what', 'where' and 'why'. Quality teaching is often inextricably linked to asking quality questions. Ask children the right questions and their answers will amaze you.

If these measures are unfruitful and a more direct approach is required, then again careful phraseology can help to turn the situation around:

'One idea could be . . .' sets the thought processes going and helps to prompt the child to an alternative solution.

'What would happen if? . . .' allows the child an input even though you have given the solution.

'Tell me what the problem is,' gives opportunity for the child to talk out a solution with you.

'If you did this, what could you do next?' helps the child safely over a difficult hurdle, with honour intact.

Design and technology is all about encouraging children to make their own choices and decisions. Continued adult support is needed to give them the confidence required to venture into the unknown and language is important for reassurance. 'Can I?' and 'Will it?' could be answered with a 'Try it and see!' 'Should I?' and 'Could I?' with 'I don't know. What do you think?' Most of all be aware that a careless response could damage a fragile confidence.

Intervention

When do we interrupt children's work to take them a step further, and how do we do it without negating what they have accomplished so far?

When little Sarah has tried for the sixth time to stick her toilet roll by glueing the cylindrical end, then it's time to say 'Let me show you this, Sarah' and begin to cut small snips around the end whilst explaining the procedure to her. If she is to fix more than one, then you do the first and she can do the rest. If not, you do half and she can continue.

Tools and equipment can be introduced by the same means. The response to 'I need a hole here' is to show the appropriate tool and to explain its use. It is an easy matter to discuss that the reason the box didn't stick was that there wasn't enough glue, or that everything slips around because there was too much.

If, from an early age, children are encouraged to work independently, the individual child will determine the pace at which they learn. As their experience broadens so does the need for a wider range of materials and their associated tools and techniques.

Designing and making across the curriculum

As was discussed at the beginning of the chapter, design and technology work in the early years offers rich opportunities for young children to engage in problem-solving activities related to many of the other areas of the curriculum. The thinking, practical and process skills developed elsewhere in the curriculum are required to be made use of in ways which deepen understandings and allow children to put skills and processes to their own purposes.

In the remainder of this chapter I want to describe some examples of work I have carried out with young children which has been stimulated by a variety of starting points linked to different areas of the curriculum.

Sound

A topic on 'sounds' was carried out with a reception class. This gave us the opportunity to investigate musical instruments, how they are constructed, how they make a variety of sounds and how those sounds are produced and transmitted. As such it grew out of scientific and musical questions, but developed into many other areas.

As a starting point the children discussed what sounds could be made by:

clicking fingers and thumbs
clapping hands together – hard and soft
stamping feet
using tongue and mouth
humming
slapping thighs.

The children then investigated a wide range of materials (some brought in specially for this purpose by myself, but others just generally available classroom materials) to see what sounds they would make.

Once the children discovered how basic sounds were made they investigated real instruments. From a comprehensive collection each child selected one instrument and returning with it to their place drew the instrument as carefully as possible and recorded the correct name, the method of playing and the materials it was made from. For example, 'A guitar, you pull the strings and it's made of wood'.

The process was repeated with as many different instruments as time permitted, children drawing and investigating between four and six instruments. The class then talked together about their findings and admired each others art work.

With all the knowledge gained from this activity the children then drew their own designs of the instrument they intended to make. Some designs were totally imaginative, some were similar to those investigated and others were exact copies of the real thing. One little boy sawed notches along a piece of wood to make a scraper stick. A little girl collected together all manner of boxes and tins and glued them together to make a drum kit. She even altered the resonance of some of the areas by stretching paper over certain surfaces (see Figure 15.2).

Figure 15.2 *Drum kit made by Harriet, aged 5*

Other children made shakers, guitars, trumpets, triangles and squeak boxes. The work produced was excellent and exciting (see Figure 15.3).

Written statements and sketches were recorded in the children's Design and Make diaries. In this way, each child was able to keep a record of research carried out, materials and tools used and techniques learned. Very often children drew what they had made after it was completed. Figure 15.4 shows a page from Oliver's diary recording the materials he used to

Figure 15.3
Horn made by Jane and trumpet made by Edward, both aged 5

make his shaker. The musical instruments the children designed and made were then used in a school assembly.

The second stage of the sound project was to give the children some experience of working together in groups and to use the knowledge they had gained to stretch them a little further. The group work was to make large instruments suitable for outdoor use in the newly designed school playground. The children decided which groups to work in, then after classroom discussion each group chose the instrument they wished to make. Suitable materials were provided but the children had to decide on how to use them.

Figure 15.4 *Extract from Design and Make Diary by Oliver, aged 5*

One group chose to make two large triangles from a long strip of aluminium. They measured its length with string and then used the string to calculate the size of each triangle. Another group strung lengths of thin bamboo cane from a woven basket to produce wind chimes.

A group of boys made a glockenspiel by testing lengths of logs for resonance and mounting them on a wooden box. Logs and box were sanded and teak oiled to weatherproof them. Metal chime bars were made by suspending different lengths of metal tent poles from a wooden bar (that group decided that the chimes sounded 'just like the Church of England').

All the instruments were tried out of doors to discover the most satisfactory material for beaters. Then the children tested each instrument in turn and made careful drawings which were mounted and displayed alongside the instruments.

The project was hugely worthwhile not only in allowing the design and technology elements and techniques to be used, but also in offering the children the opportunity of personal growth and development in the areas of co-operation and self-discipline. As well as science and music, aspects of maths and art were clearly involved and developed. Many design and technology activities lend themselves particularly well to group work, and here the development of speaking and listening skills is clearly significant. In this project, the opportunities afforded for the children to use scientific, musical, mathematical and artistic vocabularies for real, meaningful purposes were very rewarding.

Teddy Bears' Picnic

Using the song 'Teddy Bears' Picnic' as a starting point, another group of reception children were asked to make something smart for Teddy to wear to the picnic.

The children were shown a range of materials they could use – various coloured felts, coloured wools, assorted sequins and braids. Copydex was used as the fixative.

General discussion produced a list of likely articles:

Bow tie
Waistcoat
Belt
Hat

The children brought in their own teddies and decided what to make for them. Some drew pictures of their proposed designs. Appropriate teddy parts were measured with tape measures and were transferred directly onto the felt using felt tipped pens. A limited number of good quality scissors ensured that the children could cut the fabric themselves but adult help was given where required. The articles were decorated with sequins, braid and felt appliqué. Finally, the resplendent teddies were treated to a very lively picnic.

Weaving

This topic was linked to the work of a professional basket maker present in the school for one week to weave a willow hurdle in the playground. The project for the five-year-olds involved was to make branch weavings. An annotated display was mounted of examples of weaving from around the world, from which the children were to discover:

- the nature of weaving;
- the different materials used;
- the use of the woven articles;
- the countries of origin.

We plotted the various locations on a world map. Then the children carried out 'hands-on' investigations of a range of woven articles and selected an item to draw in their Design and Make diaries observing, in particular, the weaving pattern.

Fabric squares were then presented for the children to take apart (disassemble) in order to identify the 'warp' and 'weft' threads, which had been previously discussed. An Anglepoise lamp and a magnifying lens were available and the children were encouraged to use these in their investigations. Figure 15.5 shows an example of the children's recording of this activity.

Paper weaving was then introduced. Each child:

- made a 'heddle' stick; they measured 24 cms along a length of 45mm dowel, sawed it with a junior hacksaw, and sharpened the end with a pencil sharpener;
- was supplied with 'warp' sheets (made from brightly coloured A4 paper by making cuts 1½ cms apart down its length, but leaving a frame of 1½ cms around the outside) and 'weft' strips of paper 1½ cms wide;
- was asked to make two woven mats, one with the 'heddle' stick used to lift alternate 'warp' strips of paper (modelling the workings of a loom) and one just using their fingers;
- was asked to give their opinions of the two methods.

The skills learnt here were then used to create *branch weavings:* Each child:

- brought into school a small twigged branch of about 30cms in length (there was a small supply for those unable to manage this);

we have been
looking at things
that have been
woven to see how
the threads go
under and over
we looked at fabric
with a magnifying
glass and discovered
the warp and weft.

Figure 15.5 *5-year-olds investigate weaving*

- wrapped yarn around their branch to produce the warp threads;
- wove the weft threads in to make interesting and attractive designs.

Different textured yarns were used. Good 'shuttle' substitutes to draw the weft threads through are the bodkin-shaped plastic stirrers of the sort used by motorway cafés in place of teaspoons.

Birdscarers

Farming provides a wealth of learning opportunities and a design and making activity arising from this topic was birdscarers.

First the children discussed the reason for having birdscarers and the different ways in which they could work:

> mechanical . . . they could have parts that moved
> auditory . . . they could make bangs or noises
> visual . . . they could look 'scary'

The discussion progressed through the children's own experiences to ideas for individual designs. These ranged from simple scarecrows made with card and supported on sticks to cats with jaws that opened with the weight of a perched bird and to electrical fencing that 'made the birds jump but didn't kill them'. For this activity I made available to the children mainly recycled materials together with fabric scraps and 8mm × 8mm wood for the scarecrow spars. That this kind of activity provides young children with opportunities to use their own knowledge and make their own decisions (e.g., about which materials to use), in order to solve a problem, is enormously important. The highly motivating nature of this kind of work is not unconnected to the children's feelings of ownership and empowerment, and it is crucial that this aspect is fundamental.

Other starting points for design and make activities

Here are some other starting points which I have found to work very well:

1 'The Owl and the Pussycat'
   Design and make a boat to transport an animal.
2 'Hickory Dickory Dock'
   Design and make a clock.
3 'Wee Willie Winkie'
   Design and make a safe candlestick (and a candle?).
4 'Teddy Bears' Picnic'

Design and make a cart to take teddy to the picnic.

5 'Who has Seen the Wind?'

Design and make something to do with the wind, e.g. windmill, kite, glider, weathervane, birdscarer.

6 'The Nativity'

Design and make a stable for Mary's donkey. Put a hinge and a catch on the door.

Conclusion

There are no failures in design technology. An unsuccessful idea is a step forward to finding an acceptable solution. There is probably no other area of the curriculum which offers children of all ages such rich opportunities to draw upon their own experiences and resources. Design technology gives children the freedom to make their own choices and decisions, to take responsibility for their own judgements and actions. At the same time, it gives them a sense of enjoyment, confidence in their abilities and pride in their achievements.

For the educator it can be pure delight. You experience the children's excitement and as they work through and make use of the design process. You share with them in their development of practical skills and thinking abilities which will help to equip them for the rigours of their future years.

Pointers for early years design and technology

- Encourage children to make their own decisions and work independently as far as possible.
- Always use language carefully so that you do not unduly influence children's responses and give the impression that there is one 'right' solution.
- There is no such thing as a failure. An idea that does not work is a stepping stone to finding a more successful one.
- With young children the thinking processes needed may not always be reflected in the resulting work, but it is these processes that are vital.
- Ensure that there is continued progression in the activities, in children's learning and in their achievements. Children enjoy new challenges.
- Safety must be paramount. It is essential that the correct use of materials, tools and equipment is taught from the very beginning.

Acknowledgement

I would very much like to thank David Jinks for all his help and support in developing my work in design and technology with children over the past few years, and for the invaluable help he gave me with this chapter.

Useful further reading

Banks, D. (1994) *Teaching Technology*, The Educational Television Co. Ltd.

Cave, J. (ed.) (1990) *Starting Design and Technology*, London: Cassell.

DES (1987) *Craft, Design and Technology From 5 to 16*, London: HMSO.

—— (1991) *Aspects of Primary Education: The Teaching and Learning of Design and Technology*, London: HMSO.

Design Council (1987) *Design and Primary`Education*, London: Design Council.

—— (1991) *Stories as Starting Points for Design and Technology*, London: Design Council.

Jinks, D. and Kellett, J. (1993) *Design and Make Folios 1–10*, DJK Technology (photocopiable material for teachers).

Macauley, D. and Ardley, N. (1988) *The Way Things Work*, London: Dorling Kindersley.

National Association of Advisers and Inspectors in D&T (1992) *Make it Safe: Safety Guidelines for the Teaching of Design and Technology at Key Stages 1 & 2*, 3rd Edn, NAAIDT.

Williams, P. and Jinks, D. (1985) *Design and Technology 5 to 12*, London: Falmer Press.

Young, N.(1989) *Signs of Design: The Early Years*, London: Design Council.

Journals

The Big Paper, London: Design Council

Questions, Birmingham: Questions Publishing Company

CHAPTER 16

'Mrs Rainbow told us what things were like when she went to school'

HISTORY IN THE EARLY YEARS

Sallie Purkis

You may think that learning history has no place in early years education. Lively young children, full of energy, seem essentially part of the present, curious to explore the living world around them, nurturing their imagination on stories, particularly those with just a touch of magic and unreality in them. How could the past, which is dead and buried, have any relevance for them?

In this chapter we will consider how we can justify the place of history in teaching and learning in the early years, the skills, knowledge, understanding and attitudes that can be developed through learning history, appropriate resources and activities to promote learning, and how progress can be planned and monitored. Finally, since history is a statutory foundation subject in the national curriculum from the age of five, we will make reference to the programme of study for Years R, 1 and 2 and assess any contribution it might make to sound practice and effective teaching and learning.

You will encounter hostility to any suggestion that 'subjects' should be part of an early years curriculum. Until recently, many practitioners found themselves unable even to use the word 'history', putting forward three main arguments in favour of leaving it aside until the child was much older. Unfortunately these views revealed serious misconceptions about what the subject we call history actually is, but it is worth listing them in order to get them out of the way:

- history is a series of facts and dates that have to be memorised;
- it can only be learned by children who can read history books;

- young children cannot understand the concept of time, so it is pointless to introduce it in the early years.

In the light of experience, understanding and practice, most modern teachers reject these arguments and the close links between the real discipline of history, which will be examined below, and effective teaching and learning have been recognised. Exciting classroom displays, learning environments which stimulate further investigation, and resources like oral history, objects and pictures have enabled teachers to capitalise on the opportunities for developing skills and concepts across the curriculum. Many schools, through their history guidelines and policies have identified what exactly it is they want the children to learn and how they can evaluate, assess and celebrate children's progress and achievement.

What is history?

History is not a body of knowledge about what happened before we were born and not a series of facts that can be learnt by heart. While some events can be dated with a fair degree of accuracy, others cannot. The discipline of history is about analysing the fragments of evidence that people, once alive and with similar human needs and aspirations to our own, left behind. We consider the evidence and have opinions about what it means. From these opinions, history is constructed and the past reconstructed.

Historians, archaeologists and museum professionals reconstruct the past, but so do film makers, novelists and advertisers. Ordinary members of the public have their own way of interpreting the past when they join the Sealed Knot and put on a performance of a Civil War battle, dress up to attend an 'Elizabethan banquet' or make bread on a kitchen range in one of the reconstructed communities like the Beamish site in County Durham. Some reconstructions are more accurate than others and debate often rages between heritage purists, conservators, and leisure and tourist interests. Professional historians revise and re-interpret the work of a previous generation, by looking at new evidence or posing different questions. All these examples highlight the fact that there are no incontrovertible 'right' answers about the past. History is a subject where questioning and hypothesising lie at the heart and where the simple questions are the ones we all want answered whether we are five or fifty.

Some of these key questions in history are as follows:

- When did these people live ?
- What were their lives like?

- How did they feed and clothe themselves?
- What were their homes like?
- What technology did they know about?
- What was the same or different about them and us ?
- What happened to them?
- When did things change?
- Why did things change ?
- How did things change?
- How do we know?

You will not expect all these questions to be relevant for the youngest children, but each of them can be explored at different levels of understanding. They are a framework around which investigation of the past can be structured. For example, we would expect older children and adults to answer the first question with a date, a century or a period, such as Tudor; in the early years we might accept with the all-pervasive 'in the olden days', but quite soon a more accurate response, such as 'before we were born', 'in the past ' or 'twenty years ago' can be applied. The important point to keep in mind is that the methods used by a historian or archaeologist are entirely consistent with the best teaching practice in the early years. The key words are **exploration**, **investigation** and **problem solving**. The learning objectives are to enable the children to both describe and explain the past.

Is history relevant?

When I asked some early years teachers if they would include history in their schemes of work, even if they were not forced to by the national curriculum, I received positive responses. They gave a number of reasons:

- the importance of subjects concerned with questions like those above;
- the interest value of taking a 'detective' or 'investigator' approach;
- the opportunities for starting with the children's knowledge of themselves, their families and communities but the potential for extending their horizons, to learn about other people – the product model of the curriculum;
- the links with other areas of the curriculum, through the development of skills, understanding and attitudes – the process model of the curriculum.

They recognised the role of history in the growth of self-esteem, personal identity and social identity. As one early years co-ordinator commented,

'The sort of history we do is their history and it's a good introduction to a lot of other subjects'.

They further justified it by reference to the children when they first arrive at school. They have enormous energy, but they are usually egocentric, unpractised in looking beyond themselves and in some cases, bringing anti-social attitudes towards others. Part of the educational objectives of educators in the early years are to help them look beyond themselves, integrate in a group and develop tolerance and social skills. History has a role to play in this programme. The growing awareness that each of us has a past as well as a present and a future extends knowledge of self and is a psychologically healthy sign of developing maturity. Knowledge and understanding of history can help answer the two key questions 'Who am I?' and 'Where am I?' In the early years, most practitioners think that personal and local history is the most important.

Learning opportunities

History has a language of its own, the language of time, but it is also a vehicle for developing skills and concepts across the curriculum. It helps explain change, similarity and difference, not in a scientific way but in terms of human experience. In the early years, it is the learning process, linked to activities and experiences, which should take priority over any knowledge objectives. Figure 16.1 shows the 'basics' of history as a subject. As you look at it, you may like to think about the teaching strategies and resources which would engage four-, five- or six-year-olds in any of the processes and skills listed in the diagram.

The diagram is also an affirmation of the central place that talk has in early years classrooms, particularly when teaching about the past. Although the aim is to let the children do most of the talking, it is the teacher who must ensure that there is something interesting to talk about, initiate and sustain the quality of the language and steer discussion from mere observation and description to investigation and hypothesis. By understanding what history actually is and the uncertainty about conclusions, you will feel comfortable as a teacher when the children raise questions which may not have an immediate answer. You should feel able to encourage them to ask questions that they have about the topic, object or picture under discussion. As they grow older, they will become familiar with the framework of historical questions, providing there is an agreed policy about their importance in all classes in the school, and will be able to draw up their own historical questions, like those listed above.

You would not, of course, expect all children at every stage to go through

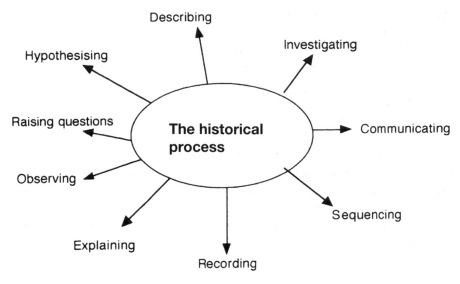

Figure 16.1 *The historical process*

the whole range of processes in Figure 16.1, but it is a framework to keep constantly in mind when planning activities in history so that you will not fall into the trap of thinking that repeating what the teacher says, describing and recording are the only objectives to plan for.

Practical implications of the process model

Let us imagine that an adult, perhaps someone's grandmother, volunteers to come into the classroom to show the children something old, such as a stoneware hot water bottle. How could even very young children be drawn into the process of learning history? Here are some suggestions for putting the historical process into action:

Observing	The hot water bottle would be carefully passed round the group, handled with the help of an adult because of its weight. The children would probably notice the screw top, but might need to have the flat bottom pointed out to them.
Describing	Vocabulary would probably include words to describe the colour (brown, grey), the weight (heavy) and the feel (cold). The length and girth could be measured.

Questioning, investigating	The children might ask what it is, where it came from and how it was used. The owner might have a story to tell about how it came into her possession and pointing out the function of the flat bottom, the place where the hot water was poured in and how it was secured.
Hypothesising	The children could be asked what they thought it was like to have a hot water bottle like this to warm the bed and why it was necessary. Some children may make guesses about the material from which it is made. Further discussion will develop from those who think it is made of stone or rock. They may also have opinions about why we do not still use them today.
Sequencing	This would only be possible if you had a modern hot water bottle in the classroom (and the children knew what it was). If you did you would then be able to introduce vocabulary like 'then' and 'now'.
Explaining	It is an object from the past, when there was no heating in bedrooms. It was last used in the Second World War, more than fifty years ago, when rubber was not available.
Communicating	The children may have more questions or express their opinions about the hot water bottle. All teachers know that it is impossible to predict, with accuracy, just what the children will notice and want to comment on.
Recording	The hot water bottle can be drawn or photographed, with the owner holding it. Four-year-olds will make an impression of the object but five- and six-year-olds will be able to write some sentences about the bottle and what they have learnt about it. The contributions can be displayed with the object or made up into a book.

Attitudes

When the teaching and learning is appropriately planned, history has an important contribution to make in the promotion of attitudes to learning and to other people. Figure 16.2 shows some of these.

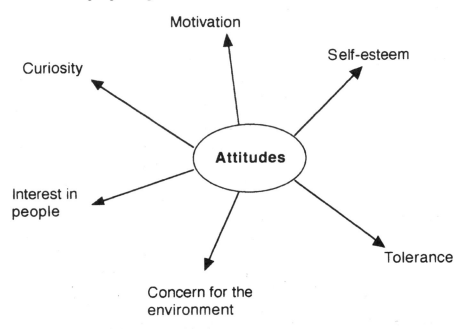

Figure 16.2 *Attitudes promoted by history*

You will not find it difficult to foster interest, enjoyment and curiosity through work in history, providing you provide an active 'hands-on' approach. As a teacher you will find yourself drawn into the excitement of historical detective work, handling objects and listening to reminiscence and able to pass on this enthusiasm to the children. Some of the other attitudes, however, may have to be deliberately selected and identified in your curriculum planning.

Unfortunately there is evidence that even small children come to school with values and prejudices towards other people and the environment which are intolerant and anti-social. They include racist attitudes that have been learnt from adults and older siblings at home and in their neighbourhood. They will find that these have no place at school. Of course, education cannot put right the ills in society, but since history is not a subject that deals in fantasy or make-believe but in the lives of people who have actually lived, one can argue that it has a responsibility to put the case for making reasoned and informed judgements, based on evidence.

Historical language

Language empowers, and in order to explain human experiences in the past, with accuracy, the children need to be equipped with vocabulary which encodes meaning. We will begin with the consideration of the language which describes time. There are many ways in which children grow to recognise and understand the passing of time. Talking accurately about *yesterday, today* and *tomorrow*, progressing to *last week, this week* and *next week* and then to some understanding of *seasons, months,* regular events that happen every year like their *birthdays,* the *summer holidays* and various *festivals* lay the foundation for describing the past, which is a very big concept indeed for the youngest children. Historical time has its own labels such as *year* and *century*. Where these are a measurement they can be part of the mathematics programme, but unfortunately history also has a series of subject-specific labels, such as *Victorian*. Experience shows, however, that by the age of seven, most children enjoy using the right label and can show that they know what it means, so there is no need to shy away from using the correct terms. It is not in the children's long-term educational interest to persist with labels like *'the olden days'*. They are perfectly able to learn to use *the past* and even the subject label *history. Before* and *after* are other concepts that become working components of the young child's vocabulary as they learn to recognise the sequence of stories and of numbers.

Many teachers introduce historical sequencing by using photographs of the children or their mothers when they were babies and discussing how they have changed. A simple timeline can be used to count back in years and language such as 'When I was a baby', 'When I was two, three or four'. These help explain the passing of time at the young child's level.

The other aspect of historical language which it is appropriate to develop before the age of seven, is the vocabulary to describe old things and age. A brainstorming session with colleagues and friends or a check in a thesaurus will reveal a list that can be used to challenge and extend children's language development. Words like *old-fashioned, ancient, antique, decayed, worn-out* all have slightly different meanings. They are applied to some things, such as people but not to others, like buildings. You would not expect everything to be introduced to all children at one time, but knowing what they mean and when they are applied are an essential 'basic' in teaching and learning about the past.

The last group of words are about the key concepts in history – *change and continuity; similarity and difference; cause and consequence*. Of these 'change' and 'difference' most frequently feature in early years history. It is important however that you always discuss their binary opposites – 'continuity' and 'similarity' – at the same time. Life in the past may have been different in degree from our own, but what is similar across the barriers of time and culture are human needs for food, clothing, shelter, security and belief. Change does not occur at the same rate in all societies.

It is important not to pass judgement too hastily on other times and cultures or to use pejorative or evaluative terms like *primitive* or *civilised*. There are still too many people in the world today who do not have access to running water or electric light. Emphasising difference between ourselves and people in the past can be another major pitfall. Care must be taken not to stereotype, but to acknowledge and respect difference. Everyone did not have servants in Victorian times and 'the Tudors' did not all dress like the privileged courtiers whose portraits give us an image of the age.

Continuity is also wide open for discussion. The evidence from the past is all around us. Some of us inhabit houses and schools built a hundred years ago. They have been changed and brought up to date over time, but they remain a living and tangible link with the past. In Britain we frequently celebrate the past, and this includes the popular 'Victorian' school day in primary schools. Even though the concepts of continuity and change are subtle, many young children are able to grasp difficult concepts. What they lack, unless you help provide it, is the language to articulate what they know and understand. It is important to have a framework of language and concepts listed in your school policy document for history, to raise awareness among staff and parents of the stages of knowledge and understanding that will help you support and monitor each child's progress.

Resources

Collecting resources to use in teaching history is not difficult or expensive and we can conveniently classify them under four headings:

    People
    Pictures
    Objects and buildings
    Books

We might also include music, but this needs other sources such as an old radio or record player to make it meaningful. Popular songs also have a place under the heading of 'people', particularly when they come as part of an older person's memories.

What follows is a discussion of issues related to the use of these various resources which I have illustrated by reference to a delightful local history project carried out by children at Harborne Infant School, Birmingham (Mauser and Reid 1990).

People

Oral history or reminiscence is one of the approaches most valued by early years educators. Its merit is that it is a contribution to history at school which children and families can make themselves. It is accessible and language-based, and need not come as English, if there is more than one mother-tongue represented in the class. It is easy to organise if you call on the school community and their contacts first. You do not need to restrict yourself to finding someone elderly or retired since everyone has a life story to tell and even 'young' people are old to a five- or six-year-old. Oral history is a winner in the classroom and makes an impact because it brings in a perspective on the past that is immediate, personal and alive. The Mrs Rainbow referred to in the title of this article was a real person (see Figure 16.3), even though her attractive name could have been a fictional invention.

When the children meet or interview someone, it is not necessary or

Figure 16.3 *Mrs Rainbow told us what things were like when she was at school*

desirable to draw up a rigid questionnaire, which might only result in stilted answers as you want to encourage the visitor to tell their story as a narrative. However, I am assuming that you will focus the session around a topic and that you will have discussed this with the interviewee so that you can tell the children the purpose behind the interview before they arrive. Most people can easily talk about their schooldays, their family life, their homes and journeys they have made. The children at Harborne Infant School interviewed past teachers about their memories of the school. The children asked questions reflecting their own interests, such as:

> What time did school start and finish?
> Did you have dinner at school?
> What was your favourite dinner?
> Did you have drinks at school?
> What lessons did you have?
> What games did you play with your friends in the playground?

Having more than one contribution on the same theme can be a positive bonus, since you will have different versions of the past which the children can discuss, describe, compare and explain. For example everyone had a childhood, but the experiences they talk about will depend how long ago it was, where it was, the size and extent of the family, gender and social class.

The oral history interview becomes more valuable in association with other historical sources such as photographs, objects or places. The history of the school, for example will make more sense for little children if they can walk round the building, look at old school photographs and listen to what it was like ten, twenty or fifty years ago from a former pupil or member of staff.

If you have a particularly good interviewee, one who talks to the point and at the children's level, you may decide to record it, saving the cassette for another occasion. This sounds useful, but you are unlikely to get the same attention from the children listening to a tape, unless they are also part of it, as you will from a real person in the classroom. It is also possible for the children, perhaps working in pairs, to make transcripts of their interviews (see Figure 16.4).

7

If we were naughty we got the cane. I got the cane for being disobedient in the corridor our parents smacked us if we were naughty at School. They slapped us and pulled our ears there were so children in my class. thera were no rewards the teacher Just said very good The toilets were outside and we used to bang the door. There was no hut.

Figure 16.4 *Transcript of an interview with an ex-pupil of Harborne Infant School*

Pictures

Pictures of unfamiliar people and places from the past are also invaluable. They too will make the past accessible, something to look at, talk about and compare. The advantages of using old photographs or paintings of familiar situations such as shopping or travelling are obvious and enable the children to work out for themselves what was the same and what was different about then and now. Figure 16.5 shows a good example of this kind of comparison from the Harborne Infant School project.

Most county libraries and local museums collect old photographs and can supply prints. You will want to select clear images, such as scenes of the milkman with his horse and cart or the ice-cream vendor on his tricycle, but there are often family groups in collections, which have unfortunately become separated from the families to which they once belonged. These show details of clothes, hair styles, gardens and objects, and have the kind of detail in them which will enable children to pick out features about the past for themselves.

Mrs Porters Room

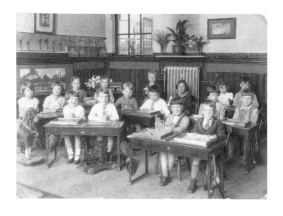 

1923   1989

The desks have changed.
In the old photograph there are
flowers and there aren't any
flowers in the new photogrph.
In the new photoyraph the boys have
different shoes then the
ones in the old photograph.
they both have a radictar.
Mrs porters classroom has changed
a lot. the windows are the
same. The old photoyraph was taken
in 1923 and the new
photogrnaph was taken in 1989

Figure 16.5 *The use of an old photograph of a familiar situation*

Objects

Objects can be collected as a result of an appeal to parents and friends as well as from car boot sales and charity shops. Like the invitation to come into school for an oral history interview, parents and friends can be asked to bring in an old object to talk about, as described in the section about the hot water bottle above. Objects collected by you can be touched and handled and presented to the children as mystery objects, something similar to the Antiques Road Show situation. They can be as contributions to topics like light, food and homes and put on display with their modern equivalents.

The environment outside the classroom

You will find good examples of museum visiting with early years pupils in the Teachers' Guides from the Ironbridge Gorge Museum (Forber, undated and 1990) listed at the end of the chapter. The success of the visits described here was almost certainly because the children were able to enter a reconstructed domestic environment; they could understand the context and make comparisons with their own experiences. A poor museum experience, however, for example where objects are in high glass cases, or where a lot of reading is involved in order to understand the display, is not really worth the effort, with very young children.

It is crucial that you make contact with a curator or education officer and assess the learning outcomes yourself, before booking a visit. The children will need to be well prepared and to have practised the skills such as close observation of objects, sketching and labelling they will need to use in the museum. You do not want to have a class of tired, restless children on your hands, particularly in a public space, so go prepared to look closely at one area, painting or object, not the whole museum. Where you do have a suitable museum near your school, consider building visits, activities and areas into your whole school policy for history, so that the children can consolidate any early years experience as they progress up the school.

Buildings

You may be in an area of old buildings, even at school in one! If your ancient buildings do not present any hazards, such as road safety, then they provide an ideal resource for many of the skills discussed earlier in the chapter, for accurate use of historical vocabulary and for drawing up a diagram of historical questions about the building. In terms of schools, the oral history potential is enormous, as can be seen from the work done at Harborne Infant

School. However, oral history is of no use in either Ironbridge or in a castle, although both can become suitable places for young children to learn.

Books

Books also have a place in resources for teaching history in the early years. Familiar stories like *Granpa* by John Burningham, *The Sandal* by Tony Bradman and Philippe Dupasquier and *Peepo* by Janet and Allan Ahlberg are about history and since the national curriculum began, some good history information books, for Key Stage 1 have been written (see list at the end of the chapter). The best bring a past perspective to familiar infant themes and use historical sources like oral history, pictures and objects to bring the past alive.

A variety of resources will contribute to the quality of teaching and learning in the early years, but cannot guarantee it. Resources are only of use when used in a planned scheme of work with a definite purpose in mind.

Activities

Activities for the children can be divided into experiences which you provide, or tasks which may be used for assessment. Whatever you choose will depend on the child or group and the skills, attitudes, concepts and knowledge you select. Below are listed some suggested activities for young children which can be adapted to particular historical projects.

Activities related to play

- Dressing up can be fun and related to the past by reference to pictures or oral memories.
- Food can be made following favourite dishes parents and older friends ate when they were children.
- Feely boxes can also be used to identify again the old objects like flat irons or candlesticks that have already become familiar from a classroom display.
- Kim's game – objects on a tray which you have to remember – will require both concentration and memory and again make your resources work for you in different situations.

Nursery songs and stories

- Many nursery songs and rhymes like 'Ride a Cock Horse', 'Three Blind Mice' or 'Ba, Ba, Blacksheep' describe an aspect of life in the past.
- Stories like those listed above and from different cultural traditions are a rich source of cultural and ethnic heritage.

Using vocabulary

- Objects can be drawn and described. Make a set of cards with some of the historical vocabulary listed above and encourage the children to put the objects in a time order and use accurate vocabulary about them.

Sorting

- Sort the objects, with modern equivalents, into categories, such as age or ownership e.g. *indoors, outdoors; men, women, children; town, country, sea-side*.
- Sort them, by relating them to a room where they were used, e.g. *kitchen, classroom, parlour* (discuss the label and how it has changed).
- Sort them into the material from which they are made, constructing descriptive phrases which can later be incorporated into sentences e.g. *the felt hat, the leather suitcase, the iron kettle*.
- Sort them into categories for display in the class museum. Write the labels and invite parents and other children to visit the museum.

Detective work

- Make time for the children to make guesses about objects, pictures and buildings.
- Provide the opportunity for them to pose their own questions such as 'I would like to know . . .'.
- Test out their guesses about an object, picture or building on another group of children. Can they work out the original from the guess?
- Introduce a collection of objects as a detective exercises by inventing a story about Granny's suitcase and what the contents tell us about her life.
- Use old photographs to 'work out' three things about the people or place in the past. What was *different* about their lives and ours? What has changed?

Time and sequence

- Use buildings around the school – you can take your own photographs of them when you go on a walk – to provide practice with sequencing activities. To begin with you might just use two categories, *now* and *then*, or *past* and *present*, but some children by the age of seven will be able to sort objects and buildings into centuries.
- Put all sorts of pictures, such as postcards that can be bought cheaply from museums, to put *homes, clothes,* or *transport* into a time order.
- Use paper timelines from published schemes (e.g. Purkis 1991), strips of paper or washing lines and pegs to and arrange the children's drawings or photographs of the locality chronologically.

Change

- Use pictures, objects, buildings and oral history to work out not only *what* has changed but *why* and *how*. (You will see that there is a hierarchy about these questions, which could be presented as a worksheet, moving from what can be seen to analysis and comparison. The questions demand thought and deduction, not just a retelling of information that has been given by the teacher.)

Oral History

Information generated in an oral history interview can be used in many ways:

- Make a book with the interviewee and their memories as the subject.
- Discuss why the book is a history book, or non-fiction book. What is the difference between the story of Mrs Rainbow, who actually came into school, and Mairi Hedderwick's fictional story of Katie Morag and the two grandmothers?
- Use part of the book to transcribe the actual words spoken by the visitor. Compare these with the account members of the class wrote about what she said.
- Draw pictures based on what the visitor told them (see example from Harborne Infant School in Figure 16.6)
- Round up the book with a special section on change, e.g. the *visitor* then and now, the *area* round the school and *how things were done*. This moves the task on beyond description to explanation and analysis.

The National Curriculum

For most of their 'early years', as defined in this book, the children's education takes place within the framework of a national curriculum. My view, shared by the educators I meet, is that it is possible to promote quality teaching and learning in history at Key Stage 1 and remain on the right side of the law. The key elements, which are about processes, not content, list the historical vocabulary already discussed and mention sequencing as a stage in the understanding of chronology. They also stipulate the use of objects, pictures and oral history as a way into the past. The level descriptions are not about content but about what the children can do and can be helpful when planning tasks which will allow the children to progress. Experience shows that few children find any difficulty in reaching the norm for their age, level 2, by the time they are seven.

In the old days the toilets
used to be by the junior gate
but now thay are by the
hall and not by the gate.
This is what I think it
might have looked like.

Figure 16.6 *The Harborne Infant School toilets 'in the old days'*

Pointers for teaching history in the early years

- Be aware of the contribution history makes to the growth of personal and social identity.
- Ensure that activities and discussion promote investigation and enquiry.
- Develop language relating to time and open-ended discussion, which helps children explain as well as describe the past.
- Collect and display resources which children can handle (objects), talk about (books and pictures) and listen to (memories of older people, old rhymes and songs).
- Have a policy for history which identifies progression in skills, knowledge and understanding, and which promotes positive attitudes to history.

Acknowledgements

I am grateful to Diane Humphreys, early years co-ordinator at Arbury Primary School, Cambridge, for talking over many of these findings with me.

Further reading

Cooper, H. (1995) *History in the Early Years*, London: Routledge

Forber, D. (ed.) (undated) *Under-Fives and Museums: Guidelines for Teachers*, Telford: Ironbridge Gorge Museum Trust.

Forber, D. (ed.) (1990) *Primary Schools and Museums: Key Stage 1*, Telford: Ironbridge Gorge Museum Trust.

Hazareesingh, S., Kenway, P. and Simms, K. (1994) *Speaking about the Past: A Resource for Teachers*, London: Trentham Books.

Mauser, M. and Reid, S. (1990) *Harborne Infant School Local History Project*, Birmingham: Education Dept., Birmingham City Council.

Pluckrose, H. (1991) *Children Learning History*, Oxford: Blackwell.

Purkis, S. (1991) *A Sense of History: Key Stage One Teachers' Book*, Harlow: Longmans.

Wright, M. (1992) *The Really Practical Guide to Primary History*, Cheltenham: Stanley Thornes.

CHAPTER 17

'If the world is round, how come the piece I'm standing on is flat?'

EARLY YEARS GEOGRAPHY

Dianne Conway and Pam Pointon

What is geography? Why teach geography?

These are questions asked by many early years educators who are not geography specialists. Comments such as 'I'm hopeless with maps!' or 'What can I do? There are no hills or mountains round here,' are heard by those responsible for ensuring geography is taught in our schools. So, what is geography?

> Geography explores the relationship between the earth and its peoples. It studies the location of the physical and human features of the earth and the processes, systems and inter-relationships that create and influence them. The character of places, the subjects central focus, derives from the interaction of people and environments.
>
> (Curriculum Council for Wales, 1991)

That geography is such a wide-ranging subject which attempts to make connections between the earth sciences and the social sciences is its strength (which other subject tries to connect the human and natural worlds to the same extent?) – but also its difficulty in commonsense understanding. How many people, if asked to explain what geography is, would refer to Trivial Pursuits knowledge of countries and their capital cities, naming of capes and bays, listing of major rivers and mountain ranges? Locational knowledge is obviously an important element of geography but if it is merely factual recall then the potential contribution is sadly diminished.

The current, more sophisticated approach includes a much broader view of what geography is about and a more active style of learning which engages children in observation, investigation, analysis and interpretation and encourages their development as young geographers. At the heart of the subject is its focus on both people and places through active exploration of their immediate environment. Their growing sense of 'their own special places' and curiosity about 'other places' is influenced by a range of experiences – both direct and vicarious through film, television, stories, music, computer games, CD-ROM etc., as illustrated in the useful model by Goodey (1973).

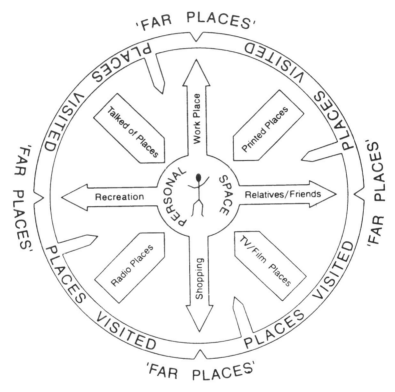

Figure 17.1 *Goodey's (1973) model of geographical experiences*

Developing learning experiences which extend the young child's knowledge and stimulates their curiosity about the wider world is important. The starting point, however, needs to be their perception of their own personal space. This is unique to them and their perceptions may be influenced by a range of variables including age, gender, class, ethnicity, disability. Young children are able to articulate thoughts and feelings about places which have meaning for them and can forcefully express their likes/dislikes of particular features in their environment, as shown by this conversation between two six-year-olds on a visit to the city:

I don't think I'd like to live in those flats. I wouldn't have a garden to play in. I think those small houses over there would be better.

Oh no. I'd rather live in the flat. The view would be great and there would be a lift to go in. Those houses are very small and squashed together.

The argument continued along similar lines for quite a while. The group were able to appreciate that everyone has their own point of view and that these views may differ. They were able to see that sometimes there are no right or wrong answers.

Broad aims for geographical education

Geography for Ages 5–16 (DES 1990) set out the following broad aims for geographical education. It should:

- stimulate pupils' interests in their surroundings and in the variety of physical and human conditions on the earth's surface;
- foster their sense of wonder at the beauty of the world around them;
- help them to develop an informed concern about the quality of the environment and the future of the human habitat;
- and thereby enhance their sense of responsibility for care of the earth and its peoples.

These broad aims need to be achieved through a range of teaching objectives which may be subdivided into those concerned with skills, knowledge and understanding, and values and attitudes (see Figure 17.2).

Geographical enquiry

Pupils should not be primarily passive recipients of information but should be given adequate opportunities to carry out practical investigations, to explore and express ideas in their own language . . . and to reflect on other peoples' attitudes and values.

(*Geography from 5–16*, DES 1986)

Involving young children in effective enquiry helps them to understand geographical concepts, develop geographical skills and explore the importance of values and attitudes in making sense of an increasingly complex and rapidly changing world.

Skills	Knowledge and understanding
• graphicacy – the making, using and reading of maps; using globes and atlases; use of photographs, diagrams, graphs • fieldwork and enquiry skills – observation, investigation, analysis and interpretation of primary and secondary sources	• general locational knowledge • specific locational knowledge, e.g. local area, contrasting localities • understanding key concepts: *location* – where is this place / feature in relation to other places / features? *patterns* – what is this place like? how are its building, parks, shops etc. organised? *relationships* – connections between different elements within a place, e.g. where people live and where people shop etc. *processes* – underlying reasons / causes for patterns and relationships which exist in the environment (local and global scale) and how they change over time *similarity and difference* – how is this place / feature similar / different to other places / features?
Values and attitudes • an interest in other people and places • awareness and appreciation of cultural and ethnic diversity within UK and beyond • concern for quality of environments • concern to value and conserve resources • awareness of different perspectives on environmental issues	

Figure 17.2 *Aims for geographical education*

What does enquiry involve?

- asking questions
- planning an investigation
- carrying out the investigation
- evaluating the conclusions.

Enquiries can be of different lengths (one lesson to a whole term), of different foci (an issue, a place or a theme) and at different scales (local to global). Identifying geographical questions can be a useful initial stage in planning an enquiry. There are seven key geographical questions which provide a framework for enquiry, each question can be a focus for an entire enquiry and further sub-questions developed:

- Where is this place?
- What is this place like?
- Why is this place as it is?
- How is this place connected to other places?
- How is this place changing?
- What is it like to be in this place?
- How is this place similar to or different from another place?

A sample enquiry is shown in Figure 17.3 (Geographical Association, 1991).

This next section offers a range of learning activities and useful resources for developing the young geographers' understanding of their world. The case study of 'Teddy's Visit ' usefully highlights how an enquiry approach can be used to explore the local area and develop a real 'sense of place'.

Developing map skills through play

All children enter school with some understanding and use of mapping skills. These skills have developed informally, directly from the child's experience. They are the result of activity and movement in and familiarity with the environment. These skills include an ability to:

- remember and find where objects are at home, e.g. their toys;
- remember where features are in the local area and take or direct you to them, e.g. the swings;
- find their way around their immediate environment, e.g. home, classroom, familiar play area;
- talk about going to places that are some distance away, e.g. 'the seaside', 'my gran's', 'on a train', 'to London'.

	Key questions	Activities
Initial perception	What is it? What do I feel about it?	Exploring the beach – a sensory walk Describing – is it warm / cold / exciting / dull
Description and definition	What is it like?	Collecting – pebbles / rocks / sand / shells Taking photographs, drawing pictures Observing / counting – different shops, building
Analysis and exploration	How do people use the beach? Why do they go there?	Analysing activities Analysing postcards Explaining why the seaside is a good place for these activities

This partial enquiry sequence could be followed by:

Collecting artefacts – children bring into school pictures, souvenirs, postcards, photographs of seaside resorts.
Comparing similarities and differences – using artefacts and personal experiences, are all the seaside resorts the same? If not how do they differ?
Questioning / finding out about a contrasting resort – children discuss what they would like to find out about a Spanish holiday resort. In groups they construct four or five questions to ask. Children invite a visitor who has been to a Spanish holiday resort and ask questions: e.g. What is the beach like? What sort of food do you eat? What do people do there? What is the weather like? What sort of shops are there?

Figure 17.3 *Exploring the seaside: a geographical enquiry. From Non-Statutory Guidance for Geography, Curriculum Council for Wales (1991) p. 42*

The most successful work will build on each child's spatial awareness and understanding and will acknowledge their experience in movement and spatial language. Much of it arises spontaneously out of traditional good practice in the early years classroom. It is important to recognise these opportunities to develop mapping skills and to think carefully about how to help children understand more from activities they naturally enjoy. Many of the activities outlined below happen in many early years classrooms as a matter of course.

Using spatial language

It is important to emphasise the *'where'* in talking with children, encouraging them to be precise about direction and location in relation to themselves, others and objects around.

- Encourage children to use locational vocabulary: 'It's behind', 'It's next to', 'It's in front of', rather than 'It's there'.
- Play games such as 'I spy' where children have to name objects where the clue may be 'It's beside a table in front of the window next to the flowers'.
- When directing children to a resource in the classroom give them directions using direction words; 'Go past the bookshelf, turn left, it is next to the red table'.
- Play games in pairs where the children have to give directions to identify objects or make journeys round the room.
- Encourage the children to give directions. Ask 'Who knows where the . . .?' If telling is difficult ask children to show others where things are.

Thinking about distances

Mapping is about how far away things are. The children should be encouraged to think about distances and to make comparisons.

- When giving directions use positional vocabulary; 'It's near the table', 'It's on the other side of the room from . . .'.
- Make comparisons of longer and shorter around the classroom and school.
- Ask 'Is it further to walk to the cloakroom or to the hall?' Ask the children to find out if they are correct.
- When making journeys talk about whether you are 'getting nearer' the destination and 'further away' from the starting point.

Using miniature world play

The activities outlined above can all be transferred to and developed further by using play equipment found in all early years classrooms.

- The wet sand can be transformed into a landscape with model houses and trees for playpeople to live in.
- Playmats of road layouts and farm layouts are representations of reality in pictorial form. They allow children to look down on a landscape and make journeys.
- Construction toys on various scales can be used to model environments in which journeys can be made.
- The dolls house provides another miniature environment where positional language can be encouraged.
- Programmable toys such as 'Pip', 'Roamer' or 'Floor Turtle' can be used to make journeys and create environments.

Using plans and pictures

Photographs taken looking vertically down on objects and places interest young children. Take photographs of objects looking vertically down: the bin, chairs, toys, everyday objects, man hole covers – anything you see.

- Send the children off to find the object in the photograph.
- Draw the shapes of the object on card and ask the children to match the shape to the photograph.
- Encourage the children to draw their own overhead or bird's eye view of classroom objects.

These activities lead easily into discussions about a birds' eye view of school or the locality and the introduction of vertical aerial photographs and plans of the school building.

Using maps

Young children are fascinated by maps of any sort. Many children enter school with experience of a variety of maps:

- the weather map on television;
- pictorial maps from theme parks, holiday resorts, zoos, forest trails etc;
- maps on postcards;
- the road atlas and maybe a street map.

The early years educator can build on this experience by introducing a wide variety of maps including the more conventional ones (see the list in Figure 17.4).

street maps	building plans
postcard maps	road maps
maps in adverts	road sign maps
housing estate maps	house plans
tourist area maps	town centre maps
Ordnance Survey maps	trail maps
railway maps	bus route maps
room plans	story book maps
board game maps	atlas maps
text book maps	guidebook maps
wall chart maps	teacher drawn maps
maps drawn by children	picture maps
land use maps	'antique' maps
resort maps	sketch maps
playmat maps	newspaper maps
building site plans	globes
teaching pack maps	walkers' maps
aerial photomaps	airline route maps
jigsaw maps	mazes
theme park maps	tea towel maps
underground maps	

Figure 17.4 *Types of maps to show young children*

A school should have copies of Ordnance Survey (OS) maps of the locality :

1 : 50,000 – 2cm on the map represents 1km on the ground.
1 : 25,000 – 4cm on the map represents 1km on the ground.
1 : 10,000 – 1cm on the map represents 100m on the ground.
1 : 2,500 – 1cm on the map represents 25m on the ground.
1 : 1,250 – 1cm on the map represents 12.5m on the ground.

Maps can be included in many activities. The youngest children will need help with orientation. Even if this is difficult, just handling the map is worthwhile.

A school plan can be used for journeys around school, for familiarisation or to carry messages. Groups of children, under the supervision of an adult, can be asked to try and follow a route marked on a school plan as a treasure hunt or/and adventure game.

Street plans or Ordnance maps can be used for walks in the local environment or planning the route the postman might take to deliver letters to the children's homes.

Aerial photographs of the local area, both vertical and oblique, can be used alongside local conventional maps. Encourage children to talk about what they see in the picture, and to recognise from where it was taken.

Pictorial maps and theme park maps from holidays and weekend visits are usually attractively presented and give children lots of ideas for creating maps of their own.

The road atlas is often one of the most popular books in the book corner. It gives exciting opportunities for discussion amongst the children. Unfortunately many atlases quickly fall apart. Regular requests to parents for their out of date road atlases, particularly the hardback ones, need to be made. One of the authors made the following observations in her mixed Year 1/Year 2 class working with atlases:

> One seven-year-old was observed engrossed in the atlas for quite a long time. When asked what he was doing his reply was 'I'm planning the route for my holiday in Cornwall.' When asked to show the teacher the route, he proceeded to find Cambridge and work his way through the atlas following the instructions to move to the next page until he arrived at the page showing Cornwall. A discussion followed about the different road colours shown on the map and he was able to pick out the motorways.

> Another group of children were to be found poring over the atlas after a coach trip to a small village 15 miles from school. They had identified the correct page and were soon able to find the village. They then spent a while trying to guess which route the coach had taken.

> The children discovered for themselves the index and how to use it. They very quickly learned how to look up the name of a place that they knew or had visited and find the correct page in the atlas.

The map of the British Isles is familiar to most young children even if they do not know exactly what it is. It is seen on the weather forecast regularly. A video of several weather forecasts is a useful tool not only when thinking about the weather but also when learning the countries of Great Britain. Most weather forecasters mention and point to the countries as they make their forecast.

The children enjoyed looking at a British Isles wall map and soon learned to spot the nearest large town, the nearest major river and where it reached the coast. They asked about the shading on the map and could think of places where there were hills and mountains.

A globe creates a great deal of discussion and is a source of fascination to young children. Every classroom should have access to one (see Figure 17.5).

A world map can be used for discussing places children have visited and countries in the news.

Making maps

Drawing is another way of representing and trying to understand movement, location and distance. Many drawings done by young children show relationships between features, for instance, parts of the body or homes and streets. Map work should involve drawing, painting, making collages and modelling.

Figure 17.5 *'If the world is round, how come the piece I'm standing on is flat?'*

- Children could draw or paint their route to school. They should be encouraged to remember landmarks and other details (See Figure 17.6).
- Drawings can be made of layouts created with playmats and construction toys such as Lego.
- 'Junk model' representations of the classroom, parts of the school, or the locality can be made. The children can finger walk routes and talk about them or even record them on paper.
- Children could be encouraged to make their own playmats and miniature worlds to use with Playmobile or Lego people and cars.
- Many children are inspired by the idea of making treasure maps.

Using stories

Children's stories often involve journeys and things happening in places e.g. *Rosie's Walk, Little Red Riding Hood* and many more. Stories need not be

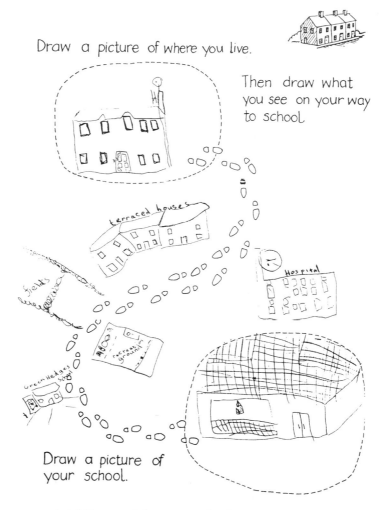

Draw a picture of where you live.

Then draw what you see on your way to school

Draw a picture of your school.

Figure 17.6 *A child's map of the way to school*

confined to story-time! They can be used as a source of geographical information to set alongside field work or mapping activities. They introduce young children to people, places and ideas. They contribute to children's understanding of and participation in the world around them. They help to foster children's curiosity about their changing world e.g. *Where the Forest Meets the Sea*.

- Some stories have maps provided by the author or artist. These can be enlarged so that the route can be followed whilst the story is read.
- If there is no map either you or the children can create one, either small individual ones or a big wall frieze.

- The story could be acted out, creating an imaginary map or using furniture to represent the physical environment.

More ideas for using stories can be found in 'Place in Story-time ' by Nicholson (1994). Suitable stories are listed at the end of this chapter.

Using the local environment

Observational walks

Most children, and indeed many adults, are not used to observing their environment closely. It is a good idea to encourage observation when out and about on any visit. Observation skills can be taught as fun activities to the youngest children.

- The children have to identify the location of photographs taken around the classroom or around school grounds.
- Photographs of the locality can be used in a similar way.
- When out on a walk children can look for various items of street furniture, post boxes, telephone boxes, bus stops, road signs, traffic signs etc. Make sure that the numbers involved are not too large and that the space to record or tally their results is large enough.
- The children might look at physical features: rivers, hills and farmland or buildings of different types and their use.
- Children can be asked to observe the quality of the environment and to discuss their likes and dislikes about places. They could be asked to list significant problems and their locations, such as dogs fouling foot paths, litter in the park and fumes in the high street. After identifying the problem they could suggest what action could be taken to improve the environment.

Choosing a context for a local geographical study

The same principles apply to selecting a geographical theme as to any other area of study.

- Is it relevant and accessible to the children?
- Does it offer the opportunity to work from first hand experience?
- Does it build on previous experience and knowledge?
- Will it enable the children to ask questions and search for answers?
- Can it be adequately resourced?

Young children should begin their geographical study in their immediate environment around themes such as 'Our School', 'Our Village', 'Journeys', 'Where I Live', 'Homes', 'A Place to Live' or 'People Who Help Us'. For the older Key Stage 1 children many of these themes can be extended to include localities further afield e.g. the nearest city or a smaller village.

Many of the practical ideas given earlier in this chapter can be used in these themes. A geographically based theme usually allows study in a cross-curricular way. There are opportunities for work in all areas of the curriculum. Below are two examples of cross-curricular projects that can be included in any locality study.

The picnic

This project involves the children asking questions and considering various possible solutions. It gives opportunities to cover areas of maths and technology as well as geography. There is also some consideration of health issues.

- Where shall we go for our picnic?
- How shall we get there?
- Which route will we take?

A local map is found. The children discuss various local picnic spots. They consider transport and maybe costs. A route is planned.

- Could we go by one route and return a different way?
- Whose route is the quickest or the most interesting?

Then comes the most important set of questions.

- What food shall we eat?
- Which foods are good to eat on a picnic?
- Where can we buy the food we need?

The children plan a walk to the local shop to find the answers. They return with some answers but also with more questions.

- How much of everything do we need to buy?
- Can we bake some cakes and biscuits ourselves?
- What will we put our picnic in?
- Could we design a lunch box?

A list of food is drawn up and each child decides what they would like. The data is gathered and sorted into a shopping list. A request is sent home for the money to cover the cost of the shopping. Recipes are found, ingredients listed, help with cooking is requested. Now there are more questions.

- When shall we go on our picnic?
- When shall we make the cakes?
- When shall we buy the ingredients to make the cakes?
- Can we buy all our food then?
- If not, when do we need to buy the other food for the picnic?

Then it is off to the shop again for the cooking ingredients.

- Perhaps we could find a different route to the shop?
- How long does it take?
- Is it a longer route than last time?

The baking is done. More shopping lists are planned and prepared so that every child can do some of the shopping. It is a good idea to warn the shop that 30 young shoppers will be coming. Try not to choose a busy time of day or delivery day. With 15 lists prepared, 30 children set off to the shop clutching their shopping bags and money.

- What do I do first when I go into the shop?
- How can I find what I want?
- How much does it cost?
- Where do I pay?
- Do I get any change? How much?

On the day of the picnic the bread is buttered, sandwiches and drink are made. Then 30 excited children carrying lunch boxes and maps set off for the picnic spot. If it is a local park or playground there could be a discussion about the play equipment, more observation work, and consideration of the quality of the environment. As a follow-up task the children could be asked to design their own play area and maybe make a model.

By using books like *Sam's Sandwich* and *Sam's Snack* by David Pelham, the children can be encouraged to write and create their own such books.

Teddy's visit

This activity is rather like a story that unfolds and develops as the weeks go by. The ideas for activities have all been tried out by a mixed Year 1 / Year 2 class. Some activities can be used by younger children.

The story begins one morning when a small suitcase or bag is found on a chair in the classroom. It has a large label saying:

'Please look after this bear'.

Inside is a small teddy bear. He has a map and a message with him saying that he is lost and needs help to find out which country he is in and to mark his location on the map (see Figure 17.7).

The map is photocopied and everyone tries to help Teddy out. Teddy spends time with each group as they work.

The next day there is another message from Teddy saying he would like to be shown round the school. So groups of children armed with route maps take him around. On another occasion he asks the children to write about themselves so that he can get to know them. His next request is to be taken on a walk around the neighbourhood. Another session with the maps and some route planning to make sure Teddy sees all the important parts of the

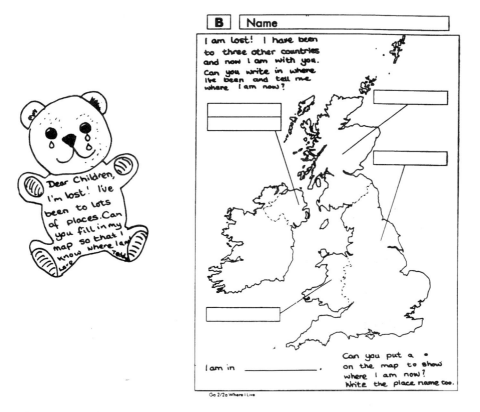

Figure 17.7 *The lost teddy bear*

area around school. Teddy is carefully carried in various pockets. He must not get lost again!

He might even request a picnic as a treat, and so we get into planning a picnic as discussed above.

Then one morning Teddy is not in his bag. He has left a note (see Figure 17.8) to say he is hiding and the children are to follow the instructions to find him but they must keep his hiding place a secret.

Hello, I'm Yellow Teddy.

I am hiding in your classroom. Can you find me? Follow the instructions and see if you can find me. Mark where you went on the map.

Start at the tape recorder –

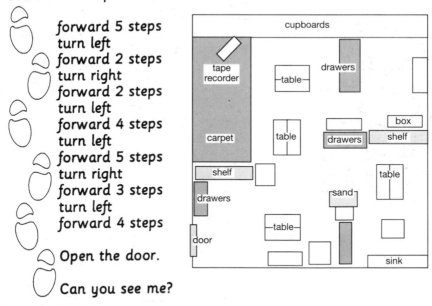

forward 5 steps
turn left
forward 2 steps
turn right
forward 2 steps
turn left
forward 4 steps
turn left
forward 5 steps
turn right
forward 3 steps
turn left
forward 4 steps

Open the door.

Can you see me?

SSHH....Don't tell anyone.

Figure 17.8 _Instructions to find Teddy_

This game can go on for several days with different hiding places. The children can devise their own instructions to new hiding places. Eventually Teddy grows tired of the classroom and asks the children to take him home to their houses to play. But before they can take him they must be able to fill in their addresses on his label, just in case he gets lost again! While he is visiting them they are asked to do some tasks:

- read Teddy the story book in his bag
- get a grown-up to read the harder story book to them both
- write Teddy's diary so he can remember his visit
- draw a route map of how to get back to school. He might get lost!

Teddy might accompany the children on other trips and visits that the class make. If it is possible he might request a ride on a train or a bus. During his stay, of course, he likes to hear stories about teddy bears, either real books or those stories written by the children. In the end Teddy receives a letter inviting him to visit a relative in another country. So out come the maps. Teddy is helped to plan his journey, his bag is labelled and then one night he disappears.

> The class became very involved with Teddy. They were enthusiastic about the tasks he gave them. They were very concerned when he really did get lost! On one walkabout he was dropped in a puddle and was left out to dry on a radiator overnight. The caretaker, thinking he had been left by a younger child, put him in the lost property bin. The search the next day was frantic. Teddy was well hugged when he returned.

> The children were particularly keen to take Teddy home. They learned their addresses quickly. His diary was carefully written. The parents played their part well and shared the children's tasks. Teddy was included in lots of the children's activities: parties, November 5th fireworks in the city, TV, computer games and meals out. There were lots of talking opportunities the next day. Even the shy children had something to say.

So geography is fun. It is happening and probably has been happening in early years classrooms for many years. Young children are fascinated by their surroundings and have the capacity to build upon natural learning experiences. Through topics like those outlined above, young children will learn from first-hand experience that there is a relationship between people and places and that they themselves can have an influence on the environment. It is important to recognise that many of the things we do have geographical possibilities. A geographical topic gives good opportunities for cross-curricular work in many subjects.

Pointers for early years geography

The following key points are important to recognise and remember when planning for geographical activities in early years classrooms:

- Young children are already active geographers.
- It is important to explore feelings about places as well as developing skills.
- Opportunities should be provided for young children to explore known and unknown worlds through play, stories, maps, photographs etc.
- Enquiry is central, especially, though not exclusively, through fieldwork investigations.
- There is a wealth of resources available locally for developing geographical awareness.

Stories involving journeys or places

The Three Bears (1985), Murdock, H., Ladybird.
Jack and the Beanstalk (1987), Hunia, F., Ladybird.
Hansel and Gretel, in *Classic Fairy Tales* (1993), Cresswell, H., HarperCollins.
Red Riding Hood (1988), Southgate, V., Ladybird.
The Three Pigs (1989), Southgate, V., Ladybird.
The Gingerbread Man (1966), Southgate, V., Ladybird.
Dick Whittington (1986), Southgate, V., Ladybird.
Town Mouse and Country Mouse (1982), McKie, A., Ladybird.
Three Billy Goats Gruff (1984), Traditional, J.M. Dent.
Fantastic Mr Fox (1970), Dahl, R., George Allen Unwin.
Winnie-the-Pooh (1926), Milne, A.A., Methuen.
Where The Forest Meets the Sea (1987), Baker, J., Julia MacRae Books.
Window (1991), Baker, J., Julia MacRae Books.
Don't Forget the Bacon (1978), Hutchins, P., Picture Puffin.
Rosie's Walk (1992), Hutchins, P., Picture Puffin.
Our Village (1988), Yeoman, J. and Blake, Q., Walker Books.
The Little Prince and the Great Dragon Chase (1994), Kavanagh, Simon & Schuster.

Penguin Small (1992), Inkpen, M., Hodder Children's Books.
Finn Family Moomintroll (1950), Janssen, T., Ernest Benn.
Enchanted Wood (1991), Hawkesley, G., Tree House Children's Books.

References

Curriculum Council for Wales (1991) *Geography in the National Curriculum: Non Statutory Guidance for Teachers*, London: HMSO/CCW.

DES (1986) *Geography from 5–16: Curriculum Matters 7*, London: HMSO

—— (1990) *Geography for Ages 5–16*, London: HMSO

Geographical Association (1991) *Response to the Draft Orders for the Geography National Curriculum in Wales*, Sheffield: GA.

Goodey, B. (1973) *Perception of the Environment: An Introduction to the Literature*, Occasional Paper No. 17, Birmingham: University of Birmingham Centre for Urban and Regional Studies.

Further reading

Foley, M. and Janikoun, J. (1992) *The Really Practical Guide to Primary Geography*, Cheltenham, Glos.: Stanley Thornes.

Geographical Association: *Primary Geographer* (quarterly magazine published specifically for non-specialist primary teachers, available from GA, 343 Fulwood Rd., Sheffield, S10 3BP).

Hulme, B., James, F. and Kerr, A. (1995) *A Sense of Place*, Twickenham: Belair.

Marsden, B. and Hughes, J. (1994) *Primary School Geography*, London: David Fulton.

Milner, A. (1994) *Geography Starts Here*, Sheffield: Geographical Association.

Nicholson, H.N. (1994) *Place in Story-time*, Sheffield: Geographical Association.

Palmer, J. (1994) *Geography in the Early Years*, London: Routledge.

Wiegand, P. (1992) *Places in the Primary School*, London: Falmer Press.

The way forward

CHAPTER 18

Whatever Next?

FUTURE TRENDS IN EARLY YEARS EDUCATION

Mary Jane Drummond

In this chapter I will explore the proposition that the ways in which we think about young children can and do affect the ways in which we provide for their learning and support their development. To put it another way, what we know about children, or think we know, shapes what we do for them in the name of education. I will examine some ways of thinking about children, and children's learning, taken from recent accounts of early years classrooms (and other settings) and try to show how we might take steps to reorganise and reshape our thoughts, our assumptions and our expectations. Future developments in early years education will, I believe, spring from an enhanced understanding of children and childhood.

Teachers teaching and children learning

One of the most challenging and entertaining books I have ever read about children's learning is *GNYS AT WRK: A Child Learns to Write and Read* (Bissex 1980). It is a detailed, vivid, first-hand narrative account of how five-year-old Paul became an accomplished writer and reader; what makes it different is not just its puzzling title (taken from a notice Paul pinned over his work-bench–desk at the age of 5 years 6 months) but its insider's viewpoint: the author, Glenda L. Bissex, is Paul's mother. She was also, when the story began, an educator studying for her master's degree in education. One afternoon, when she was trying to read, Paul wanted to play with her. Frustrated in his attempts to make her put down her book, Paul disappeared for a few minutes, returning with a piece of paper, on which he had printed, with rubber stamps from his printing set, the letters RUDF (Are you deaf?) His mother was dumbstruck and, in her own words, 'Of course I put down my book.'

The bulk of the book comprises Bissex's regular observations of her son's acts of writing and reading, illustrated with copious extracts from the written material that Paul produced over the six years of the study: there are excerpts from stories, lists, notices, books of jokes, report cards for his pets (including marks for PEING) and, in due course, when he starts school (at 5 years 10 months) his first written texts from the classroom, sadly stilted, after the richness of his earlier output. For example, at 6 years 10 months at school he writes: 'This is my reading book', whereas at 6 years 7 months, in just one day at home, he had written four newspapers, complete with cartoons, news, advertising and weather (THE SAFTERNEWN IT'S GOING TO RAIN).

Bissex's commentary and conclusions are based on her privileged position as both mother and educator. With a kind of binocular vision, she sees some disconcerting truths about how educators intervene in children's learning. In one memorable passage she writes:

> We speak of starting with a child 'where he is', which in one sense is not to assert an educational desideratum but an inescapable fact; there is no other place the child can start from. There are only other places the educator can start from.
>
> (Bissex 1980, p. 111)

I hope I am not alone in finding this insight an uncomfortable one. Bissex seems to me to be suggesting, all too credibly, that educators do (sometimes? often?) start in 'other places', and that the consequences for children's learning are frequently undesirable. Furthermore this suggestion seems to be an alternative version of the proposition with which I began: that how we think about children – or 'the child' – is of crucial importance in how we educate them – or him, or her. And this proposition, however we phrase it, raises questions worth worrying about. If early years educators do not, as Bissex suggests, start 'where the child is', with a coherent and principled understanding of the child's learning, then where do they start? And why? Can we learn to move closer to a more desirable starting point? What would it look like? What do we really mean by this 'educational desideratum', or an enhanced understanding of children?

My suspicions that Bissex is telling us something important about teaching and learning are based on two distinct sources of evidence: first, my own experiences as a educator and observer in early years classrooms, and secondly, other accounts and research studies of what early years educators actually do, and how they conceptualise the relationship between teaching and learning.

My own first-hand experience tells me, that, all too often, my carefully prepared activities, my lovingly drawn-up topic webs, my finely adjusted schemes of work, have failed to connect with children's pressing intellectual concerns, or with their energetic and enquiring minds. My observations in other classrooms have, over the years, confirmed my awareness of what I think of as 'the curriculum gap', the distance, sometimes a hair's breadth, sometimes a yawning chasm, that stands between what educators teach and what children learn.

If there is such a gap, and I am certain that there is, at least some of the time, in every classroom, I am equally certain that it cannot be attributed to malice or apathy in the hearts and minds of early years educators. Nor do published studies of children's experiences at school (Wells 1987, or Hughes 1989, for example) resort to the language of blame to account for what they see in classrooms. These authors do not mince words in identifying the mismatch between the educators' benevolent and educational intentions and the children's learning. But nor do they suggest that educators deliberately disable learners, or consciously create dysfunctional learning environments. So what is going wrong? And what can we do to put it right?

Some of the evidence suggests that part of the problem lies in the weakness of the language in which we describe and justify our work. In an early study of infant teachers' thinking (or, rather, a study of what infant teachers say about their work to investigative sociologists), Sharp and Green (1975) report an interview with 'Mrs Carpenter', a teacher of a vertically grouped class of rising-fives to rising-sevens. The discussion turned to the need for structure in teaching.

The interview proceeded as follows:

Interviewer How do you mean?

Teacher I mean we all, well, I have a little plan but I don't really . . . I just sort of, mmm, try and work out what stages each child is at and take it from there.

Interviewer How do you do this? How does one notice what stage a child is at?

Teacher Oh we don't really know, you can only say the stage he isn't at really, because you know when a child doesn't know but you don't really know when he knows. Do you see what I mean? You can usually tell when they don't know [long pause]. [There was a distraction in the interview at this point.] What was I talking about?

Interviewer Certain stages, knowing when they know –

Teacher   – and when they don't know. But even so, you still don't know, when they really don't (pause) you can't really say they don't know, can you? . . . That's why really that plan they wanted wouldn't have worked. I wouldn't have been able to stick to it, because you just don't . . . you know when they don't know, you don't know when they know.

Interviewer   How do you know when they don't know?

Teacher   How do I know when they don't know? [pause] Well, no, it's not so much that you don't know. I know when they're not ready to know, perhaps that's a better way of putting it.

(Sharp and Green 1975, p. 168)

The disarming candour of these statements should not blind us to the poverty of the understanding they express. This teacher, for all her good intentions, which I am willing to take for granted, is unlikely to be able to start 'where the child is'. She does not, on the evidence of this interview, have a way of explaining, even to herself, what it is that the educator knows when she or he knows where a child is, or what it is that the educator must then do with that knowledge.

Sharp and Green's work has been succeeded by other enquiries, less ideologically driven, but reaching similarly worrying conclusions. For example, Bennett *et al.* (1984) investigated the match between tasks and pupils, and identified a chronic weakness in educators' skills of diagnosis. In this carefully planned and cautiously quantified study of 'the quality of pupil learning experiences', the researchers found that more than half the observed tasks were badly matched to the child's level of understanding and achievement. High attainers were regularly underestimated and low attainers overestimated (ibid., p. 65).

The diagnostic skills of a group of 17 experienced infant teachers were studied in detail. As part of an in-service course, they were asked to examine transcriptions of some of the mismatched tasks recorded in the early part of the study. They were invited to discuss what seemed to be going on, to hypothesise about the children's understanding, and to explore any questions raised by the observations. The authors report that the teachers were extremely unwilling to respond to the classroom material in this way. 'They saw all problems as self evident . . . (they) made no use of the notion of hunch or hypothesis . . . all problems were to be solved by direct teaching' (ibid., p. 197). It seems as though these teachers' prime concern was with the quality of teaching, and that they had correspondingly little interest in learning.

Evidence from studies such as these suggests that there is indeed a problem. The professional language of the early years educator does not seem to be robust enough to frame adequate or effective descriptions of children and their learning. It is, I believe, not just the looseness and vagueness of the words we use that let us down, but a more fundamental issue. Starting 'where the child is', for all its familiarity as a slogan, as an 'educational desideratum', is simply not the best place to start; it is not an effective way of conceptualising the enterprise of early years education.

'To have' and 'to be'

I am influenced in this suggestion by the work of Erich Fromm, sociologist and psychoanalyst, who suggested in *To Have or To Be?* (1976) that the human condition in general is suffering from the dominance of western society's desire 'to have', at the expense of our understanding of what it is 'to be'. Applying this distinction to early years education, to its curriculum, its pedagogy, and its most idealistic aspirations, suggests to me that there is a need to re-emphasise our understanding of *what* children are, rather than *where* they are, or what we want them to *have*. Since, as Fromm says, 'there is no being that is not, at the same time, becoming and changing' (p. 25), it follows that, if we know what we want children to *be*, in the first four or five years of their educational lives, then we are likely to be effective in helping them to *become* the well-educated seven or eight-year-olds who will move into the next stage of their education. We will be well placed too, during their years of early education, to support to the utmost their present 'powers to be', another of Fromm's memorable phrases (in *Man for Himself* 1949, p. 84).

Since reading and re-reading Fromm, I have been drawing on his concept of children's 'powers to be' in my thinking and writing, and I am slowly becoming convinced of the strength of this starting point in thinking about the future of early years education. This vital phase of education straddles the non-statutory / statutory divide; the children we work with in the early years have attended a bewildering variety of settings, as well as living and learning in their homes for five solid years, before they enter the orbit of the national curriculum's statutory orders. But even after the children's fifth birthdays, we, their educators, are still at liberty to think about our pupils in ways that match our philosophy and our principles. In terms of teaching, coverage and content, we will, for the next five years at least, be working with core and foundation subjects, and religious education. But in terms of children's learning, we are still at liberty to think for ourselves. And I am arguing here that we cannot do better than to think in terms of what we know for certain about children's powers – their powers to do, to think, to feel, to know and understand, to represent and express. There is no compulsion on us to think of children in the early years as, exclusively, students of history, geography, science and so on. There are, if children's learning is our priority, more effective ways to *be* their educators than by surrendering our own powers to the curriculum we *have*, by statute, to accommodate.

By way of encouragement, we might turn to an exciting curriculum document, recently published in New Zealand, which sets out draft guidelines for the education of children from birth to six (the age of starting school). The Maori title of their bilingual document, *'Te Whāriki'*, refers to a traditional hand-made mat, which can be woven in an infinite variety of patterns; it represents the idea that the planned curriculum, based on commonly agreed goals and principles, can have a different pattern for every kind of early years service, in every individual early years centre. This in itself is a stimulating approach from the perspective of this country, but even more challenging is the set of ideas embodied in the five goals that run through the guidelines.

These goals are:

- **well-being**
  (the health and well-being of the child are protected and nurtured)
- **belonging**
  (children and their families feel a sense of belonging)
- **contribution**
  (opportunities for learning are equitable and each child's contribution is valued)
- **communication**
  (the languages and symbols of their own and other cultures are promoted and protected)
- **exploration**
  (the child learns through active exploration of the environment).

Early years educators in New Zealand, in whatever kind of setting, are invited to commit themselves to these goals for children; some of them may seem to go almost without saying, but others are well worth thinking about more carefully. The goal of *well-being* fits securely within the British tradition; we are still proudly conscious of the legacy from the great pioneers of early education – Rachel and Margaret McMillan, for example, working in the back streets of Bradford and Deptford to bring health and hygiene into the lives of young children (Steedman 1990). The goal of *communication* is equally likely to receive general assent from early years educators here, though it may be some years yet before the British government publishes its curriculum guidelines in two languages. But the goals of *belonging* and *contributing* are radical departures from our familiar ways of thinking.

In these goals, it seems to me, the New Zealand educators are setting out their aspirations for children's 'powers to be'; they are explicitly prioritising their belief that children can, and should, *be* members of a harmonious community, in which they have a place, to which they can make a contribution. This is a way of thinking about young children, and the education they deserve that, I believe, we might enthusiastically try for ourselves.

The New Zealand representation of children's powers set out in '*Te Whāriki*' reads easily enough across onto a model of children's learning that is proposed in a series of questions set out in *Making Assessment Work: Values, and Principles in Assessing Children's Learning* (Drummond, Rouse and Pugh 1992). In this discussion pack, the authors argue that effective assessment is predicated on the educator's principled understanding of the purposes of early years education. Practitioners are invited to ask themselves about their aspirations for children. What do we want our young children:

- to do?
- to feel?
- to think?
- to know and understand?
- to represent and express?

Answering these questions, is, I believe, part of the way forward for early years education in this country. And there are, fortunately for us, many sources to which we can turn to support us in our thinking. In this volume too, other authors have written of their personal experiences of children's powers, and the versatility and enthusiasm of children's learning in appropriately structured classroom environments. There is a healthy emphasis, throughout this collection, on the range of children's powers, and an accompanying emphasis on the context – children's play – in which so many of these powers are exercised.

Play and imagination

This emphasis on play is an important element in the argument to be made for a distinctive approach to early years education. But it is also a particularly challenging part of the task that lies ahead. Every early years educator, it is safe to assume, has at some time been made painfully aware that the importance of play in educational settings is not universally acknowledged. Although numbers of recent publications have taken up the challenge, and defended the educational value and outcomes of play, perhaps we have put too much professional energy into defending the contentious verb 'to play', which in some quarters is used as the polar opposite of the verb 'to learn' –

see Michael Fallon's notorious speech about pre-school play groups, for example (Note p. 347). Perhaps we would do better to emphasise 'play' in its noun form, and to construct our arguments around a full description of what, in the *context* of play, children think, feel, do, understand and express. What kinds of thinking and feeling characterise play? Are they important? Might it not be easier to make a case for the imagination, or for empathy, or for experiment and exploration, than for play?

In making such a case in my work as an in-service educator, I have found it salutary to see the confidence and the zeal with which other educationalists, outside the early years community, argue a position that I find thoroughly convincing. Mary Warnock, for example, moral philosopher as well as educational reformer, argues in *Schools of Thought* (1977) that the imagination is good in itself. Being more imaginative, like being more healthy, needs no further justification (p. 153). In *Imagination* (1976), Warnock makes even bolder claims:

> I have come very strongly to believe that it is the cultivation of imagination which should be the chief aim of education, and in which our present systems of education most conspicuously fail, where they do fail . . . in education we have a duty to educate the imagination above all else.
>
> (p. 9)

She characterises imagination as the human power 'to go beyond what is immediately in front of (their) noses', to 'see into the life of things'. It is a power which is not only intellectual: 'its impetus comes from the emotions as much as from the head'. Imagination is both necessary and universal; as part of human intelligence, it needs educating, and this will entail 'an education not only of the intelligence but, going along with it, of the feelings' (p. 202).

The need for high expectations

Warnock's aspirations for the human condition, even in this briefest of summaries, seem to me to illuminate some exciting possibilities within an early years education programme. If we can recognise, as I believe we can, the young child's powers to think and to feel, we can see clearly the weight of our responsibility to educate those powers.

In recent years, there has been considerable interest in an approach to early years education practised in the Emilia-Romagna district of Italy. A touring exhibition of their work, *The Hundred Languages of Children*, testifies to the extraordinary richness of their educational programme. 'The corner-stone of our experience' says Carlina Rinaldi, consultant and co-ordinator in the region (in Italian *pedagogista*), is an understanding of children as 'rich, strong and powerful'. She spells out what this means:

> they have . . . plasticity, the desire to grow, curiosity, the ability to be amazed, and the desire to relate to other people and communicate . . . Children are eager to express themselves in a plurality of symbolic languages . . . [they] are open to exchanges and reciprocity as deeds and acts of love which they not only want to receive but also want to offer.
>
> (Edwards *et al.* 1993, pp. 101–2)

There are interesting parallels here, I think, with the New Zealand educators' categories of belonging and contributing. But the Italian educators are not exclusively interested in the social dimension of learning; they go on to describe a central feature of their provision, the *atelier*, a creative workshop, rich in materials and tools, in which children from birth to three, as well as from three to six, become masters of 'all the symbolic languages' (such as painting, drawing and working in clay). In the atelier, 'children invent autonomous vehicles of expressive freedom, cognitive freedom, symbolic freedom and paths to communication' (ibid., p. 120). In the atelier, surely, they are exercising the powers that Warnock describes: 'to see into the life of things' – and not just to see, but to represent and express what they see.

The Reggio Emilia approach to early childhood education has, I am arguing, much to teach us in this country. I am not suggesting that we should follow their prescriptions to the letter, or that we should swallow, wholesale, their priorities and perceptions. But I am convinced that their way of seeing children, from birth, as strong to do and feel, skilled in learning, powerful in communicating, has profound effects upon the curriculum they provide, a curriculum that is sensitively and challengingly matched to the children's developing 'powers to be'. Their expectations of what children can do, and think and feel, are, to English eyes and ears, extraordinarily high. But the children in their schools rise to these expectations, as they explore both the world that is opening out in front of them, and their own interior worlds of feeling and imagination. As one reads the detailed account of their class-room projects, given in Edwards' book, one wonders what these Italian educators would make of some of the experiences provided in early years classrooms in this country.

My own observations of four-year-olds in their first terms in primary schools in several local authorities suggest that, in some classrooms, children's powers are seriously undervalued. The demands made on the children – to follow instructions, to complete worksheets, to cut and stick and colour in, as required by their educators, do not do justice to the children's energetic and enthusiastic minds. In one classroom, as part of a local authority evaluation programme (Drummond 1995), a child was observed using a template to draw a shape representing a T-shirt on a square piece of wallpaper. The T-shirt was one of twenty similar cutouts, destined for a frieze of teddy bears, who were being changed from their winter outfits to their summer clothes as part of the classroom topic on 'The Summer'. The child followed his teacher's directions as best he could, but the scissors were far from sharp and the wallpaper prone to tear. After some frustrating minutes had passed, the child looked up at the teacher who was leading this activity and said 'I can sew, you know'. I take this child's comment seriously, as a gentle – even forgiving – admonition to his educators. It is as if he were telling them to think again, to question their motives in asking him to perform this meaningless and unrewarding task. It is as if he were pointing out, most politely, that his powers to think, and do, and feel, were not being nourished or exercised by a curricular diet of templates and teddy bear friezes.

Bennett *et al.* (1984), we have already noted, found evidence that teachers both overestimated and underestimated children's abilities to complete language and number tasks. One particularly interesting finding from this study is that the problem of underestimation, when the task set was too easy for a child, seemed to be 'invisible to teachers in classrooms' (p. 49). The teachers in the study did not identify any tasks as beneath the child's attainment level, not challenging enough, or as a waste of a child's time. Bennett *et al.* explain this finding by reference to the emphasis placed on procedure, rather than product, in number and language tasks. When teachers saw children correctly following these procedures (using full stops in their writing, for example, or carrying a ten in an addition task), they 'did not compare the child's product with his actual level of understanding' (p. 63). They appeared to be satisfied with the children's compliance with the procedures they had been taught. This explanation seems reasonable enough, but it may only be half of the story. If one piece of the puzzle is excessive concern for procedures as defined by the educator, then another, equally important, element in the picture is a serious lack of concern for what children can do for themselves. It appears that the teachers in this study were not interested in the possibility that the children could do *more* than was required of them. They seemed to be blind to children's inventiveness, their individual ways of seeing, their personal explorations into the unknown.

By contrast, in another classroom in the evaluation study cited earlier (Drummond 1995), a group of young children spent 25 minutes absorbed in water play. The nursery nurse had, at their request, added some blue dye to the water, and the children were intrigued by the different shades of blue they could see: paler at the shallow margin, and darker at the deepest, central part of the water-tray. One child was even more interested in another, related phenomenon. He spent nearly ten minutes of this period of water play observing his own shoes and how their colour appeared to change when he looked at them, through the water and the transparent water tray. The child seemed to be fascinated by what happened when he placed his feet in different positions; he leaned intently over the tray to see what colour his shoes appeared to be at each stage. He did not use the words 'experiment' or 'observation', but that was what he was engaged in, nonetheless. After each trial, he withdrew his feet into the natural light of day, as if to check that they retained their proper colour. Had the dye stayed in the water, where he had seen it put? Or had some of it seeped out, into his shoes?

At the end of the morning session, the teacher and nursery nurse announced that it was time to tidy up. The children worked together to empty the water tray of the sieves, funnels and beakers they had been using. They took out the jugs, the teaspoons and the ladles, emptied them, and put them away. When they had nearly finished, the boy stopped and asked aloud, of no one in particular, 'How do we get the blue out?'

I think this is a remarkable question, showing as it does, this young scientist's mind at work. Only further conversation with him would reveal his present understanding of the concepts of light, colour, and reversibility; but his question is incontrovertible evidence of his urgent desire to find out how the world works, how its regularities and unpredictabilities can be accounted for. It is evidence too of his already firmly established knowledge that, as an active member of the world, he can experiment with it, act on it, and reflect on it, on the way to understanding it.

This child's question offers his educators exciting opportunities for development, but only if they respond to what he can do, and is doing. If they focus on what he does not know, or does not fully understand, they will miss the chance to feed and exercise his growing powers to hypothesise and experiment. The way they conceptualise this child's question – as genuine enquiry, or unthinking ignorance – will directly affect the experiences they go on to provide for him.

Conclusion

I have been arguing that the way forward for early years education is in a re-examination of some of our taken-for-granted assumptions and expectations. If educators, without any ill-will, think of young children as immature, incapable, illiterate, or ignorant pupils, then the experiences and activities they provide will not give children opportunities to prove themselves for what they really are: accomplished learners, passionate enquirers, loving companions. The classroom and its tasks will simply not be spacious enough for the exercise of children's powers to be : to be scientists, artists, dramatists, moralists, constructing and reconstructing the world.

But if early years educators can free themselves from any notion that because the pupils they work with are the youngest children in school, they are therefore the least capable, and least competent, then the future looks bright. There is then a real possibility that we can provide experiences, time and space, food and exercise, for learners who are already, long before they start school, capable, competent, imaginative and eloquent.

The founder and, for many years, director of the Reggio Emilia programme is Loris Malaguzzi. In a long interview about the principles underpinning their developing pedagogy he describes how, in Italy too, pressure from later stages of education threatens to distort and deform early years practices.

> If the school for young children has to be preparatory, and provide continuity with the elementary school, then we as educators are already prisoners of a model that ends up as a funnel. I think, moreover, that the funnel is a detestable object, and it is not much appreciated by children either. Its purpose is to narrow down what is big into what is small. This choking device is against nature.
>
> (Edwards *et al.* 1993, p. 86)

But Malaguzzi is optimistic, visionary even, in his determination that early years education will not choke or be choked. His fundamental position is a succinct summary of the argument I have proposed here: 'Suffice it to say that the school for young children has to respond to the children.' I have suggested that for schools to do this, our starting point must be a thorough understanding of what children are, in order that we can support their being and becoming. And if we can achieve such an understanding, we will be well placed to share in the glory of Malaguzzi's vision of the future. 'The continuing motivation for our work', he claims, is

> to liberate hopes for a new human culture of childhood. It is a motive that finds its origin in a powerful nostalgia for the future and for humankind.
>
> (ibid., p. 88)

Note

Michael Fallon, then Minister for Schools, spoke to the National Primary Conference of the NAHT on 1 November 1991. His speech included these words:

> At worst, this kind of practice (topic work) turns primary schools into pre-school playgroups where there is much happiness and painting but very little learning.

References

Bennett, N., Desforges, C., Cockburn A. and Wilkinson, B. (1984) *The Quality of Pupil Learning Experiences*, London: Lawrence Erlbaum Associates.

Bissex, G. L. (1980) *GNYS AT WRK: A Child Learns to Write and Read*, Cambridge, Mass: Harvard University Press.

Drummond, M. J. (1995) *In School at Four*, Hampshire's earlier admissions programme, final evaluation report, Spring 1995, Hampshire County Council.

Drummond, M. J., Rouse, D. and Pugh, G. (1992) *Making Assessment Work: Values and Principles in Assessing Young Children's Learning*, Nottingham: NES Arnold/National Children's Bureau.

Edwards, C., Gandini, L. and Forman, G. (1993) *The Hundred Languages of Children: The Reggio Emilia Approach to Early Childhood Education*, Norwood, New Jersey: Ablex Publishing Corporation.

Fromm, E. (1949) *Man for Himself*, London: Routledge and Kegan Paul.

—— (1976) *To Have or To Be?*, London: Jonathan Cape.

Hughes, M.(1989) 'The child as learner: the contrasting views of developmental psychology and early education' in C. Desforges, (ed.) *Early Childhood Education* (*British Journal of Educational Psychology* Monograph Series No. 4) pp. 144–57.

Ministry of Education (1993) *Te Whāriki: Draft Guidelines for Developmentally Appropriate Programmes in Early Childhood Services*, Wellington, New Zealand: Ministry of Education.

Sharp, R. and Green, A.(1975) *Education and Social Control: A Study in Progressive Primary Education*, London: Routledge & Kegan Paul.

Steedman, C. (1990) *Childhood, Culture and Class in Britain: Margaret McMillan, 1860–1931*, London: Virago.

Wells, G. (1987) *The Meaning Makers: Children Learning Language and Using Language to Learn*, Sevenoaks: Hodder & Stoughton.

Warnock, M. (1976) *Imagination*, London: Faber & Faber.

—— (1977) *Schools of Thought*, London: Faber & Faber.

Index